Writing Strategies for

All Pri lents

JOSSEY-BASS TEACHER

Jossey-Bass Teacher provides educators with practical knowledge and tools to create a positive and lifelong impact on student learning. We offer classroom-tested and research-based teaching resources for a variety of grade levels and subject areas. Whether you are an aspiring, new, or veteran teacher, we want to help you make every teaching day your best.

From ready-to-use classroom activities to the latest teaching framework, our value-packed books provide insightful, practical, and comprehensive materials on the topics that matter most to K–12 teachers. We hope to become your trusted source for the best ideas from the most experienced and respected experts in the field.

Writing Strategies for All Primary Students

Scaffolding Independent Writing with Differentiated Mini-Lessons, Grades K–3

Janet C. Richards

Cynthia A. Lassonde

JOSSEY-BASS
A Wiley Imprint
www.josseybass.com

Published by Jossey-Bass
A Wiley Imprint
989 Market Street, San Francisco, CA 94103-1741—www.josseybass.com

Library of Congress Cataloging-in-Publication Data

Richards, Janet C., 1936–, author.
  Writing Strategies for All Primary Students : Scaffolding Independent Writing with Differentiated Mini-Lessons, Grades K–3 / Janet C. Richards, Cynthia A. Lassonde.
    p. cm
  Includes bibliographical references and index.
  ISBN 978-0-470-61071-8 (pbk.)
  1. Composition (Language arts)—Study and teaching (Primary) 2. English language—Composition and exercises. I. Lassonde, Cynthia A., 1957–, author. II. Title.
  LB1576.R518 2011
  372.62′3–dc22

                                                                                          2010045579

Printed in the United States of America
first edition
PB Printing 10 9 8 7 6 5 4 3 2 1

Contents

Foreword

Most of us are familiar with the age-old adage for preparing children to be successful in school and beyond. Teachers need to focus on the "three R's"—reading, 'riting, and 'rithmetic. Yet in recent years one of these skills has received significantly less attention—writing. Even though we know one of our most important tasks is to introduce young students to written language—how to use it creatively and effectively to communicate—for the most part we have neglected strategies to develop students' writing. This book offers an array of strategies on which K–3 teachers can rely to ensure their students develop as able writers who can self-regulate their independent writing.

Whether you teach primary or upper-elementary grades, administrators and school districts count on you to teach your students to quantifiably improve their writing skills. You need to offer strategies to help them along the way, from the initial draft to polishing and bringing their unique voices to their writing tasks. In the mini-lessons described in this book, you'll see concrete, research-based ways to scaffold students' writing that make writing more pleasurable and successful for English language learners, writers who struggle, emerging writers, and students with advanced writing abilities.

All children want to write. In fact, through their pretend play, drawing, and conversations about storybook plots and characters, children try to use and understand writing long before they can actually write conventionally. What is truly remarkable is that these early writing activities tend to be even more visible than children's early reading attempts. As young children scribble and draw, they often begin to experiment with making wavy lines and letter-like shapes. In their early experiments, children demonstrate their knowledge about and desire to use writing. They find writing can be useful in their social relationships: in making requests, in defining and labeling their world, and in expressing their feelings of friendship and love. In these early activities, before children even go to school, they are beginning to construct such literary forms as notes, letters, stories, and poems.

Once children enter school, how do we corral their enthusiasm and creative minds so their writing is coherent, engaging, and purposeful? One important way is to screen your class to determine who would benefit from what strategies, then model and teach chosen strategies to small groups of students, and finally support students as they execute strategies independently. The strategies described in this book help students generate and organize their ideas for writing, translate their ideas into written texts, and review and reread parts of the texts to revise their work. All of these strategies are designed to place students in control of their writing.

To develop as writers, students need to find a balance between "doing it myself" and knowing when to ask for assistance and collaboration from others. Writing strategy mini-lessons fit this model. Teachers do not teach strategies that students cannot developmentally handle. In the same way, teachers do not offer certain strategies to those students who are already proficient in particular aspects of writing. These students have no need to learn strategies they already use with ease.

It has been my pleasure to write a foreword for this much-needed book. It is the first of its kind, and as a teacher you will refer to the wide range of chapters throughout the school year. If you need strategies to help your students begin to write, think of ideas about what to write, draft stories or content pieces, revise writing, or edit spelling, or if you need strategies to guide students from the beginning to the end of the writing process, you will find the answers in this book. Congratulations to Janet Richards and Cynthia Lassonde!

SUSAN B. NEUMAN
University of Michigan

Writing Strategies for All Primary Students

Introduction

Along with reading comprehension, the ability to write well is a predictor of academic success and a basic requirement for participation in civic life and in the global economy.
Graham & Perin, 2007, p. 1

There are many exceptional books that focus on writing instruction, and each offers a different comprehensive approach or program. However, as a senior acquisitions editor of literacy publications recently told us, ''Despite the number of volumes available on writing instruction, there are still not enough good books that explicitly address how teachers might teach writing.'' We concur with the senior acquisitions editor. Furthermore, numerous teachers and teacher educators have told us they want more ideas about writing instruction because no single writing approach ''will meet the needs of all students'' (Graham & Perin, 2007, p. 11).

Every year, large numbers of students in the United States graduate from high school or drop out of school unable to write at the most basic level (Kamil, 2003; Snow & Biancarosa, 2003). The reality is that most teachers have little time to deviate from their school districts' requisite pedagogical objectives and curriculum goals to offer small-group or even whole-class writing instruction based on students' immediate writing requirements. As one teacher commented, ''Because of all the state mandates for subjects like reading, math, P.E., and more, I don't have time to teach specific writing lessons'' (''Drawing Kids into Writing,'' 2008, p. 7). Indeed, teachers in our graduate language arts and writing methods classes tell us they are only allowed to offer forty minutes of writing instruction per day. Therefore, they have little time to devote to students' distinctive writing needs. In our own recent experiences as teachers of primary students, and now as supervisors of our apprenticing teacher candidates and professors of master's and doctoral education students, we have been frustrated by the disparities among the writing needs of primary students; the perceived time restrictions of a busy academic agenda; and the absence of a resource, such as this book, that could help educators incorporate meaningful writing strategy mini-lessons into the core of their daily writing and curriculum goals. Teachers feel restricted by an overemphasis on one-size-fits-all, rigid, formulaic writing lessons that leave little room for differentiated instruction and are designed by those who are far removed from students' specific writing requirements.

1

Yet, as teachers know, the majority of primary children benefit from carefully planned, individualized writing instruction based on what they need to know next about writing (Tompkins, 2008). For example, for the most part, many primary students may write well but lack proficiency in certain areas of writing. They therefore need some supplementary instruction tailored to their specific writing requirements. And, as Gail Tompkins (2008) and Lisa Delpit (2003) note, explicit writing instruction is especially important for children from minority cultures who may not be familiar with "certain knowledge and strategies not made explicit in their classrooms. Explicitness is crucial because people from different cultures have different sets of understandings" (Tompkins, p. 71). Another area of concern is that for various reasons an entire class of students may need customized lessons that focus on particular aspects of writing.

So how do teachers of writing who are challenged by lack of time and inhibited by mandated programs find time to teach explicit writing lessons that fit students' needs? We propose, based on our personal teaching experiences, our research, and our extended study of writing theory and pedagogy, that an effective, pragmatic solution for teachers is to offer writing strategy mini-lessons based on the needs of individual students, small groups of students, or perhaps an entire class. "Strategy instruction involves the explicit teaching of behaviors" (Guthrie, 2009, p. 7). Mini-lessons are made up of fifteen- to thirty-minute direct-instruction sessions designed to help students become strategic, skilled writers (Atwell, 1998; Tompkins, 2008). Brief strategy lessons easily fit within the framework of any required school district's writing approach or program. As Tompkins notes, "The question is not whether to teach strategies . . . but how and when to teach them" (p. 71).

This book, *Writing Strategies for All Primary Students: Scaffolding Independent Writing with Differentiated Mini-Lessons, Grades K–3,* has the potential to change writing practice. It offers easy-to-understand descriptions of writing strategy mini-lesson instruction for all K–3 writers, including students in need of some occasional help, those who benefit from frequent supplemental writing instruction, those who struggle daily with aspects of writing, and advanced writers. Specifically, the book offers an array of strategies that teachers can model, help students learn in an interactive setting with peers, and assist students to apply independently to enable them to take control of and self-regulate their writing. This book is particularly needed because although it is acknowledged that writing workshops and process-oriented teaching methods have introduced many positive changes to writing instruction, these approaches do not support students in need of some additional help in one or more dimensions of writing and those who are challenged daily by writing assignments (Collins, 1998).

K–3 WRITERS

Students in kindergarten through grade 3 represent a wide range of writing skills. This book aims to meet the needs of students at all developmental levels of writing in grades K through 3, from emerging writers to advanced writers, including those who struggle and those for whom the English language is a second language.

Emerging Writers

The writing process begins from the time children can hold writing utensils and draw scribbles, symbols, and pictures that represent meaning to them (Soderman, Gregory,

& McCarty, 2005). In this book, we recognize that writing strategies benefit emerging writers and also transitional and conventional writers (Sulzby, 1990). Over time, students begin to differentiate between drawing and writing as separate symbol systems (Dyson, 2001). We have provided writing strategies for each part of the writing process for emerging writers in the scribble, prephonemic, and semiphonemic stages (see Gentry, 2008). In these stages, students use pictures as mock writing, and move into using strings of letters and then some letters for phonemes they hear in words. This book identifies students who inconsistently use letters to represent phonemes as emerging writers. Each writing strategy mini-lesson includes suggestions for adapting the strategy for use with emerging writers.

Writers Who Struggle

There is no single profile of a struggling writer. Often we identify those who struggle by comparing them with those who are more proficient. For an in-depth discussion of writers who struggle, how to identify them, and how to instruct them, please see Chapter Five, Writing Strategy Instruction for Struggling Writers by Eva Garin and Rochelle Matthews-Somerville. Adaptations for writers who struggle can also be found at the end of each writing strategy mini-lesson chapter in Sections Two through Five.

English Language Learners

English language learners may need support with vocabulary, sentence structure, and syntax that exceeds the type of assistance required by other primary writers. As you model and teach writing strategies to English language learners, you will want to rely and expand on the language and writing abilities students already possess in their first languages. All mini-lessons provide adaptation ideas for teaching writing strategies to students whose second or third language is English that will help them become proficient writers.

Advanced Writers

Advanced writers excel in writing. You will have your own standards for identifying your advanced writers based on your grade level and students' abilities. They may be students who love to write and write prolifically. The content of their writing may show maturity. The mechanics of and spelling in their work might be exceptional. You may recognize your advanced writers by the themes they select, their engagement in writing, the length of their sentences, their word choices, or the intricacy of details in their writing. All mini-lessons include adaptation ideas for challenging advanced writers.

HOW THIS BOOK IS ORGANIZED

We have designed this book to help you develop as a strategic teacher of writing and to help your students become strategic writers. There are five main sections in this book. Each major section begins with an overview to help you know what to expect as you read its chapters. The overviews summarize each of the chapters and, therefore, assist you in determining what strategies in the book are most relevant to you and your students.

Section One, Developing Understandings About Writing Strategy Mini-Lessons, includes five chapters that provide background information about how to screen and assess students to help you teach writing strategy mini-lessons that meet the individual needs of your students in your classroom and that correlate with your existing writing program. Section One also provides a comprehensive description of the theories that undergird writing strategy mini-lessons and how to offer these mini-lessons. For a brief introduction of each chapter, see the Section One opening pages.

Sections Two through Five categorize the nature of the writing process we hope students develop as they work their way through the strategies. Each chapter in these sections portrays a strategy. Section Two includes strategies for inventing. Section Three offers mini-lessons on drafting. Section Four provides strategies for revising, polishing, or editing writing and moving toward a final draft. Finally, Section Five presents comprehensive strategies students can employ as they work through all of the phases of the writing process. Each of the strategies in Sections Two through Five is offered in a uniform format so readers can easily predict where to find specific information. Here is the outline of the components:

Introduction—This provides a brief overview of the strategy's objectives.

Why This Strategy Is Important—This section narrates an informal, contextualized purpose for the writing strategy mini-lesson.

The SCAMPER Model for the Strategy—In this part of the chapter, authors follow the SCAMPER model (fully described in Chapter Two) to portray a writing strategy mini-lesson.

Adapting the Strategy—Here you will find suggestions, following the SCAMPER model, for how to adapt the mini-lesson to meet the diverse needs of emerging writers, writers who struggle, English language learners, and advanced writers.

Extending the Strategy—Ideas for extending the strategy are shared in this helpful section.

Evidence Connections—This section offers two annotated, relevant reading suggestions that connect to the ideas presented in the chapter.

References—A list of useful texts completes each strategy so you can seek out further readings on the ideas discussed in the chapter.

Furthermore, some of the strategy chapters contain survey and assessment forms that you can duplicate and use in assessing your students. And many share samples of students' writing and illustrations.

HOW TO USE THIS BOOK

This book is different from other writing instruction books. You will first want to read it from start to finish to learn all about what writing strategy instruction entails. Then you will want to revisit particular sections and dip into the ideas and strategies presented. This book will be a practical resource tool for you. It will be a writing book you will keep on your professional bookshelf, to consult when you need informed ideas to help your students improve their writing.

LET US HEAR FROM YOU

We want to hear from our readers. Therefore, we have provided our e-mail addresses below. Tell us how you have implemented the strategies in this book and about your students' independent, self-regulated writing achievements as they employ writing strategies. Perhaps you have extended or altered the strategies presented, or maybe you have devised some writing strategies on your own because you wanted to meet your students' particular writing instruction needs. Tell us about your uses and adaptations of our model and the strategies presented in this book. Teachers who understand the theory behind writing strategy instruction and the SCAMPER model for teaching writing strategies possess the knowledge and ability to offer best practices in writing instruction for all students in grades K through 3.

JANET
(JRichards@coedu.usf.edu)

CINDY
(Lassonc@oneonta.edu)

REFERENCES

Atwell, N. (1998). *In the middle: New understandings about writing, reading, and learning.* Portsmouth, NH: Heinemann.

Collins, J. (1998). *Strategies for struggling writers.* New York: Guilford Press.

Delpit, L. (2003). Effective white teachers of black children: Teaching within a community. *Journal of Teacher Education, 54,* 413–427.

Drawing kids into writing. (2008, October 17). *St. Petersburg Times,* p. 7.

Dyson, A. H. (2001). Where are the childhoods in childhood literacy? An exploration in outer (school) space. *Journal of Early Childhood Literacy, 1,* 9–39.

Gentry, J. R. (2008). *Step-by-step assessment guide to code breaking.* New York: Scholastic Press.

Graham, S., & Perin, D. (2007). *Writing next: Effective strategies to improve writing of adolescents in middle and high schools* (Carnegie Corporation Report). Washington, DC: Alliance for Excellent Education. Retrieved September 7, 2007, from www.all4ed.org/publications/WritingNext/WritingNext.pdf.

Guthrie, J. Contexts for engagement and motivation in reading. *Reading Online, 4*(8). Retrieved February 19, 2009, from www.readingonline.org/articles/art_index.asp? HREF=/articles/handbook/guthrie/index.html.

Kamil, M. (2003). *Adolescents and literacy: Reading for the 21st century.* Washington, DC: Alliance for Excellent Education.

Snow, C. E., & Biancarosa, G. (2003). *Adolescent literacy and the achievement gap: What do we know and where do we go from here?* New York: Carnegie Corporation of New York.

Soderman, A. K., Gregory, K. M., & McCarty, L. (2005). *Scaffolding emergent literacy: A child-centered approach for preschool through grade 5.* Boston: Allyn & Bacon.

Sulzby, E. (1990). *Writing and reading instruction and assessment for young children: Issues and implications.* Paper commissioned by the Forum on the Future of Children and Families of the National Academy of Sciences and the National Association of State Boards of Education, Washington, DC.

Tompkins, G. E. (2008). *Teaching writing: Balancing process and product* (5th ed.). Upper Saddle River, NJ: Pearson/Merrill/Prentice Hall.

Section

Developing Understandings About Writing Strategy Mini-Lessons

The five chapters in Section One provide foundational understandings about what it means to teach writing effectively in today's primary classrooms. They will help prepare you to deliver writing strategy mini-lessons through the SCAMPER model, explaining the rationale for teaching writing strategies and exploring how to teach them, how to connect writing strategy instruction and mini-lessons to your writing program, the central features of evaluation, and how to meet the needs of all primary writers.

Chapter One, Teaching Writing Strategies in the Classroom, an invited chapter written by Steve Graham, focuses your attention by describing the strategic facets of students' skilled writing, such as planning and gathering suitable ideas and information for writing, reflecting and revising as they work through their writing, and self-directing their work and environment in productive ways. In the remainder of the chapter Graham explains why writing strategy instruction is beneficial for young writers and how writing strategies should be taught.

Chapter Two, Incorporating the SCAMPER Writing Strategy Mini-Lesson Model into Your Writing Program, provides an overview of the SCAMPER model and how to fit it into the writing program your school uses. It also discusses how the SCAMPER model addresses the principles of Response to Intervention (RtI) and offers ideas for contextualizing the model within a meaningful environment.

In Chapter Three, Architecture of a Mini-Lesson, Anne Marie Juola-Rushton identifies the function of the writing strategy mini-lesson as the vehicle for young writers to learn the purposefulness of writing and the value of being a writer. The author then shares an example of a mini-lesson using the SCAMPER model format. She also provides suggestions for maintaining new strategies over time through the use of an ''if-then'' strategy reinforcement chart.

Jane Hansen presents the four central features of evaluation in Chapter Four, The Role of Teachers' Evaluations: (1) teachers evaluate the ways they use their own lives and writing to ensure their young writers value their own lives and writing; (2) teachers evaluate by observing and conferring with their students while they write among their classmates; (3) based on their in-context evaluations, teachers provide strategy lessons in which they show children how much confidence they have in them; and (4) teachers establish networks of supportive evaluators among the children in their classrooms.

In Chapter Five, Writing Strategy Instruction for Struggling Writers by Rochelle Matthews-Somerville and Eva Garin, the authors answer the questions Who are the struggling writers? and How do we know our students are struggling with writing? They then suggest general accommodations and strategies for writers who struggle.

We urge you to read these chapters thoroughly before you offer writing strategy instruction using the SCAMPER model. What makes educators exemplary writing teachers is their understanding of theories related to writing instruction, teaching, and learning, and of how to connect these theoretical perspectives to practical applications. By aligning writing strategy mini-lessons with sound theory, you will be better able to make sound choices about what specific writing strategies to model and teach.

Chapter 1

Teaching Writing Strategies in the Classroom

STEVE GRAHAM

Writing is a self-directed, effortful, and strategic activity (Graham, 2006; Zimmerman & Risemberg, 1997). This is clearly evident when skilled writers talk about how they compose. One point they often emphasize is the goal-directed nature of writing. One of my favorite examples of this involves the famous critic and author Robert Benchley (Hendrickson, 1994). When he was a college student at the beginning of the twentieth century he was asked to write about the arbitration of the international fisheries problem from the point of view of either the United States or Great Britain. He decided to set his own goal for this task, and addressed the question from the point of view of the fish!

Skilled writers also maintain that they spend time preparing in advance what they plan to do and say. This was evident in the case of J. K. Rowling, author of the *Harry Potter* books. Before writing the first volume in this series, she spent several months planning it, filling several boxes with notes and ideas (Shapiro, 2000). Likewise, R. L. Stine, creator of the popular *Goosebumps* and *Fear Street* thriller books, indicated he relies heavily on the traditional strategy of outlining (Associated Press, 1995). He creates very complicated and detailed chapter-by-chapter outlines for a book before writing it, claiming that knowing what will happen in advance makes writing the book more enjoyable.

In addition to spending time preparing ahead of time what they will write, skilled writers continue to plan as they write. Ray Bradbury, the celebrated science fiction writer, for instance, first decides what his hero or heroine wants, and then fills in the details while writing (Bradbury, 1992). The playwright Harold Pinter often started with an idea of what might happen, and sometimes the story remained true to this possibility, but sometimes it veered off into new terrain as Pinter worked on it (Kazin, 1967).

Further, skilled writers are strategic when gathering information for their texts. If they do not readily have the needed information at hand, they know how to get it. Sometimes this involves a common strategy, such as consulting an authoritative source; conducting an interview; or retrieving information from a primary source, like a diary. In other instances, this process involves a more innovative method. Sue Hubbell, who writes children's books about bugs, employs both approaches. When writing the book *Broadsides from the Other Orders,* she obtained information about her main characters—silverfish, katydids, daddy longlegs, and so on—by visiting the Library of Congress and reading everything that she could find (Hubbell, 1996). She then called leading experts on each bug to obtain even more interesting facts. For some bugs, such as camel crickets, however, there was little information and no living expert, so she raised and observed these bugs herself.

Skilled writers further employ effective and sometimes innovative strategies for organizing the information and material they generate or collect when writing. This can be as simple as organizing ideas categorically. Shelby Foote, the historian featured in Ken Burns's television series *The Civil War,* noted that for one writing project he arranged ideas on large cardboard posters, making a column for each year of the civil war and rows for such concepts as diplomacy, military, and politics (Lamb, 1997). After he had entered the relevant facts and observations on the poster, he could tell at a glance what was going on in a particular year.

Still other skilled writers organize their ideas around a basic writing schema. In the *James Bond* novels, Ian Fleming repeatedly used the same organizational pattern from one book to the next, with minor variations (Eco, 1982). Robert Pirsig, the author of *Zen and the Art of Motorcycle Maintenance,* used a more freewheeling organizational strategy. He placed the ideas for his book on index cards, shuffling them about until he found an arrangement that suited him (Burnham, 1994).

Skilled writers engage in other fundamental strategic activities, such as monitoring, evaluating, and revising their texts. Truman Capote repeatedly revised what he wrote (Cowley, 1958). Once he had produced a first draft by hand, he would completely revise it again in longhand. He followed this with a second revision typed on yellow paper. Capote then set the paper aside for a suitable period of time before reading it cold, now making revisions on a retyped version—this time on white paper. Sometimes this was still not enough to suit Capote's sensibilities, and he threw away quite a few manuscripts at this point. Similarly, Raymond Carver, the great short story writer, would produce as many as twenty or thirty drafts of a story (Burnham, 1994).

In addition to planning what to do and say; gathering or generating suitable ideas and information; and evaluating and revising their plans, ideas, and texts, skilled writers take great care to arrange their working environments in ways that are productive for them. Sometimes they go to extremes to accomplish this goal. Victor Hugo, the author of *Les Miserables* and *The Hunchback of Notre Dame,* ensured that he wrote regularly by confining himself without clothes to his study each day (Wallace & Pear, 1977). George M. Cohan employed perhaps the most extravagant strategy of all time, renting an entire Pullman car on a train and traveling in it until he finished writing his book (Hendrickson, 1994).

Although these examples do not exhaust the many strategic facets of skilled writing, they clearly illustrate that an important element in becoming a skilled writer is to become a strategic writer. In contrast, young developing writers typically employ an approach to writing that minimizes the use of such strategic processes as monitoring, evaluating, planning, revising, and so on (Graham, 1990; McCutchen, 1988; Scardamalia & Bereiter, 1986). They compose by drawing from memory a relevant idea, writing it down, and using each preceding phrase or sentence to stimulate the next idea. This knowledge-telling approach to writing is dominated by a single composing process—generating writing content. Information that is somewhat topic appropriate is created or retrieved from memory and turned into written language. Developing writers make little attempt to evaluate or rework these ideas or to consider the constraints imposed by the topic, the needs of the audience, or the organization of the text.

It is also important to stress that motivation plays a key role in whether or not young students are strategic (Alexander, Graham, & Harris, 1998). This is aptly illustrated in a Calvin and Hobbes cartoon by Bill Watterson in which Susie, the little girl who lives next door, is staying at Calvin's house after school. Calvin sees her looking at one of her schoolbooks and asks her what she is doing. She tells him that she didn't understand a chapter in the book, so she reviewed her notes on the previous chapter and is rereading the chapter that was unclear. Calvin can't believe it. "All that work," he gasps. Susie explains that she now understands the chapter, but Calvin dismisses her explanation, shaking his head and smirking, "I used to think you were smart."

Contrary to Calvin's opinion, however, Susie's behavior is smart because it is strategic, thoughtful, reflective, and self-directed. These are the same types of characteristics that underlie skilled writing. Consequently, an important goal in writing instruction for young developing writers is to help them become more strategic when composing. This involves helping them learn to do the same types of strategic things that more skilled writers do, including increasing how often and how well they plan, monitor, evaluate, revise, and so forth. One way of doing this is to tackle this problem head-on by directly teaching young developing writers the same kinds of strategies used by their more skilled counterparts. Of course, this does not mean that the strategies you teach children will be exactly the same as the ones used by more experienced and competent skilled writers. Instead, most of them will be simpler but designed to accomplish the same kinds of goals.

The good news is that directly teaching developing writers strategies for planning, revising, and regulating the writing process is very effective (see Graham & Perin, 2007; Rogers & Graham, 2008). This is true in the primary grades for typically developing writers (see Tracy, Reid, & Graham, 2009) as well as children who experience difficulty learning to write (see Graham, Harris, & Mason, 2005; Harris, Graham, & Mason, 2006). I next consider what a strategy is and why teaching writing strategies is beneficial for young developing writers.

WHAT IS A WRITING STRATEGY?

In an earlier book (Graham & Harris, 2005), I applied the collective wisdom of two different children to help me define the attributes of a strategy. The first comment was from a young boy who frequently played "army" with his friends and defined a strategy as not letting the enemy know you are out of ammunition by pretending to keep on firing. This child's definition by example illustrates a basic attribute of a strategy: it is purposeful. Strategic actions involve consciously deciding that a course of action is needed to meet a desired goal. For this youngster, the unstated goal was to stay alive, and the plan for accomplishing this goal was to trick the enemy.

The second comment came from a child who indicated that he would like to know how to invent a pair of glasses with open eyeballs painted on them so he could sit in class and look like he was listening. This child's comment highlights that strategies require procedural or how-to knowledge for accomplishing the target goal. A major obstacle for our young inventor was a lack of knowledge about how to build the special glasses. This procedural know-how can take the form of algorithms, which are step-by-step techniques for accomplishing a specific goal. In writing, this may include knowledge about how to write a certain type of poem, like a haiku. This knowledge can further take the form of a more general guideline or heuristic, such as how to brainstorm ideas for writing.

Two other attributes of a strategy are illustrated in a Calvin and Hobbes cartoon in which Calvin tells Hobbes he has a strategy for reading an entire chapter in his history book. He explains that the secret is to break the task down into manageable chunks and deal with each chunk one at a time. Despite this excellent plan, he tosses the book away saying, "I first ask myself, do I even care?" As Calvin demonstrates, strategies involve more than goals and plans. They require the motivation to carry out the designated courses of action and the effort to see them through.

Strategies, including writing strategies, therefore, are purposeful, procedural, willful, and effortful. Each includes a procedure or plan for accomplishing a desired goal. Strategies must be deliberately activated, and they require commitment and effort to be effective.

WHY IS WRITING STRATEGY INSTRUCTION A GOOD IDEA?

Part of what children require to become good writers is strategic know-how. Employing strategies is essential to becoming a competent writer. No one can become an effective writer without learning how to acquire, organize, and transform ideas for writing, as well as how to regulate writing processes and behaviors (Alexander et al., 1998).

This doesn't mean that strategic knowledge is needed for every writing task. Many writing tasks that occur as a part of everyday life, such as writing a brief note to a friend, usually do not require strategic solutions or a great deal of effort. This is not the case, however, for many of the more important writing assignments children encounter at school. Crafting a story, writing a report, or persuading others through writing are not easy or routine tasks for most young children. Such writing benefits from a deliberate, systematic, and strategic approach by students.

How do writing strategies help young developing writers accomplish such tasks? For one thing, a strategy specifies a course of action for successfully completing the writing task or some part of it. This helps the child organize and sequence his or her actions, thoughts, or behaviors. Consider the process of revising. To revise, a child must first recognize that a change is needed. The child diagnoses the problem (although this is not mandatory), makes a decision on how to change the text, and then carries out this decision (Bereiter & Scardamalia, 1987; Hayes & Flower, 1980). Beginning writers may not be particularly adept at directing their attention to each of these actions in this order (Graham, 1997). This can be addressed by teaching them a strategy that ensures that the separate actions involved in revising are activated and occur in an organized and regular fashion.

A second advantage of teaching writing strategies is that such instruction makes visible and more concrete the mental operations that occur during composing. A writer's strategic behavior is usually hidden from view because it occurs in the "head." When teachers model how to use writing strategies, they make these mental actions more transparent to children by demonstrating verbally and visually how to apply them. In essence, hidden and relatively abstract processes, such as generating ideas for writing, become more tangible.

Another benefit of strategy instruction is that developing writers learn new approaches to composing. Learning new ways of planning, revising, or regulating the writing process is critical for young writers. Contemporary approaches to teaching writing, such as the highly popular Writers' Workshop, for instance, stress the use of predictable routines for writing, encouraging students to plan, draft, edit, revise, and publish their written work. Surprisingly little attention is devoted to teaching these processes in many classrooms (Cutler & Graham, 2008). Such instruction should provide young writers with the tools needed to carry out these processes successfully and effectively.

Finally, an often unrecognized benefit of teaching writing strategies is that it increases children's knowledge about writing, the writing process, and their capabilities as writers (Graham & Harris, 1993). For example, when young students are taught a strategy for planning a story (see the example later in this chapter), they acquire information on the content and structure of stories as well as procedural knowledge about how to generate and organize possible ideas for writing. As they use the strategy, they obtain additional information about the value of the strategy and their competence as writers (Zimmerman & Risemberg, 1997). If the strategy improves children's story writing, their confidence or sense of efficacy concerning writing is likely to improve as well. Enhanced efficacy, in turn, boosts motivation for writing, increases effort, and serves as a catalyst for more strategic behavior. As a result, writing strategies not only influence immediate writing performance but also can contribute to students' overall writing development (Scardamalia & Bereiter, 1985).

HOW SHOULD WRITING STRATEGIES BE TAUGHT?

Because writing strategies are so important to young children's writing development, we must carefully consider how they should be taught. This famous Chinese proverb provides useful guidance in this regard: "I hear and I forget. I see and I remember. I do and I understand" (Kelly-Gangi & Patterson, 2002, p. 87). Describing a writing strategy, its purpose, how to use it, and why it is effective is an essential first step, but this is only the start. Students need to see how the strategy works and practice using it themselves.

For some students, however, hearing, seeing, and doing will not be enough. These students will require even more for writing strategy instruction to be effective. They may require further assistance, including

- Additional explanations about the strategy, its parts, and how it works
- Extra modeling on how to apply it
- Extended feedback and support as they practice using the strategy
- Help with developing mnemonic devices and charts for remembering the steps of the strategy
- Teaching of prerequisite skills and processes needed to use the strategy effectively
- Identification of roadblocks that interfere with mastering the strategy
- Guidance in applying such procedures as self-monitoring and goal setting to help them better regulate their use of the strategy

To be effective with all students, writing strategy instruction must be responsive to individual students' needs and characteristics. A one-size-fits-all approach will not ensure that all children will become strategic writers. An equally important point is that strategy instruction must be substantial enough that students not only gain control over their use of the strategy but also come to value it. Although some writing strategies may be simple enough that young developing writers can master them in a single lesson or mini-lesson, this will not be the case for other strategies. In essence, it is not enough to provide a single lesson for the mastery of a strategy. Instead, strategy instruction will be more effective if you devote a series of related lessons (or mini-lessons) to its mastery, so that it can be adequately explained, modeled, and practiced. Teaching some complex writing strategies, such as how to plan a report, will require longer lessons and even more time.

As noted earlier, strategic behavior involves more than just knowledge and skill. It also involves will. This is captured in the following Chinese proverb: "Teachers open the door, but you must enter yourself" (Kelly-Gangi & Patterson, 2002, p. 45).

The use of a new strategy by students requires both intention and effort. In the case of writing, students are asked to set aside their typical approaches to composing (with which they probably have had some success) and purposefully apply a new procedure. For many students, making the switch to using a new strategy is not easy to do. However, effective writing strategy instruction promotes students' will to use a new strategy by

- Establishing that effort is important in learning and using a new strategy
- Reinforcing students' effort and use of the strategy
- Providing opportunities for students to see how the strategy improves their writing
- Involving students as active collaborators in learning the new strategy (including fostering students' ownership of the strategy)
- Enthusiastic teaching on the part of the teacher

Mastering a new writing strategy is not just dependent on learning how to apply it in a single situation and being motivated to use it—it requires knowing when and where to apply it as well as how to adapt it to new situations (Salomon & Perkins, 1989). Writing strategy instruction should therefore incorporate procedures to promote both maintenance and generalization of strategy use (in other words, using the strategy in, and adapting it for, new situations). These include

- Identifying opportunities to use the new writing strategy
- Setting goals to use the strategy with new tasks
- Considering how to modify the strategy so that it will work in new situations
- Evaluating with students the results of using the strategy with these tasks

Another key principle in effective strategy instruction is to involve students in authentic writing tasks aimed at a real audience. Children are much more likely to apply a new strategy to tasks that are legitimate. This was evident in a class I observed a couple of years ago. They had decided to clean up a local stream. Part of the children's effort involved writing letters to local newspapers as well as the mayor, city council members, and other influential citizens. They wrote for and obtained a local grant to help them clean up the stream. The students in this class were enthusiastic about the project, and it showed in what they wrote and what they did. They were self-directed, and needed little help from their teacher. Moreover, they used planning and revising strategies they were taught earlier in the year without prompting or reminders.

Teachers can also increase the likelihood that students will use newly taught writing strategies if their classrooms are supportive, pleasant, and nonthreatening places. Children are less likely to exert the effort needed to apply a new strategy if they view the classroom as chaotic, unfriendly, or punitive (Graham & Harris, 1994). Listed below are some things you can do to make the writing classroom an enjoyable and supportive place, where students are more likely to use the writing strategies they are taught:

- Establish a classroom in which students feel free to take risks when writing.
- Create an exciting mood during writing time.
- Encourage students to arrange their own writing spaces.
- Develop writing assignments that reflect students' interests.
- Allow students to make decisions about what they write.
- Praise students for their effort, use of strategy, and accomplishments
- Conference with students about their writing goals, advances, and setbacks on current projects.
- Encourage students to help each other as they plan, write, and revise and edit their work.
- Ask students to share their work with each other.

Finally, no writing strategy is effective in all situations and with all students. Just because a writing strategy improved children's writing in a research study or someone else's classroom does not guarantee that it will be effective with all students in your classroom. This makes *evaluation* a critical, but often overlooked, component of strategy instruction. Evaluation, in addition to providing confirmation that the writing strategy worked as intended, is beneficial for three other reasons. One, teachers who closely assess the effectiveness of what they do are better able to take charge of the teaching process, making modifications and adjustments as needed.

Two, ongoing evaluation of writing strategy instruction allows teachers to learn more about themselves and their students. This provides teachers with considerable insight into how effective their teaching is and what types of adjustments in teaching their students need. Three, ongoing evaluation is important to students' growth as writers. If instruction is ineffective and not modified, students will likely devalue the strategies they are learning and may interpret their lack of progress as an indication of their incompetence.

AN EXAMPLE

I illustrate the principles of effective strategy instruction with an example in which a writing strategy for planning and drafting a story was taught to young children (Danoff, Harris, & Graham, 1993). The strategy involved generating ideas for each basic part of a story in advance of writing. The teacher encouraged students to embellish and upgrade these initial plans as they wrote. The steps of the strategy are presented below:

Step 1. Think of a story that you would like to share with others.

Step 2. Let your mind be free.

Step 3. Write down the story part reminder:

W-W-W

What = 2

How = 2

Step 4. Make notes for each question below:

Who is the main character; who else is in the story?

When does the story take place?

Where does the story take place?

What does the main character want to do; what do the other characters want to do?

What happens when the main character tries to do it; what happens with the other characters?

How does the story end?

How does the main character feel; how do other characters feel?

Step 5. Write your story—use good parts; add, elaborate, or revise as you write; and make good sense.

The class was taught conjointly by a general education teacher and a special education teacher. The teachers worked directly in the classroom with students with special needs and other children who required additional assistance. After reviewing students' writing portfolios, the teachers decided to teach the strategy above. The portfolios indicated that some of the children in the class, including those with special needs, wrote stories that were incomplete. Other students could improve their story writing by including greater detail and elaboration as well as more action. The teachers also wanted to help several students who were anxious about writing to establish a stronger sense of motivation, or an "I can do it" attitude. This included all of the students with special needs and two students struggling with writing.

The two teachers decided that the special education teacher would take the lead in teaching the strategy, but both teachers would play an active role in instruction, allowing them to better respond to individual needs. The strategy was taught during Writers' Workshop, which included students' consulting with their peers when planning and revising their papers, conferencing regularly with teachers about their work, sharing their in-progress and completed work with classmates, selecting papers for publication, and reflecting on their writing accomplishments and challenges in their journals (Atwell, 1987; Graves, 1983). Although students typically chose the topics for their papers, the teachers selected the genre (in this case story writing). Initially, the strategy was taught as an extended series of mini-lesson sessions, lasting approximately twenty to thirty minutes each. Once students started to apply the strategy by themselves (with teacher assistance as needed), mini-lesson sessions for the whole class ceased and the children practiced using the strategy as part of the regular Writers' Workshop approach.

The first session involved a conference with the entire class. The class discussed what they knew about story writing, including identifying the common parts of a story (in other words, setting, characters' goals, actions to achieve the goals, ending, and characters' reactions). The teachers described the target writing strategy, and the class talked about how including and expanding story parts improve a story. The teachers established the goals for learning the strategy (to write better stories that are more fun to read and write), and explained how they planned to teach it, emphasizing students' roles as collaborators (including the possibility that they might serve as tutors for other students learning the strategy in the future). They also stressed the importance of effort in mastering the strategy. Each student made a commitment to learn the strategy.

During the next session, the class focused even greater attention on the basic parts of a story, concentrating on the setting (characters, place, and time) and story episodes (precipitating event, characters' goals, actions to achieve goals, resolution, and characters' reactions). They examined several familiar stories to identify these elements and discussed the different ways authors use and develop these parts. They further considered how knowledge of story parts helps the reader understand the author's message. To make sure students understood each story element, the class generated ideas for story parts using different story lines.

Students also selected stories they had previously written from their portfolios and determined which parts they had included, with the teachers showing them how to graph the number of parts they included. At this point, the teachers explained that students would keep a graph showing the number of parts in each story they wrote as they learned to use the strategy. This would allow them to monitor the completeness of their stories and the effects of learning the strategy. For students who included all or nearly all story parts in previously written stories, the teachers stressed that more detail, elaboration, and action would improve these parts.

In the third session, the teachers reintroduced the planning and drafting strategy described above. Each student was provided with a chart listing the strategy steps and a mnemonic (W-W-W; What = 2; How = 2) for remembering the questions for the parts of a story (Step 3). They discussed the purpose for each step as well as where and how to use the strategy (for example, when writing stories, book reports, and biographies).

During the fourth session, which was expanded to last the full class period, the special education teacher modeled (while "thinking out loud") how to use the strategy. Students participated in this activity by helping the teacher as she planned and made notes for each story part, and as she wrote the first draft (in which the initial plan was also modified and upgraded). Before starting, the teacher set a goal to include all story parts and "think of a lot of ideas for each one." She explained that students should set similar goals before writing their stories and check to see if they had met them once they were finished. Once the modeled story was completed, the class looked to see if it included and fully presented all the parts. The teacher verbally congratulated herself for achieving her goal and graphed the results, noting that she was able to do so as a result of using the strategy and working hard. At the end of this session, the teachers asked the students if they could suggest any changes that would make the strategy better. Although the students did not suggest any changes, the teachers revisited this issue in later lessons.

In the next session, students memorized the mnemonic and the strategy steps. The teachers explained that it would be easier to use the strategy if students did not have to spend time looking up the steps, mnemonic, and so forth. Most students practiced memorizing these items with partners, and had mastered them in less than twenty minutes. Several students needed additional time and help from one of the teachers to fully memorize them.

Students now began to use the writing strategy as they wrote their own stories during Writers' Workshop, receiving assistance from the teachers as needed. The students with special needs and a few other children received an additional session, during which they collaboratively planned a story with the special education teacher. This allowed the teacher to ensure that they correctly understood how to use the strategy, mnemonic, and self-regulation procedures (goal setting, counting, and graphing story parts) correctly. The other students in the class also planned and wrote their first stories collaboratively, but with peers. The general education teacher provided them with help if they needed it.

As students continued to practice applying the strategy during Writers' Workshop, the two teachers modified the amount and intensity of their support. Assistance included additional explanation about the strategy and remodeling of how to use some parts of it. In some instances, help concentrated on planning for greater detail and elaboration or increasing the goals and actions of the characters in the story. As soon as possible, such support was faded, and teachers emphasized students' independent use of the strategy.

Most students were able to apply the strategy and accompanying self-regulation procedures correctly and efficiently after writing three stories. Students who needed additional assistance received it from the teachers until they could use the strategy easily and independently.

As a wrap-up, the teachers held a conference with the whole class to evaluate the strategy. Students told the teachers they were glad that they had learned the strategy because it helped them write better stories. The class also identified opportunities for applying what they had learned, and they agreed to hold a review session once a month to revisit the strategy and their successes in using it, and to modify it if needed.

A LAST COMMENT

All children are capable of writing well. To do this, however, they need to learn how to use the same tools as good writers. The writing strategies presented in this book provide a bridge for young developing writers to begin their journey toward competence, providing them with vehicles for becoming more thoughtful, reflective, and self-directed writers. Although developing writers also need to master a variety of other writing skills (for example, handwriting, spelling, and sentence construction), becoming more strategic is essential to becoming a good writer.

REFERENCES

Alexander, P., Graham, S., & Harris, K. (1998). A perspective on strategy research: Progress and prospects. *Educational Psychology Review, 10,* 129–154.

Associated Press. (1995, December 27). This man gives children "Goosebumps" and "Fear Street." *Valdosta Daily Times,* p. B1.

Atwell, N. (1987). *In the middle: Writing, reading, and learning with adolescents.* Portsmouth, NH: Heinemann.

Bereiter, C., & Scardamalia, M. (1987). *The psychology of written composition.* Hillsdale, NJ: Erlbaum.

Bradbury, R. (1992). *Zen and the art of writing.* New York: Bantam Books.

Burnham, S. (1994). *For writers only.* New York: Ballantine Books.

Cowley, M. (1958). *Writers at work: The Paris Review interviews.* New York: Viking Press.

Cutler, L., & Graham, S. (2008). Primary grade writing instruction: A national survey. *Journal of Educational Psychology, 100,* 907–919.

Danoff, B., Harris, K. R., & Graham, S. (1993). Incorporating strategy instruction within the writing process in the regular classroom: Effects on the writing of students with and without learning disabilities. *Journal of Reading Behavior, 25,* 295–319.

Eco, U. (1982). The narrative structure in Fleming. In B. Wattes, T. Bennett, & G. Martin (Eds.), *Popular culture: Past and present* (pp. 245–262). London: Croom Helm.

Graham, S. (1990). The role of production factors in learning disabled students' compositions. *Journal of Educational Psychology, 82,* 781–791.

Graham, S. (1997). Executive control in the revising of students with learning and writing difficulties. *Journal of Educational Psychology, 89,* 223–234.

Graham, S. (2006). Writing. In P. Alexander & P. Winne (Eds.), *Handbook of Educational Psychology* (pp. 457–478). Mahwah, NJ: Erlbaum.

Graham, S., & Harris, K. R. (1993). Self-regulated strategy development: Helping students with learning problems develop as writers. *Elementary School Journal, 94,* 169–182.

Graham, S., & Harris, K. R. (1994). The role and development of self-regulation in the writing process. In D. Schunk & B. Zimmerman (Eds.), *Self-regulation of learning and performance: Issues and educational applications* (pp. 203–228). New York: Erlbaum.

Graham, S., & Harris, K. R. (2005). *Writing better: Teaching writing processes and self-regulation to students with learning problems.* Baltimore: Brookes.

Graham, S., Harris, K. R., & Mason, L. (2005). Improving the writing performance, knowledge, and motivation of struggling young writers: The effects of self-regulated strategy development. *Contemporary Educational Psychology, 30,* 207–241.

Graham, S., & Perin, D. (2007). A meta-analysis of writing instruction for adolescent students. *Journal of Educational Psychology, 99,* 445–476.

Graves, D. (1983). *Writing: Teachers and children at work.* Exeter, NH: Heinemann.

Harris, K. R., Graham, S., & Mason, L. (2006). Improving the writing, knowledge, and motivation of struggling young writers: Effects of self-regulated strategy development with and without peer support. *American Educational Research Journal, 43,* 295–340.

Hayes, J. R., & Flower, L. S. (1980). Identifying the organization of writing processes. In L. Gregg & E. Steinberg (Eds.), *Cognitive processes in writing* (pp. 3–30). Hillsdale, NJ: Erlbaum.

Hendrickson, R. (1994). *The literary life and other curiosities.* San Diego, CA: Harcourt and Brace.

Hubbell, S. (1996, October 27). News from an uncharted world. *Washington Post: Bookworld,* pp. 1, 8.

Kazin, A. (1967). *Writers at work: The Paris Review interviews.* New York: Viking Press.

Kelly-Gangi, C., & Patterson, J. (2002). *The gift of teaching: A book of favorite quotations to inspire and encourage.* New York: Barnes & Noble.

Lamb, B. (1997). *Booknotes: America's finest authors on reading, writing, and the power of ideas.* New York: Random House.

McCutchen, D. (1988). "Functional automaticity" in children's writing: A problem of metacognitive control. *Written Communication, 5,* 306–324.

Rogers, L., & Graham, S. (2008). A meta-analysis of single subject design writing intervention research. *Journal of Educational Psychology, 100,* 879–906.

Salomon, G., & Perkins, D. (1989). Rocky roads to transfer: Rethinking mechanisms of a neglected phenomena. *Educational Psychologist, 24,* 113–142.

Scardamalia, M., & Bereiter, C. (1985). Fostering the development of self-regulation in children's knowledge processing. In S. Chipman, J. Segal, & R. Glaser (Eds.), *Thinking and learning skills: Current research and open questions* (Vol. 2, pp. 563–577). Hillsdale, NJ: Erlbaum.

Scardamalia, M., & Bereiter, C. (1986). Written composition. In M. Wittrock (Ed.), *Handbook of research on teaching* (3rd ed., pp. 778–803). New York: Macmillan.

Shapiro, M. (2000). *J. K. Rowling: The wizard behind Harry Potter.* New York: St. Martin's Griffin.

Tracy, B., Reid, R., & Graham, S. (2009). Teaching young students strategies for planning and drafting stories: The impact of self-regulated strategy development. *Journal of Educational Research, 102,* 323–329.

Wallace, I., & Pear, J. J. (1977). Self-control techniques of famous novelists. *Journal of Applied Behavior Analysis, 10,* 515–525.

Zimmerman, B. J., & Risemberg, R. (1997). Becoming a self-regulated writer: A social cognitive perspective. *Contemporary Educational Psychology, 22,* 73–101.

Chapter

Incorporating the SCAMPER Writing Strategy Mini-Lesson Model into Your Writing Program

CINDY LASSONDE AND JANET RICHARDS

Thoughtful, flexible use of strategies when writing is a chief characteristic of skilled writers and should be an instruction goal of all teachers (Lenski & Nierstheimer, 2002). In this book, we define the term *strategy* as an intentional "sequence of cognitive steps designed to accomplish a particular outcome" (Collins, 1998, p. viii). Students who use strategies as writing tools to improve their ability to solve problems and accomplish writing tasks or goals learn to trust their decisions, ask clarifying questions, self-monitor and evaluate their accomplishments and mistakes, develop personal processes for learning, and set personal goals as they improve their writing (Beckman, 2002). Strategic writers learn how and when to use strategies effectively and how to imbed strategic behaviors into their schemata so strategies become automatic resources for learning.

As educators, we are responsible for teaching students the value of learning and applying multiple writing strategies according to their needs. These strategies include the following (Beckman, 2002):

- **Making associations**—"I can spell *caught* because I know how to spell *taught*."
- **Planning**—"I'll use this graphic organizer to think about what I want to write."
- **Questioning**—"When my friends read this, will they think it's funny or boring?"
- **Visualizing**—"Let's see. What would a person look like here if she were scared?"

- **Accessing cues**—"I remember that secret song that tells me how to sound out a word."
- **Using mnemonics**—"I'll use CSPS (characters, settings, problems, solutions) to help me remember the four main parts of a story."
- **Revising**—"This checklist will help me make my story better so others will understand what I want to say."
- **Checking and monitoring**—"Does this make sense?"
- **Verbalizing**—"I'm going to read this to you. Tell me how it sounds."

Strategy instruction focuses on the learner's needs and helping the learner become automatic in his or her use of multiple strategies across content areas and learning situations (Beckman, 2002). "Explicit strategy instruction includes teacher modeling, scaffolding, and coaching, with direct explanation for why strategies are valuable and how and when to use them" (Guthrie, 2001, p. 7). In this chapter, we introduce you to the SCAMPER writing strategy mini-lesson model, which represents an intentional set of components designed to promote K–3 students' learning and effective application of writing strategies.

YOUR K–3 STUDENTS' WRITING

Take a moment to think about your K–3 writing program.

- What does it look like?
- Do you use a writing workshop approach?
- Do you teach a variety of writing genres?
- Do you integrate writing instruction with reading and within such content areas as science, social studies, and math?
- Do you follow a required writing program?
- Do students understand and use the writing process?
- Do students observe you as you compose?
- When and how do you assess what students know about writing?
- How do you provide individualized attention to students' writing needs?

Now, reflect on students' writing in your class.

- Are they developing strategies they can apply across writing contexts? How can you tell?
- How much time each day do you devote to students' collaborative or independent writing?
- Are they all engaged and confident writers?

Thoughtful reflection about your writing program and students' writing in your class will help you identify and analyze the goals you want to achieve with young writers. No matter what approach you use to teach writing, your overall goal, undoubtedly, is to equip students with the tools they need to become self-regulated, independent, strategic writers. That is, you want your students to develop personal learning schemata or sets of writing strategies that they use and self-monitor automatically with self-assertion and confidence (Beckman, 2002). You want your students to go on to the next grade level having learned and practiced the thinking processes they will use to address future writing challenges. Whether students compose invitations or notes to friends, create stories or poems, complete homework assignments, or respond in writing for assessment purposes, you want young writers to possess a repertoire of effective strategies they can readily access with the ease and confidence of an accomplished archer reaching for arrows from a quiver. And, of course, you want them to know how to use these strategies appropriately in various contexts for the best results.

We know teachers' and students' time is in high demand. Educators are overloaded with teaching requirements. Students may think they don't have time to learn even one more thing (Beckman, 2002). There are never enough hours in the day or days in the school year to achieve all of the learning goals and reach all of the expectations you and your students set for their writing. Of course, you don't want to waste time. You don't want to teach writing strategies students already know. Students lose interest when they are already familiar and proficient with an aspect of writing you might teach. You also don't want to have writers struggle with writing strategies they are not yet developmentally ready to understand and apply. They lose confidence when instruction is beyond their current developmental stages and needs. We know you want to improve students' writing performance results through effective, time-efficient intervention and problem-solving processes. That is why we developed the SCAMPER model of teaching writing strategies.

WHAT IS SCAMPER?

The SCAMPER model is based not only on the theoretical frameworks and knowledge-based themes previously outlined in the introduction to this book but also on our combined extensive experiences writing with primary students and noting what strategies help them improve their writing and their writing confidence. The SCAMPER model represents a learning process tailored to the instruction of writing strategies in a mini-lesson format. Each of the strategy chapters in this book represents a series of several sequenced mini-lesson sessions that you can schedule into your writing curriculum. The mini-lesson format allows you to meet your students' writing instruction needs through fifteen- to thirty-minute, differentiated, direct-instruction sessions that can be connected to any district, school, or class writing program.

SCAMPER is an easy-to-remember acronym that will help you and your students remember all of the parts of an effective model for teaching writing in a problem-solving way. Each of the strategies included in Sections Two through Five of this book is structured according to the SCAMPER model. We describe the components of the SCAMPER model here; but, as you read through and begin to integrate the writing strategy mini-lessons into your writing curriculum, you will come to understand the power of SCAMPER clearly. SCAMPER stands for

Survey and Assess
Confer
Assemble Materials
Model

Practice

Execute

Reflect

You will want to read each strategy fully before you schedule your mini-lesson sessions for the week. We recommend you devote a fifteen-minute whole-class session just to **survey and assess** your students, the first component of the SCAMPER model; this will allow you to select a small group of students with whom you will work on the chosen strategy. The next day, spend another session to **confer** with your small group, the second component of the model. Then, **assemble materials** you will need, and plan to **model** the strategy the following day. The remaining components of the model—**practice, execute, and reflect**—may be combined into one or two mini-lesson sessions or planned for three separate sessions. You know your students and their writing and learning needs; this model allows you to decide how much to teach of a particular mini-lesson on a certain day. Determine which parts of the SCAMPER model you want to combine and which you want to plan as separate mini-lesson sessions. Then, as you proceed with each session, observe to determine if you will need to repeat one of the components of the model. For example, your students might need more practice before they can independently execute the strategy. The model is flexible and should be adjusted as necessary.

We think it is important to restate that a particularly essential aspect of the SCAMPER model is that both teachers and students understand what students need to learn next about writing, so teachers do not waste valuable time teaching facets of writing students already know and use with proficiency. SCAMPER promotes self-regulated learning; that is, through the SCAMPER process, students reflect on the strategies they have learned and use, and the benefits of these strategies. When teachers survey and assess students' writing requirements, they become familiar with their students' zones of proximal development (ZPD) and do not present writing lessons that surpass students' current understanding and exceed their existing ZPD (Vygotsky, 1978). The model also coincides with the key elements of Response to Intervention (RtI), which we discuss later in this chapter. In the following sections, we describe each of the components of SCAMPER in more detail.

(S) Survey and Assess

The initial component of SCAMPER, in which you **survey and assess,** allows you to quickly determine your students' specific writing instruction needs. How would you evaluate whether or not students would benefit from learning to use a designated strategy at this stage in their writing development? Perhaps some of your students already use the strategy or are not at the appropriate zone of proximal development in which being exposed to this strategy would benefit them. You would not teach these students the designated strategy. Be purposeful and specific as you survey and assess students' writing needs. The Survey and Assess section of each strategy chapter in this book provides contextualized suggestions for how to go about determining which students would benefit from learning the designated strategy.

Your immediate task is to determine exactly what aspects of composing individual students need to learn next about writing. Jot down the names of students and what they need to learn next in your Writing Strategies Notebook.

Then categorize students' writing needs so you can form small groups of students who are ready to learn the same strategy. You will see in the mini-lessons that we describe specific observable behaviors to look for in students' responses and writing to determine what strategies would be helpful in teaching them to improve their work. For example, if you observe that some of your students struggle when they attempt to write nonfiction pieces, they may be ready to learn the strategy in Chapter Twenty-Five, Comprehensive, Step-by-Step Composing for Nonfiction Writing. If they are not ready to learn the entire comprehensive strategy, you might model and teach them parts of the strategy, such as how to determine what they know about a topic prior to writing. In the same way, if you see that some of your students forget to include a basic story feature in their stories, you might decide to teach them the strategy in Chapter Eight, Let's Tell a Story. Once you are familiar with all of the strategies in this book, you will undoubtedly become adept at recognizing what will fit your students' needs. Your strategy instruction will develop continuity and flow. And your students' writing will benefit!

(C) Confer

Following surveying and assessing, **confer** or talk with students about a strategy's purpose. Each strategy chapter provides contextualized recommendations for focused, intentional conversations. In general, encourage your students to talk about their perceived writing goals and needs. Then explain how a particular strategy will help them improve their writing. This is an important part of the model because it inspires students to become engaged, self-regulated, and self-motivated writers. When students understand the purpose and rationale behind these strategies, their learning becomes authentic and meaningful. They develop confidence in themselves as writers and take control of their independent writing.

(A) Assemble Materials

To be well prepared, you want to **assemble materials** before actually beginning the remaining components of the mini-lesson. We like to have a basket of common writing and instruction materials at hand for small-group writing times. The basket might include a few markers of different colors, scissors, a ruler, Post-it notes in a variety of colors, transparent tape, and correction tape. Also, within your small-group writing area, have a supply of large sheets of paper, wall-size chart paper, and an easel. Before you begin the modeling part of the lesson, check to see what additional materials you will need.

The "A" in SCAMPER presents your opportunity to transition from conferring (a listening and conversational mode) to modeling (a more structured, direct-instruction mode). Organize the resources you and students will need when you model the strategy. Arrange your necessary tools (which previously were out of sight to avoid distracting students), focus students, and take a deep breath as you collect your thoughts. Prepare to present a clear, sequenced think-aloud as you demonstrate and model the new strategy.

(M) Model

"Modeling writing is an important element in guiding students' writing toward success" (Karle, 2005, p. 2). This component, in which you **model** the strategy, involves demonstrating how to use the strategy as you share your thinking processes aloud in front of students. For example, consider Chapter Twenty-Four, Making Pictures. You might model your thinking processes by telling a short story or nursery rhyme, and then closing your eyes and sharing all the images you have about the story or rhyme. For example, you might tell the rhyme "Jack and Jill." Then, with your eyes closed, you might say,

> *I saw green grass, a hill that was not too tall, two children holding hands as they went up the hill, a well with a triangular top over it, a bucket or pail used to scoop up water from the well, and a large spoon to enable people to ladle water from the pail....*

Strategies are cognitive processes, so this part of the model encourages students to follow your train of thought as you meet, problem solve, and resolve writing challenges while they watch and listen. You may find you need to model your thinking with more than one example, or you might need to repeat this component within different contexts (such as in various content areas or genres). Therefore, you might decide to repeat this component of the strategy by planning two modeling sessions on consecutive days. You will make these kinds of decisions based on your students' needs and your understanding of their learning and writing abilities.

(P) Practice

Next, help students **practice** the strategy. Provide repeated chances as needed for students to practice the strategy under your supervision and guidance. During this part of the model, confirm and redirect as needed to facilitate students' success with the strategy. With each practice example, step back a bit more to lead students toward independent and self-regulated use of the strategy. "Supportive scaffolds ... are learner-centered events that provide students with situations in which students can co-construct learning with an adult or a more knowledgeable other" (Lenski & Nierstheimer, 2002, p. 130). Bruner (1978, p. 19) explains that when a more knowledgeable individual scaffolds a learner, the learner "can concentrate on the difficult skill she is in the process of acquiring." The key to this component of the model is that you are right beside the students, working through the practice examples with them. Be attentive as you continue to observe and assess students' needs. If you find students need more practice before moving on to applying the strategy independently in the next part of the model—executing the strategy—schedule a second practice session for the following day. The SCAMPER model encourages this type of flexibility in scheduling and teaching.

You may decide during this step to have students record something in their Writing Strategies Journals.

What Is a Writing Strategies Journal?

A Writing Strategies Journal is a personal, informational writing resource that each student develops. Students regularly add to and consult their journals as part of assignments across content areas. In their journals, students

- Store or create personally meaningful notes, diagrams, graphic organizers, pictures, examples, and other cues to help them remember and apply specific writing strategies when they are writing independently across content areas
- Save effective and meaningful teacher-provided resources and handouts (such as sample graphic organizers to use for planning writing or illustrated mnemonic devices)
- Practice using and executing various writing strategies
- Reflect on their writing progress

We recommend that each entry in the journal be meaningful to the student. The journal should not become a place for the student just to copy and store notes. Within the strategy chapters in this book we have included recommendations for the types of cues, responses, and resources your students will find helpful and that are most likely to make meaningful additions to their journals. Each student's journal should reflect his or her writing development, individual needs, and personal learning schemata. Allow students to use and add to their Writing Strategies Journals across content areas and learning situations, not just during writing strategy mini-lessons.

(E) Execute

Scaffold and support students as they **execute** the strategy in authentic writing. This component of the SCAMPER model provides opportunities for peers to write together, collaboratively teach one another, develop confidence, and become independent and self-regulated in their uses of the strategy. Vygotsky (1978) proposed that true learning takes place in the natural exchange of language between students and peers and students and adults in an interactive, social environment. This position supports collaborative writing groups in which primary writers have considerable opportunities to talk with peers and the teacher about how they are using a given strategy (National Council of Teachers of English, 2004). The cognitive benefits of peer discourse and the active role of students as participants in their own learning have been the subject of numerous studies (Haneda & Wells, 2000; Van Slys, 2003). All of our strategies offer creative ideas for collaborative implementation.

(R) Reflect

Help students **reflect** on how they use the strategy in their independent writing. Encourage and guide students to talk about their writing and their uses of the strategy to confirm the strategy's effectiveness and the likelihood they will apply it in the future. This piece provides closure for the mini-lesson, leading the teacher and students in a full circle back to the conferring phase. Students' reflections will lead them to understand how applying the strategy improved and enhanced their writing.

SCAMPER AND RESPONSE TO INTERVENTION (RTI)

SCAMPER and RtI go hand in hand. RtI is defined as "the practice of providing high-quality instruction and intervention matched to student need, monitoring progress frequently to make decisions about changes in instruction or goals, and applying child response data to important educational decisions" (National Association of State Directors of Special Education and Council of Administrators of Special Education, 2006). RtI principles include

- Evidence-based instruction that supports learning
- Differentiated instruction that allows intervention to be delivered immediately, instead of waiting for students to "fail"
- Time for practice
- Use of assessment data to inform instruction

The SCAMPER model is based on education research that is key to best practices in teaching writing. Also, each chapter in this section and each strategy chapter cites current research applicable to this model. When you assess students' strengths and needs and select appropriate strategies, you will be equipped to differentiate instruction to meet students' needs. They won't have to struggle endlessly with their writing, because you will confer with them and support and scaffold their progress. SCAMPER provides opportunities for teacher-student practice and student-student practice as students execute strategies during supervised mini-lessons. Furthermore, SCAMPER provides structure through a systematic approach that matches instruction to needs. The goal of the process is to accelerate learning for all. When SCAMPER is incorporated into the structure of writing strategy mini-lessons, all students can learn to write.

Finally, SCAMPER is appropriate for intense intervention as a core instruction model (see RtI's Tier 1), which represents the majority of students; as a small-group model (see RtI's Tier 2); and as an individualized model (RtI's Tier 3). (See National Association of State Directors of Special Education and Council of Administrators of Special Education, 2006, for a description of each tier.) The inherent structure of the SCAMPER model is adaptable to all levels of instruction; however, this book focuses on small-group intervention (Tier 2), in which teachers coach writers and closely guide them through practice, scaffolding, and reflection. (For more information on RtI and Tier 2, we recommend a comprehensive guide offered by Renaissance Learning. This guide, "Making RTI Work: A Practical Guide to Using Data for a Successful 'Response to Intervention' Program" (2010) is available at no cost from www.renlearn.com.)

THE RECURSIVE NATURE OF SCAMPER

The writing process—inventing, drafting, conferring, revising, editing, and publishing—is recursive, and the steps of the process are intertwined. When students write, you will note that sometimes they return to brainstorming even after they have drafted. Or they might revise first drafts, then step back in the writing process to draft new sections. Conferring could be repeated during or after each step.

Similarly, although we present the steps to SCAMPER in a linear model, we don't think of SCAMPER as a prescribed instruction paradigm. For example, as you follow the SCAMPER model you will find that you won't necessarily always move from P to E (Practice to Execute). You may discover, as you observe students trying out a strategy, that you need to provide more modeling before students can comprehend how to apply the strategy to a new example. Or you might need to reassess students' application of the strategy as they work with their peers toward using it confidently and independently. Conversations with peers might reveal gaps or misunderstandings in learning. Through close coaching, you will adjust the structure of the SCAMPER mini-lesson to fit students' needs. In the next section, we offer further suggestions for matching SCAMPER to your students' requirements and your classroom community.

CONTEXTUALIZING SCAMPER IN YOUR CLASSROOM COMMUNITY

The background chapters in Section One and the strategies in Sections Two through Five integrate and contextualize the SCAMPER model. The third chapter in this book, Architecture of a Mini-Lesson by Anne Marie Juola-Rushton, portrays how Anne integrates the SCAMPER model into her young students' daily writing.

One of the wonderful benefits of the SCAMPER model is that it makes students aware of the components of learning to write. They become metacognitive about their learning and application of writing strategies. When they know the model, they are aware that during the conferring phase, the teacher values their input. They recognize the use of modeling as a teaching approach to which they should pay attention. They understand that practice and reflection include monitoring their learning and thinking processes, and talking about them with others. They develop ways to talk about writing and writing strategies.

We invite you to think of various contexts that might fit your classroom and community culture and the SCAMPER model. For example, you might set up a city-based atmosphere in your classroom in which students move from one strategy station to the next. Each strategy station is set up with props so each center represents a different city building, such as the public library (with stacks of books), the city bank (with a play cash register and money in the center of the table), and the post office (with mail slots and delivered mail). You could also add other dramatic props, such as special hats children wear at each station to represent something the workers at that site might wear. You might even place the stations around the school. If you have consulting teachers working with your students, you could move a group of students to the principal's office (city hall) or the nurse's office (city hospital) to work at a special strategy station. Or you could integrate a content area theme into the SCAMPER model. Wouldn't it be exciting for students' successes at the strategy stations to move them through a sequence in which each develops from a chrysalis into a monarch butterfly? You could artistically create a way to visually represent to each child his or her progress through the centers. How about a SCAMPER Strategy Day in which the entire primary division in your school celebrates strategic writing? Use your imagination. The key is to contextualize the learning experience for students without overshadowing the objective of learning helpful writing strategies through SCAMPER.

TO *SCAMPER*

In closing, we'd like to leave you with these thoughts. To *scamper* means to run quickly or to playfully run about as a child does ("Scamper," n.d.). We like to use the definition of *scamper* as a metaphor because it relates to the objectives behind the creation of our SCAMPER acronym in several ways:

- SCAMPER aims to make the most of valuable instruction and learning time so that writing development progressively moves forward. Students' writing development cannot help but advance steadily, rather than stall, when teachers follow the structure SCAMPER offers.

- The SCAMPER model is flexible and can be adapted to meet the needs of your students. While teaching a strategy you can scamper from one mini-lesson component to another as needed.

- Writing programs that effectively incorporate the SCAMPER mini-lesson writing strategies promote writing in a supportive way that students can comprehend and enjoy. They become more at ease and successful with strategic writing than they have ever been before, due to the support and reinforcement they experience through SCAMPER.

- The SCAMPER model only takes about fifteen to thirty minutes from each day. The strategies presented in this resource are meant to be direct-instruction mini-lessons that are just a part of your writing program.

- When strategies are taught through the SCAMPER model, they become quick shots of instruction students need to improve their writing.

We think SCAMPER will give your students and you the confidence you need to scamper about playfully with your writing! Enjoy!

REFERENCES

Beckman, P. (2002). *Strategy instruction*. ERIC Clearinghouse on Disabilities and Gifted Education (ERIC ED). Digest #E638. Arlington, VA. Retrieved September 7, 2010, from www.ericdigests.org/2003-5/strategy.htm.

Bruner, J. S. (1978). The role of dialogue in language acquisition. In A. Sinclair, R. J. Jarvella, & W.J.M. Levelt (Eds.), *The child's conception of language* (pp. 241–256). Berlin: Springer-Verlag.

Collins, M. (1998). *The parents' and teachers' guide to helping young children learn*. Cutchoque, NY: Preschool.

Guthrie, J. T. (2001). *Preparing students for high-stakes testing in reading*. Newark, DE: International Reading Association.

Haneda, M., & Wells, G. (2000). Writing in knowledge-building communities. *Research in the Teaching of English, 34*, 430–459.

Karle, C. (2005). Unlocking the mystery of writing. In G. Tompkins & K. Blanchfield (Eds., pp. 1–3). *50 ways to develop strategic writers.* Upper Saddle River, NJ: Pearson/ Merrill/Prentice Hall.

Lenski, S., & Nierstheimer, S. (2002). Strategy instruction from a sociocognitive perspective. *Reading Psychology, 23*, 127–143.

Making RTI work: A practical guide to using data for a successful "Response to Intervention" program. (2010). *Renaissance learning.* Retrieved September 22, 2010, from http://doc.renlearn.com/KMNet/R004336320GJBD8A.pdf.

National Association of State Directors of Special Education and Council of Administrators of Special Education. (2006). *Response to intervention: NASDSE and CASE white paper on RTI.* Retrieved June 23, 2009, from www.nasdse.org/Portals/0/ Documents/Download%20Publications/RTIAnAdministratorsPerspective1-06.pdf.

National Council of Teachers of English. (2004). *NCTE beliefs about the teaching of writing.* Received September 22, 2010, from www.ncte.org/positions/statements/ writingbeliefs.

Scamper. (n.d.). *Collins English dictionary—Complete and unabridged 10th edition.* Retrieved September 30, 2010, from http://dictionary.reference.com/browse/ scamper?&qsrc=.

Van Slys, K. (2003). Writing and identity construction: A young author's life in transition. *Language Arts, 80*(3), 176–184.

Vygotsky, L. (1978). *Mind in society: The development of higher psychological processes* (M. Cole, Trans.). Cambridge, MA: Harvard University Press.

Architecture of a Mini-Lesson

ANNE MARIE JUOLA-RUSHTON

I remember one morning watching my two-year-old daughter Olivia play. She had papers of all sizes spread across her bedroom floor. With pencils, crayons, and markers, she had scribbled notes in an effort to use written text as a tool to communicate with her world. Olivia had proudly written ''letters'' by stuffing scribbled notes into envelopes and stacking them with meticulous care. When I caught her glance, she gleamed with pride about her work. I carefully captured the moment within my memory bank, not wanting to forget the dedication, fervor, and joy she packed into each writing piece.

When I became a primary educator, it was my hope to develop a community of writers filled with the same confidence and joy Olivia had about her writing that day I had observed her writing letters in her bedroom. I was apprehensive about the writing mandates, packaged curriculum, and testing pressures that awaited me as a classroom teacher. However, I reminded myself that it was my responsibility as a teacher to design a writing approach to meet the needs of all my students.

During my first years of teaching, as I worked on my master's degree, I attended professional development workshops and read everything I could get my hands on to increase my ability to provide a framework for success in my writing classroom. Overwhelmed at first by the vision of transforming all my new learning into a working curriculum, I gradually began to recognize common threads that writing researchers offered. Balancing the selections of writing curricula from which I had to choose, over time I integrated writing theory with pedagogy. The SCAMPER model in which I incorporate those writing ideas is infused with a sense of priority, passion, and grace: priority to commit to writing instruction, passion to develop curious authors, and grace to connect my writing instruction seamlessly to not only the school day but also life.

Every day I bring to my students all the conversations about writing I've ever had and my commitment and awareness to learn from each student. In the end, the teaching of writing happens in small, intimate moments just like the time I caught my daughter creating her written masterpieces. What I've learned as a writing teacher is that these small, intimate moments of authorship intertwine with curriculum preparation I bring to instruction. In this chapter I will introduce you to the architecture of a mini-lesson as a bridge to connect the development of writing instruction with the personal experiences about which students yearn to write.

PURPOSE OF THE WRITING STRATEGY MINI-LESSON

All of the students are gathered in our cozy meeting area. In my classroom, I use the classroom library area because it provides the environment of cooperation and collaboration for our writing instruction. The purpose of gathering students together in a whole-class or small-group format is to teach a strategy they can use as writers not only during their independent writing time in class but also in their writing lives. It is through the mini-lesson that young authors recognize the usefulness of writing in their world. Children learn that there are genres of writing, from lists for the grocery store to thank-you letters for holiday gifts or other modes of communication, and begin to use these genres as additional modalities through which their voices can be heard. The mini-lesson is the forum in which these brief, explicit teachings are delivered (Calkins, 1983). It is the mini-lesson—with its explicit instruction from the writing teacher—that teaches students the value of being a writer. Implemented at the beginning of a writing workshop, the mini-lesson connects past learning with deepened or new learning to be introduced. Be sure to keep each mini-lesson session short and focused so the strategy-learning process can begin.

This book recommends the use of the SCAMPER model of a series of mini-lesson sessions to teach primary writing strategies. As Lassonde and Richards describe in Chapter Two, there are seven components to the SCAMPER model: surveying and assessing, conferring with students, assembling materials, modeling, practicing with scaffolding, executing the new strategy in independent work, and reflecting on the benefits of the strategy. These components may be combined and adapted as needed into a series of sessions to meet students' learning and writing needs. Each component serves a purpose and sets the stage for the day's work and future writing initiatives. The following presents a sample writing strategy mini-lesson, Growing Ideas. This section will both provide you with the foundation for getting writers started and demonstrate what the SCAMPER model looks like in a primary classroom.

SAMPLE WRITING STRATEGY MINI-LESSON: GROWING IDEAS

One of the most frequent requests from teachers is for a writing strategy mini-lesson to present at the beginning of the school year that will get students to write. Growing Ideas is one such essential strategy that is equally important to revisit throughout the school year.

The sample series of mini-lesson sessions that follows represents all I have learned about teaching writing through mini-lessons. Although in this chapter I describe how I teach this strategy to a small group of students, in my classroom I have also presented it in whole-class and one-on-one conferences. It is equally effective with various group sizes. The following series of writing strategy mini-lesson sessions is designed for a small group of first-grade students and presented using the SCAMPER model.

Survey and Assess

Before you enter my classroom to observe our daily mini-lesson, be mindful of the accumulation of surveying and assessing that has brought us to this teaching point. The coordination of a writing strategy mini-lesson requires much more than recognizing the state learning standards and the curricular unit of focus. What matters most and can be incredibly daunting at the same time is that all students can learn something to transfer into their writing lives. I find the focus strategy or objective of the mini-lesson evolves from a pattern of needs and accomplishments that I recognize when I meet with my students for small-group work or for individual writing conferences about their work (Calkins, 1983; Graves, 1994). By having the focus or objective of the mini-lesson in the forefront, I am better prepared as a teacher to guide the instruction of my writers.

A daily source I use to **survey and assess** for the mini-lesson focus is student work samples. I have students place their writing work on their tables before lunch. If I know meetings or other obligations will deter me from capturing their understandings of our new learning, I will ask the students to place sticky notes at their stopping points from their previous writing allotment so I can review their most current writing. This provides me with a snapshot of whether the students might need more practice before they can independently execute the strategy.

Confer

Organizing notes from conferring can be intimidating for even the most accomplished teachers of writing. Carl Anderson (2005) demonstrates the use of simple record-keeping techniques throughout his book *Assessing Writers*. The system I have found most useful for recording my conferences is a checklist format adapted from Anderson's work. I use my checklist as a sort of cheat sheet as well as a record-keeping tool.

I keep a checklist in my Writing Strategies Notebook and refer to it to review the progress of my students' writing. The checklist is composed of a set of carefully selected focus strategies (see Figure 3.1). The strategies align with developmentally appropriate goals I have determined for the school term and the learning standards my district and state require. The checklist provides me with a graphic display of who has mastered and who is struggling with particular strategies so I can efficiently support students' growth. I pull only the students who are struggling with a particular strategy for small-group instruction and reteaching. Students are not pulled for reteaching of strategies they have already mastered. I look to those students who have mastered certain strategies to mentor others through collaborative writing. Sometimes these students even participate with me in the modeling component of the SCAMPER model.

When I **confer** with students, I think of it as comparable to eating Sour Patch Kids candy. The intensity of the sour flavor is brief but has a lasting impression. This is also true for an effective conference. The use of students' writing time should be minimal, yet powerful. With a strategy to generate ideas for writing, I can guide and support my students during my conferring sessions by providing a purpose for each student through the strategy.

Writing Standard 1: The student uses writing processes effectively.

_______ Recognizes the need for details that support the central idea

_______ Demonstrates an organizational structure in writing

_______ Uses spelling approximations and some conventional spelling

_______ Recognizes the appropriate use of capital letters

Figure 3.1 Writing Checklist

In the following conference, I provide contextualized recommendations to the student by having her do all the work while I prompt and offer tips along the way. The student writer, Anna, is trying the Growing Ideas strategy using a mentoring text. I am inspiring her to generate ideas. In this example, *My Best Friend* (Rodman & Lewis, 2007) is the story she has chosen as her favorite book. I approach Anna as she is flipping through the pages of her book with paper and pencil at her side. Anna is visually ''walking'' through the pictures, studying each page for details.

''I notice you taking a picture walk through your book. Can you tell me about the character you connect with the most?'' I ask, kneeling down next to Anna.

''Well, there's Lily and she's my age, but then there's also Tamika and she is so cool! I don't really like Shaunice because she's hogging Tamika,'' Anna says.

''When I look at your face it seems like you have some feelings about Shaunice's hogging Tamika,'' I suggest.

''Yeah, my cousin Abby is always hogging my sister,'' Anna says.

''That's an idea you could grow,'' I explain.

''There was this time they both went for ice cream and I didn't get to go. I was so mad!'' Anna declares.

I tap my hand on the paper. Anna is already sketching an ice cream cone with a sad face as I move on to confer with another student. In this coaching conference, I gave Anna the prompts to assist her in connecting with the characters of the story. I kept my language specific to our strategy for the day and allowed Anna to provide me with the details. After all, my goal was not to provide Anna with ideas to write about but to guide her in growing ideas on her own.

To continue from the surveying and assessing and conferring components, below I focus on using authors as mentors as one way to grow writing ideas. I approach modeling, practicing with scaffolding, executing the new strategy in independent work, and reflecting on the benefits of the strategy through a facilitative role. The purpose here is to support students with independence and transference of the newly introduced strategy. Before I begin, however, I need to assemble the materials that will best suit my teaching focus.

Assemble Materials

I **assemble materials** based on the projected outcome of my mini-lesson. The selection of a mentoring text can be overwhelming if you do not keep your focus and age group in mind. For the purpose of this mini-lesson, I selected a favorite picture book of mine, *Dandelion* by Don Freeman (1977). We read this book previously when we shared our favorite stories in Reading Workshop, so students are already familiar with it. Selecting a mentor text with which students already have a familiarity is important because they can use the book as a tool for learning rather than becoming lost within the content. Additional materials necessary for me to have on hand include chart paper and markers. Along with their favorite books, the students bring either their writing journals or a single page of paper per student. I have a drawing of the storybook outline on the chart paper with which to model, and the students can transfer the storybook outline onto their personal papers.

Model

This mini-lesson occurs at the beginning of the school term to kick off our writing sessions. This is one of a handful of mini-lessons that will establish our community of writing and accomplish my goal of having students independently choose topics for their writing, which correlates with our district and state standard of selecting a focus for writing and following it through.

A small group of students who have been identified as needing to learn and practice how to grow ideas are sitting on their favorite picture books. Preestablished vocabulary includes such concepts as *author, examine,* and *strategy.*

I begin the session by providing students with something familiar they can connect to their upcoming work. I say,

> *Writers, all of our lives we have been enjoying the writing of our favorite authors. One thing I love about writing is how we get to know our favorite authors by what they share with us. This year we're going to really get to know each other through our writing, because each one of us is an author too.* (I make eye contact with each student.) *I am so excited! Let's get started. Today, we are going to look at what it is that we like about our favorite authors.* (I really mean it. I hug my favorite book in front of me to **model** for the students how precious this author's work is to me.)

I continue modeling by overemphasizing my strategy focus. I say,

> *Today we are going to grow our own writing ideas by examining the writing of our favorite authors. This is important because it gives us a starting point for our own writing. Watch me* (pointing to the storybook outline encompassing the entire sheet of chart paper) *as I think about what it is I like so much about the story and place it in my own storybook outline so that it becomes a planner for my work as an author.*

(See Figure 3.2.)

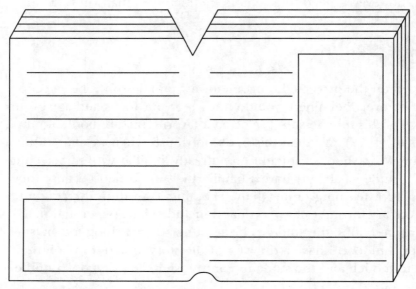

Figure 3.2 Storybook Outline

I take a picture walk through *Dandelion,* with stopping points where I jot and draw things that are significant to me or that remind me of personal childhood memories on the chart paper that is housing my storybook outline. I place these items on the page in the sequence of how they come to mind, and I use them more as starting points from which to build than to provide sequence.

> *Wow! Don Freeman has given me some great ideas to grow as a writer. Look!* (I point to the single words, phrases, and sketches that are now on the storybook outline.) *I can write about when I played dress up as a little girl, a stormy day when I got caught in the rain, or my sixth birthday.* (I continue to read the ideas and share the words to the pictures I sketch.) *I am so excited to start writing! Wait, since you are all working on growing ideas for writing by examining your favorite authors, why don't you give it a try?*

To this point, students' engagement has been verbal. The connection provided the students with prior learning from which to build and the teaching point opened the pathway to extend that learning. The practice portion of the mini-lesson will not only provide the students with an opportunity to try out their new learning but also allow me to see students attempt the focus strategy before playing it out independently. This is important because I can get a heartbeat on the strategy's effectiveness.

Practice

It is essential for students to **practice** the new strategy. We have a trial run before we leave the more explicit portion of the writing strategy mini-lesson.

> *All right, writers, now it's your turn. I want you to take a picture walk in your favorite book to see what ideas you can grow. I will give you the signal when I want*

you to finish. Please take your book out from underneath you now, and take your picture walk to grow your ideas. (Students do this individually as I observe them by circulating through their rows on the rug. Then I return to my chart paper at the front.) *Writers, I want you to turn to a partner and share two or three ideas you will sketch or write in your storybook outline.*

This is an essential step because it gives accountability to the students. Not only do I listen in while they share but also their partners now know what ideas they will use to build their storybook outlines. These ideas become the seeds, or plans, for their future writing pieces.

While students practice the strategy of growing ideas for writing from mentor texts, I circulate to listen to some conversations. This is the first experience students have with the strategy, and their responses allow me to gain an understanding of how it's going for them. Then I call the students back to me.

One, two, three, eyes on me. (I have all students sit on their books and face me.) *I heard some amazing ideas sprouting. I heard David sharing with Mary that his character is a superhero and he is going to jot in his storybook outline about the time he was a superhero for Halloween. I also heard Benjamin sharing with Tyler that his favorite book takes place in the city. He has been to Washington, DC, with his parents and is going to draw the White House in his storybook outline. Wow! Let's get started!*

I lead the students to their writing spaces by repeating how we are going to accomplish learning our new strategy for the day.

Today and any day that you are stumped for a great idea to write about, one thing that you can do is return to your favorite book to grow ideas. That way you will never be left without an idea to write about. Let me see a show of thumbs from those of you who are ready to try it. Great! Writers, off you go.

Now that students have had the opportunity to connect this new learning to their prior understandings as writers and receive additional support in what the strategy looks like as part of the teaching point, the practice portion of the mini-lesson architecture has allowed for a secure comprehension of the strategy. Each of these three components of the architecture of the mini-lesson prepared the writers for independent execution of the strategy.

Execute

The next day I review the strategy with the students, and they **execute** the strategy independently, each using a new book. I know some students may need extra guidance before they are ready to add this strategy to their tool chest, whereas others may grasp the concept without hesitation. I find that giving students a chance to share at the conclusion of writing time allows them to wrap the bow around their gift of a new strategy. I encourage them to collaborate with their classmates during writing time to continue developing their strength in using this strategy to grow their ideas.

Reflect

The strategy needs to be meaningful and transferable. Because the time to **reflect** culminates the strategy and sets the stage for the next day's work, I value the important role it plays in my students' application of their new learning. I keep the time allotment short, five minutes or less, and I use language consistent with the mini-lesson sessions from previous days. A short reflection time along with clarity of language provides the students with something consistent to transfer to their writing lives.

While students are busily writing away, putting their new strategy into practice, I confer with individuals. Because this is their first experience with using favorite authors to grow ideas as writers, there are two parts to our reflection. The first part of the reflection focuses on the helpfulness of the new strategy. The second part of the reflection focuses on each student's sharing what he or she gained from implementing the strategy. After reminding students that our stopping time is drawing near, I direct their attention to our starting chart that houses my original storybook outline.

> *Writers, I am so amazed by the great ideas your authors gave you for potential stories. I wish they were here for us to thank* (sigh of disappointment). *Since they're not, I want to give each of you a chance to hear some of what I saw. I saw Amanda growing an idea about fishing with her grandpa.* (I quickly tap the chart with my storybook outline as a reminder that it was written down on hers.) *Another thing that I saw was Anna connecting to an experience her author shared through a character hogging the attention of another character.* (I tap the storybook outline again.) *Now I want each of you to hear the great ideas this group has grown. After I give this direction, person number one will share the ideas he or she jotted or sketched. Each person will thank him or her for sharing, and we will continue with the person on his or her right.*

While students share with each other, I listen in on the sharing and add to my checklist or conferring notes. I record which students appear to be secure and which might need reteaching. I don't want to over-teach a strategy or make it so mundane that students lose interest in applying the strategy to gain the skill. The reflect portion of the mini-lesson is often the most overlooked component of the architecture. It is an essential component because it demonstrates the significance of the strategy while ensuring effective implementation.

REINFORCEMENT OVER TIME

I find generating story ideas an essential strategy for helping students develop the personal belief that they are indeed authors. Nothing can cause a writing session to flat-line more quickly than assigned topics, so I integrate assigned topics sparingly. To reinforce this strategy over time, I look at the students as writers through an "if-then" lens. Table 3.1 provides some examples of scenarios for this specific strategy of focus. If a student demonstrates a particular behavior, I implement its corresponding reinforcement through another mini-lesson. I go through the SCAMPER model again, surveying, assessing, conferring, and gathering a small group or pairing the students with others who can complement where they are in their writing process.

Table 3.1 If-Then Strategy Reinforcement

If I see a student ...	Then I reinforce by ...
Copying the author's ideas and not growing his or her own	Providing a follow-up mini-lesson the next day in which I chart a storybook outline that mirrors students' pieces with a reformed teaching point (to maintain privacy). "Today the goal as a writer is to revisit ideas from a favorite author, which I do by providing a real-life example of what the experience I am going to write about was like for me. This is important because for me to truly invest in a writing piece, it needs to grow from my heart."
With so many ideas that many of them are actually repetitions of the same experience	Conferring with a student by revisiting his or her storybook outline. "Hey, you really grew a lot of ideas from your favorite author. Sometimes when I have so many I will start to organize them by color. Look, you wrote the words "ice cream" and the word "pie," and you drew a picture of a watermelon. Why don't you take that blue crayon right there and draw a line through each of those things? What connection can you make among them?" The student will continue categorizing the items, noticing at the end that he or she really has a few strong pieces from which to write.
With a blank page	Pulling a small group of students with nothing written down or minimal connections to the mini-lesson helps the students to not feel deflated. With this small group, I take a book that is already familiar to all of us and has a common school-related topic (such as *The Recess Queen,* O'Neill, 2002) and repeat the same teaching point of growing ideas as writers by examining our favorite authors.
Writing short stories in his or her storybook outline	Pairing the student with a partner who not only exemplified the goal of the mini-lesson but also has strong communication skills to "teach" the student how he or she jotted and sketched.

TIPS FOR SUCCESSFUL MINI-LESSONS

Finding the structure to format my writing strategy mini-lessons was more than an accomplishment for me to add to my teaching practices. Using mini-lessons as architecture for my writing instruction opened my world to how much the quality of students' writing can improve when I pay attention to the structure of my instruction. Each component is the root of success for students who are growing as authors. I hope you find the final section, Things to Consider, to be not only the culmination of this chapter but also a reference in planning for the implementation of mini-lessons with strategy focuses.

THINGS TO CONSIDER

The architecture of a mini-lesson can provide the guide you've been looking for to keep your writing sessions productive. Some essentials covered within the components of the architecture that should not be overlooked include the natural flow of teacher-to-student and student-to-student interaction. It is important to keep your connection component of the mini-lesson brief and teacher directed. The same holds true for the teaching point. Both of these rely heavily on what you know about your writers and what you want these writers to gain from the mini-lesson experience. It is during the practice and execute portions of the architecture that students' active engagement occurs. To culminate the mini-lesson, reflection calls for equal participation of teacher and students.

> **Things to Remember**
>
> - **Connection**—teacher directed
> - **Teaching point**—teacher directed
> - **Practice**—student directed
> - **Execution**—student directed
> - **Reflection**—teacher and student directed

As primary educators, it is through the structure of the mini-lesson that we can teach young students how to plan and organize their ideas. In her book *First-Grade Writers: Units of Study to Help Students Plan, Organize, and Structure Their Ideas,* Stephanie Parsons (2005) recognizes the need to provide structure for primary students' writing. The sample mini-lessons in this book complement the limited pool of resources in the field of writing instruction for primary students. This book provides a starting point for educators to meet the needs of their growing writers.

REFERENCES

Anderson, C. (2005). *Assessing writers.* New York: Heinemann.

Calkins, L. (1983). *Lessons from a student: On the teaching and learning of writing.* New York: Heinemann.

Freeman, D. (1977). *Dandelion*. New York: Puffin.

Graves, D. (1994). *A fresh look at writing*. New York: Heinemann.

O'Neill, A. (2002). *The recess queen*. New York: Scholastic Press.

Parsons, S. (2005). *First-grade writers: Units of study to help students plan, organize, and structure their ideas*. New York: Heinemann.

Rodman, M., & Lewis, E. B. (2007). *My best friend*. New York: Puffin.

Chapter 4

The Role of Teachers´ Evaluations

JANE HANSEN

A writing teacher's ultimate goal is to teach students to evaluate themselves. Self-evaluation is a necessity if students are to intentionally become better writers. The SCAMPER model encourages students to self-regulate their learning and writing progress as they monitor and evaluate their accomplishments and mistakes.

Young writers learn to identify the ideas and skills that matter to them, and the techniques to use to be effective writers. They experiment with their drafts and letter formations, and they consider their peers' ideas and teachers' lessons as they compose. Using their sense of what they want to accomplish, young writers pursue the intentional task of announcing themselves to their world, as you will see in the case studies in this chapter.

One case is Alexi, the only English language learner in his kindergarten class. A shy, hesitant boy, he initially hides behind his difference, saying little and writing little. Sue Harris, his teacher, realizes that in order to write in a strong voice, Alexi needs to feel comfortable; he needs to value his entire self in this classroom. Ms. Harris and the students need to value both of Alexi's voices—English *and* Spanish. Eventually, we see this young writer intentionally use his writing to proudly tell his classmates who he is.

The other case is Tavin, a prekindergarten boy who, like everyone else in his classroom, began the year not knowing how to write his name. We see his teacher model this skill, in the context of a class writing event, by showing her students the importance of placing their names at the tops of the writing pieces they create each day. Tavin finds this difficult, but one day we see him intentionally rewrite his name until he masters this important task of placing himself on paper.

I will use these cases to exemplify four features of evaluation that I have observed in my more than two decades as a researcher of children's writing. These features are engrained in the SCAMPER model to enable the purposeful progress of young writers:

First, teachers of writing evaluate the ways they use their own lives and writing to ensure their young writers value their own lives and writing.

Second, teachers of writing evaluate their students by observing and conferring with them while they write among their classmates, and by providing in-context strategy lessons in which they provide the confidence the students need to intentionally enter new territory as writers.

Third, based on their in-context evaluations, teachers of writing provide strategy lessons in which they show the students how much confidence they have in them, and provide them with the assurance they need to intentionally enter new territory as writers.

Fourth, teachers of writing establish networks of supportive evaluators among the children in their classrooms. In the next section I will present the four features in more detail and incorporate the case studies into them.

THE CENTRAL FEATURES OF EVALUATION

1. *Writing teachers evaluate the ways they use their own lives and writing to ensure their young writers value their own lives and writing.*

Sometimes, as we will see, teachers find experiences in their own lives with which certain hesitant children can identify, and which thus pique their interest in writing. And, as the second teacher in the upcoming section, Robyn Davis, shows, the format of a teacher's writing can influence his or her students' growth. In our example, the teacher creates a piece of writing each day as a demonstration lesson, and the particular way in which she begins it helps her young writers develop an important skill.

This second teacher is particularly important in that the vast majority of teachers fear writing and therefore do not use their own writing as part of their teaching. Often their fears are the result of evaluation practices their own teachers used, whereby their teachers did not focus on what their students yearned to say. Instead, their teachers tended to focus on noncentral aspects of writing, such as punctuation and spelling. We now know, however, that a focus on what writers want to say is what brings students into writing.

As Shagoury (2009, p. 13) states,

> *Approaching child writers ... mean[s] learning to listen to children in new ways, not with the intent of correction, but of providing the right kind of support. This support may take a variety of forms, from providing examples, [to] modeling, [or] extended listening.*

Watching and listening serve as the foundation of teachers' evaluations of their writers. When we provide writing instruction, we primarily base it on (1) what writing processes we see students use as they write, (2) what we hear when they interact with their classmate-writers, (3) what we learn when we confer with them among their friends, and (4) what we see when we study their work.

In February, Ms. Harris decided she had to do something about Alexi, the boy in her kindergarten class who came from El Salvador. To be a writer with a strong voice, he needed to use both of his voices (Norton, 2005). Until he values who he is, Alexi will not step forth, as writers must do; writers are persons who want others to hear their voices.

Ms. Harris chose to use an upcoming event in her life to try to show the class and Alexi the importance of his home country. She used a map of the Americas to show Ecuador, where she intended to travel, and El Salvador, a country over which she would fly. Alexi, a quiet boy, beamed. Before long, as you will see, he intentionally used his writing to proudly establish his identity.

In the prekindergarten classroom of Tavin, the boy who intentionally learns to write his name, we see Robyn Davis teach this skill within the context of her own writing demonstration. Miss Robyn opens their daily writing block by reading a children's book to the class; then, on an easel, she creates her own piece of writing for the day. Regardless of what she writes about, Miss Robyn always begins by carefully writing *Miss Robyn* at the top of the paper, a strategy that shows the children, all of whom came from families of poverty, the importance of their writing and the significance of their written names.

None of her four-year-olds could write their names when they arrived in the fall, and none of them knew their names could appear in written form. These very young writers learned to treasure their name cards and themselves (Solley, 2005). Miss Robyn's daily demonstration showed them the value of learning how to write their own identifiers, a task she wisely taught in an important context—as their way to claim possession of their daily writing.

In the next section we see the young writers in these two classrooms as they work at their tables, and we observe their teachers as they evaluate and teach them in that context.

These two teachers share an overall view of evaluation that guides their instruction decisions. Specific examples of writing strategy mini-lessons are detailed in following chapters, and this evaluation chapter provides the framework within which those mini-lessons fit. When put into practice, the features of evaluation shown in this chapter enable the overall camaraderie mandatory for any mini-lesson to take root.

2. *Writing teachers evaluate their students by observing and conferring with them while they write among their classmates, and by providing in-context strategy lessons in which they provide the confidence the students need to intentionally enter new territory as writers.*

These teachers create classrooms in which their students write daily, and the teachers in this chapter work in settings in which everyone realizes the importance of young writers' making their own decisions about what to focus on each day. These teachers do not, in other words, follow a scripted curriculum (Dutro, 2009). While their students write, the teachers move about among them, stop beside them, sit with them, observe them, and confer with them. They listen for what is important to each young writer, and what each one needs to move forward. These teachers set the stage upon which the students will think about what they want to do next as writers.

In Ms. Harris's kindergarten class, the children write about whatever they want four days a week. They all write about their current unit of study (apples, nocturnal animals, and so on) on the fifth day. One afternoon in Ms. Harris's class, shortly after the map lesson in which she pointed out El Salvador, a researcher in the classroom, Ms. Evertson, who circulated as Ms. Harris did, sat beside quiet Alexi for several minutes. As she sat, Ms. Evertson wrote some Spanish words in her journal (Hansen et al., in press). She wrote about her husband going off for a ski trip, drawing herself at the door calling, ''Adios!'' and her husband replying, ''See ya mañana!''

This tickled Alexi, and the next day he met Ms. Evertson with excitement. ''I'm writing Spanish words today!'' He tells her the story he wants to write: ''There's a snake and a dragon, and they're best friends. They . . . hang out together . . . . I want to write this: 'Una colavra y dragon—a snake and a dragon.' '' He writes those words, and says, ''That's the title. Now I want to write the rest in English.'' He writes, ''Let's get ice cream,'' followed by ''Finished'' (see Figure 4.1).

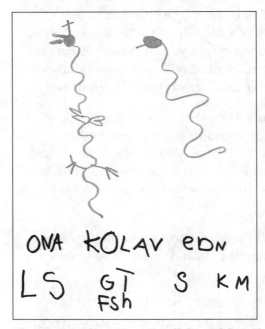

Figure 4.1 Alexi Uses English and Spanish Words

The importance of what the adults do in conferences to show young writers they value them cannot be overemphasized. The worth Ms. Evertson placed on Alexi as a person who speaks Spanish played a huge role in his ''coming out'' as a writer.

Now we return to the prekindergarten classroom in which the children also write daily, and in which they can always write about whatever they want. As they settle in at their tables, they choose pieces of paper and begin by writing their names. As they do so, Miss Robyn circulates among them, close at hand, listening to their talk.

''I'm gonna write about my dad today.''

''I'm not. I'm writin' 'bout a truck.''

''Why you always writin' about trucks? I'm writin' a elephant.''

Despite their talk, the first marks on their papers are not drawings that may resemble elephants or letters that may become ''dad.'' The first marks are their names.

As they write these important words, Miss Robyn offers tidbits of support. "Your 'o' in your name is nice and round," and, to another child, "You carefully drew the curve for your 's.'" At another table she refers to the name game they play every day, saying, "Do you remember what that first letter in your name is called?" At another table, a child whose name begins with a "Q" says, "My name was on the Bingo cards yest'day."

She notices Tavin has tried to write his name. The "T" is in place, but the "a" looks like an upper-case "Q." A lower-case "a" is difficult for Tavin, but he always tries. When it doesn't satisfy him, he leaves "Ta" as his signature, and moves into his writing for the day. On this day, as on most days at this point in time, his self-appointed writing task, like that of his friends, is to create a treasure map. Miss Robyn sees how engrossed he is in his work, and does not comment, on this day, on his name. As we will see, however, Tavin does learn to write it.

Sometimes, of course, as Miss Robyn circulates, she hears students express frustration as they try to write their names, and she quickly steps in. Name writing cannot become a negative; one's name is too important to be anything but beautiful. When Marquarius writes his "M" but almost cries because his "a" does not please him, Miss Robyn says, "You know what, Marquarius, an 'a' is very hard, and your 'M' is as handsome as you!" He smiles a careful smile, and Miss Robyn adds, "Your 'M' looks proud! You can write more of your name some other day. What is it you want to write about today?"

Miss Robyn is there, and she directs her writers into a successful day by providing the quick in-context strategy lessons they need to remain intentionally at work. These students will experience more pleasure than pain. When Brian Kissel (2008) was a researcher in this classroom for two years, he never heard one child complain about writing. Miss Robyn evaluates each writer daily, in person, with "kid gloves"—careful to preserve their little, fragile selves.

Whereas the in-context lessons the teachers provide as they circulate among the writers are of ultimate importance, the teachers also use their observations to provide them with ideas for strategy lessons.

    3. *Based on their in-context evaluations, writing teachers provide strategy lessons in which they show the students how much confidence they have in them, and provide them with the assurance they need to intentionally enter new territory as writers.*

The teachers base their strategy lessons on their evaluations of the young writers as they observe and confer with them while they are in the process of writing. Typically, Ms. Harris and Miss Robyn conduct these lessons within the context of their own writing, after they have read to the class. In general the teachers create lessons that may strengthen what the writers try to do on that day. Always, however, whether or not the writers use a strategy on a given day depends on what they each decide to accomplish that day.

We return to Alexi's kindergarten, in which Ms. Harris is writing a chapter book, one chapter per day, as her strategy lesson. Many of her young writers have started to create fiction, and she thinks their story lines could be more coherent. They are involved in her ongoing saga, and are learning to think ahead, to consider what makes a sensible, fun piece of writing.

Ms. Harris's story is about an evil giant who threatens their school, and today she wonders what should happen next. Cassie suggests, "We can save ourselves! And we can save the whooooooole school!" Of course! Kindergarten heroes!

After Ms. Harris completes her short chapter, we follow Alexi to his table. One month has passed since his first foray into his Spanish self, and he has continued to explore his identity. Today he adds a new twist. He begins by saying, "I'm going to be a hero, too." His oral story is about a giant troll who intends to invade the school, and Super Alexi hears about it when he is watching television at home. "I have to save them!" he exclaims, referring to the students, and draws himself, the superhero, wearing a blue cape.

As he begins his piece of writing, we hear influence from Ms. Harris's lesson, although her point was not for the children to necessarily write about an invasion of the school. Regardless, Alexi was listening and thinking ahead to his own writing. His teacher's story not only influenced his topic, but also his twist—to have heard the topic on television—may be a result of his attention to the details the students had been discussing as they helped Ms. Harris create her story.

It is significant that Alexi creates a special role for himself. He is gaining strength; his voice is becoming strong. Knowing her various students will be influenced by her writing in different ways, Ms. Harris is particularly pleased when Alexi uses it as an opportunity to intensify his sense of self. For this young writer to see himself as someone who can influence his own destiny is her prime goal. Stay tuned! In the next section of this chapter, we will see what Super Alexi does next!

For now, we return to Miss Robyn's prekindergarten class for an example of what appears to us adults as the somewhat simple writing task of learning to write their names—but that is one of the most difficult tasks for very young writers. At the beginning of the year, most of her writers experimented with markers, because these were new tools for their small hands to control. They gradually created specific shapes, and soon created the important people and ideas in their lives.

On the day we are now observing, before the writers settle in at their tables to write, they meet with Miss Robyn to interact with her while she reads the book *Caps for Sale* (Slobodkina, 1966). The students love the illustration of the man with many hats on his head. Then, turning to the easel, Miss Robyn writes her name on her piece of writing for the day. Knowing that some of her writers continue to find this a difficult task, she misprints one of her letters, and starts her name over, under her first attempt. As she does so, her comments tell them of the name's importance: "This is MY writing for today. No one else will write exactly what I write, so I try to write my name carefully. It tells everyone that this is what I am thinking about today."

After she finishes her piece of writing, the children scatter to their tables to write. We focus on Tavin, who starts with his name on the top, and then tries again and again and again. Then he turns to his writing/drawing, and creates a man with several hats (see Figure 4.2).

Both of his teacher's lessons influenced him. The book Miss Robyn read influenced his topic choice, which is often the case for a few students every day. Professional writers intrigue the young writers. When Miss Robyn reads something they love, she talks with them about it, asking, "What did this writer do? How come I love this book?"

Figure 4.2 Tavin Rewrites His Name

Writers, young and old, study their craft—they want to know about illustrations and words that foster the delivery of important messages.

Also important, Tavin rewrote his name, a strategy Miss Robyn has always sanctioned. This, however, was his first day to use that strategy. Somehow, he decided this is something important for a writer to do. For him to do. Today.

With many possible sources for ideas—books, their teacher's writing, their classmates, their lives, and their ever-active young minds—Miss Robyn's writers always (yes, always) are able to decide what to do as writers each day. Plus, we see in the next section the particular influence of the network among the young writers on their intentional growth.

    4. *Writing teachers establish networks of supportive evaluators among the children in their classrooms.*

Supportive evaluation and response create the sense of ''We are all writers!'' that keeps students' energy high. Writing is hard work, and the students' sense of value in themselves and each other strengthens their resolve. Their camaraderie is imperative for their intentional growth.

We now return to Alexi for our final look at this young writer. When we left him, he had drawn himself as Super Alexi. At that point he wondered aloud to his tablemates, ''I got two ideas to get the troll. One to have fire coming out of my mouth. Or throwing magic Spanish songs out of my mouth to make him sleep.'' Alexi is trying to decide whether he wants to promote his Spanish identity or his American one. His examples not only involve the two languages but also show very different means by which to solve a problem.

Kalia, a tablemate, has no difficulty, however, deciding between Alexi's options. ''Do the English one,'' she says. Alexi looks at her with wide eyes and says, ''Nope. Spanish.'' Done. He draws the notes and writes: ''I throw magic Spanish songs. The troll fell asleep. Khurk School was safe today'' (see Figure 4.3).

Alexi immediately asks Ms. Harris if he can read his story to the class, a setting in which she has taught the students to provide supportive response/evaluation. It is a place

Figure 4.3 Super Alexi Throwing ''Magic Spanish Songs'' at the Troll

where Alexi now feels he will be confirmed. He reads, and then asks, ''What are your questions?'' Marquis asks, ''Why did you write about Spanish?'' Alexi does not hesitate: ''That's my language.'' The discussion continues, and Alexi's classmates learn about his story as he explains and reexplains it—in his words (Parker & Pardini, 2006).

The power of his friends' evaluations—and his power to overcome them when he so chooses—are important to Alexi. He is now a full-fledged member of this class of writers, much to Ms. Harris's relief. Alexi had come new to her classroom in the middle of the previous year, and it had taken a lot of work on her part for this boy to become a writer with a strong voice. He needed much validation, and her approach to evaluation convinced this uncertain child of his value.

Finally, we return to prekindergarten, where we see Tavin once again. He sits at a busy table of male writers, all intent on creating treasure maps, a hot task for a period of time. The maps, however, become increasingly complicated, and Tavin starts to lose interest.

On this day, not in a hurry to engage in treasure hunts or to write about a book or something else, he devotes his energy to his name. He not only writes it several times, as he has done previously, he perfects it. When it doesn't look right, he writes it again and again—and again! Using his well-worn name card as a mentor text and recalling the brief strategy lesson his teacher offers the class each day, he decides, ''This is my day!'' and he succeeds (see Figure 4.4).

On his first attempt, Tavin didn't like the long tail on his ''a.'' His second attempt shows that he drew a line on the right of the ''a,'' but the two lines did not please him. His third attempt was at the bottom of the paper, and he didn't like his ''n.'' Finally, he printed a version that pleased him—the third line. Yes, it clearly says, ''Tavin.''

Figure 4.4 Tavin Succeeds at Writing His Name

This day becomes a landmark. Tavin's diligence brings him to a new place. With his ability to write his name to his own satisfaction, he has become, in his mind, a writer. With extra energy he works at his writing, challenging himself, as his classmates have started to do. Each student finds a place of recognition.

These young creators build bigger and better structures with their blocks, create longer and longer snakes with clay, and try harder and harder things as writers. On day one, they entered their Writers' Workshop—and their block corner—ready to create (Ray & Glover, 2008). On all successive days, as they learn of options, they sometimes glide with ease across their papers, and sometimes decide to step into new territory—to intentionally become increasingly proficient.

In particular, Miss Robyn's daily, brief name-writing strategy lesson influences each child, one-by-one. They are at very different motor-skill levels, and they have widespread thoughts about what is important in writing—regardless of what Miss Robyn says. Week-by-week, or month-by-month, they all learn to write their names. At the beginning of each month, Miss Robyn files a copy of each child's current version of his or her name. Their growth throughout the year, from lines and shapes to clearly formed letters for both first and last names, shows the total success of Miss Robyn's name-writing strategy lessons.

The differences among the children, and their investment in their writing, keep their community alive. They constantly look at what their peers are doing, look for what they admire, and try what they think they can do. To be able to evaluate themselves so they can make wise decisions about what to try next is vital to their growth.

THE WRITING TEACHER'S ULTIMATE GOAL

Daily, the young writers in these case studies sit, think, write, read, and walk about among one another. They love the company they keep and seek resources to move them forward. They thirst for support. Writers thrive in the midst of evaluators who see value in them and their work. They understand, likewise, the value of providing others with the support they may seek.

Their support often comes from Ms. Harris or Miss Robyn, two teachers who understand the inner workings of writers, their insecurities, and the importance of the development of a strong voice in order to be heard.

These teachers—as the Super Evaluators—evaluate their writers with these thoughts in mind:

"What can I say, do, and teach that will strengthen my students' inner voices and place them in positions in which they know—without being told—that they are competent writers?"

"What can I say, do, and teach that will keep these young writers engaged and on the lookout for ways to advance their work?"

And so I end this chapter as I began, hoping that the four features I have observed in my research generate ideas for you to contemplate. A writing teacher's ultimate goal is to teach students to evaluate themselves. Self-evaluation is a necessity if students are to intentionally become better writers. Use of the SCAMPER model for writing strategy mini-lessons promotes the development of self-regulation and self-evaluation in young writers.

REFERENCES

Dutro, E. (2009). Children writing "hard times": Lived experiences of poverty and the class-privileged assumptions of a mandated curriculum. *Language Arts, 87*, 89–98.

Hansen, J., Davis, R., Evertson, J., Freeman, T., Suskind, D., & Tower, H. (in press). *The preK–2 writing classroom: Growing confident writers*. New York: Scholastic Press.

Kissel, B. (2008). Apples on train tracks: Observing young children reenvision their thinking. *Young Children, 63*(2), 26–32.

Norton, N.E.L. (2005). Permitanme hablar: Allow me to speak. *Language Arts, 83*, 118–127.

Parker, E., & Pardini, T. (2006). *"The words came down!" English language learners read, write, and talk across the curriculum, K–2*. Portland, ME: Stenhouse.

Ray, K. W., & Glover, M. (2008). *Already ready: Nurturing writers in preschool and kindergarten*. Portsmouth, NH: Heinemann.

Shagoury, R. E. (2009). *Raising writers: Understanding and nurturing young children's writing development*. Boston: Pearson.

Slobodkina, E. (1966). *Caps for sale*. NY: HarperTrophy.

Solley, B. A. (2005). *When poverty's children write: Celebrating strengths, transforming lives*. Portsmouth, NH: Heinemann.

Chapter 5

Writing Strategy Instruction for Struggling Writers

ROCHELLE MATTHEWS-SOMERVILLE AND EVA GARIN

Meet Ethan. Ethan is a first-grade student who is bright and articulate, and who enjoys school. That is, he enjoys school until he has to write about something he has read or experienced. Ethan can talk about ideas, opinions, and recollections; and he can tell a story with detail and expression. Ethan struggles with putting his ideas on paper, not formulating his ideas or knowing what to write.

WHO ARE THE STRUGGLING WRITERS?

We as teachers know the most challenging part of identifying struggling writers is that they can be any of the students in our classrooms! There is a common misconception that only students who struggle academically or those who struggle in reading, in general, struggle with the writing process. This is not the case. Some struggling writers compose very little considering the time allocated for writing; others lack awareness of how to organize the writing and therefore produce papers that are less coherent. There are still many students who have difficulty with adding details to a composition and with word choice, handwriting, mechanics, and identifying and correcting errors. As educators, we must remember that students like Ethan who struggle with writing do not necessarily have general deficits in language learning abilities. Instead, teachers must consider that some of the tasks (for example, cognitive and cultural) requested of young students are not appropriate given the developmental learning stages of many of them. (See Vygotsky's work on zones of proximal development, 1978.) Furthermore, many of these primary students may simply prefer or need to learn strategies for writing that are often overlooked or not considered in the early grades.

EVIDENCE CONNECTIONS

Over the years many studies have shown that well-designed strategy instruction can produce substantial gains in writing quality for struggling writers (Graham, 2006; Graham & Harris, 2003; Graham & Perin, 2007; Zimmerman & Risemberg, 1997). But what does well-designed strategy instruction entail?

A well-designed program includes strategies for inventing, drafting, and polishing, as well as self-regulation and self-efficacy strategies (Santangelo, Harris, & Graham, 2007). Despite the potential gains students can make with appropriate strategy instruction, it is still not surprising that many primary students experience continued challenges with writing, because self-regulated learning (for example, goal setting, self-evaluating, self-monitoring), which is clearly needed to write effectively and independently, develops much later in an individual's life. (See Zimmerman, 2000, for a discussion on attaining self-regulation from a social cognitive perspective.) It is quite likely that for many struggling writers, development of self-regulated learning takes place during the middle and high school years. This chapter offers suggestions about how to use the SCAMPER model for writing strategy mini-lessons to help primary students who struggle with writing acquire the self-regulated writing behaviors that lead to the independent writing for which we aim.

ASSESSING STUDENTS: HOW DO WE KNOW WHO IS STRUGGLING?

How do we identify struggling writers and their areas of weakness? On the surface, surveying and assessing students to identify the areas in which they struggle may seem like an overwhelming task. One way teachers can identify struggling writers is to compare and contrast the abilities of proficient writers with those of struggling writers. Proficient writers are able to set goals and subgoals based on audience and task. They organize their writing using knowledge of text structure. They generate sentences, transcribe mechanics, evaluate using extensive criteria, and select and monitor strategies productively. Some struggling writers may possess some of these abilities with limited proficiency; however, in general, many of them have difficulty coordinating all of these complex writing tasks. The good news is there are four broad areas for strategy instruction that teachers can observe and identify:

1. **Inventing**—listing and developing ideas
2. **Drafting**—putting ideas on paper
3. **Polishing**—rewriting
4. **Self-regulation and self-efficacy**—checking one's own work and seeing oneself as a writer

Many struggling writers have great difficulty at the very beginning stages of the writing process. For those students, creating a plan to get started is the most daunting task. They have little thought of audience or goals for writing, and they lack understanding about how to generate ideas. Invention or preplanning is often absent. Many teachers may also notice that students who struggle to write often have limited knowledge about mechanics; therefore, the polishing or revising stage may be the most challenging. Quite a few struggling writers have poor reading skills, limiting knowledge of evaluation processes, which leads to difficulties fixing errors. These students are also more challenged when the writing is linked to something they have read. (We offer teachers two books: *Strategies That Work* and *Interactive Writing and Interactive Editing*, to support such students in the Resources section below.) Finally, outside of all the technical aspects of writing, many students have poor self-regulation and low self-efficacy.

To identify student weaknesses, we use these simple techniques:

1. *Keeping checklists of potential problem stages.* Checklists are great tools to get a quick visual snapshot of students' areas of need. A checklist can be general or it can be individualized for each child. Both the student and the teacher can use well-designed checklists for different purposes. The teacher can use them as diagnostic or progress-tracking tools, and students can use them as self-reflective revising tools. Allowing students to collaborate in the creation of their checklists will further assist them with understanding the process of writing from beginning to end. Using checklists can also put the focus back on the process of writing as opposed to the product. The extensive writing checklist in Figure 5.1 will help you inventory students' writing skills.

Directions: Use this checklist to inventory the student's foundational writing skills.

Area of Need?	Observed or Not Observed Writing Skill	Sample Intervention Ideas
Physical Production of Writing		
__Y __N	*Writing speed.* The student writes words on the page at a similar pace as peers.	Teach keyboarding skills. Allow the student to dictate ideas to a peer who will transcribe.
__Y __N	*Handwriting.* Handwriting is legible to most readers.	Teach keyboarding skills. Provide systematic handwriting practice.
__Y __N	*Handwriting.* The student leaves white space between words.	Teach keyboarding skills.
Mechanics and Conventions of Writing		
__Y __N	*Grammar and syntax.* The student's knowledge of grammar rules and syntax is appropriate for age and grade level.	Teach rules of grammar and syntax. Have the student compile an individualized checklist of his or her own common grammar and syntax mistakes to use to edit and revise his or her work.
__Y __N	*Capitalization.* The student uses both upper- and lower-case letters.	Teach capitalization rules.
__Y __N	*Capitalization.* The student capitalizes proper nouns.	Assign a peer buddy to support the student's revision processes.
__Y __N	*Punctuation.* The student uses punctuation at the end of each sentence.	Have the student type written pieces with an editing program.
__Y __N	*Punctuation.* The student uses apostrophes in contractions and possessives.	Provide the student with written rule reminders in a notebook. Assign a peer buddy to support the student's revision processes.

Figure 5.1 Writing Skills Checklist

Area of Need?	Observed or Not Observed Writing Skill	Sample Intervention Ideas
__Y __N	*Spelling.* Skills are age and grade appropriate.	Provide the student with a list of commonly misspelled words. Teach dictionary skills.
__Y __N	*Spelling.* The student uses standard spelling.	Teach dictionary skills.
Writing Content and Production of Writing		
__Y __N	*Vocabulary.* The student uses age- and grade- appropriate vocabulary.	Provide the student with a vocabulary notebook with commonly used words.
__Y __N	*Word choice.* The student distinguishes word choices that are appropriate for informal written discourse versus formal discourse.	Teach thesaurus skills. Teach rules for word choice.
__Y __N	*Word choice.* The student uses synonyms for words.	Teach thesaurus skills.
__Y __N	*Word choice.* The student uses the right action word forms with nouns.	Refer to a word wall or a word bank.
__Y __N	*Word choice.* The student begins sentences in different ways (sentence diversity).	Provide the student with a list of "story starters."
__Y __N	*Audience.* Identifies targeted audience for each writing assignment and alters written content to match needs of projected audience.	Compile sample written pieces that specifically focus on varying language use for target audiences.
__Y __N	*Structure.* Sentences go from left to right.	Provide the student with written rule reminders in a notebook.
__Y __N	*Oral versus written work.* Dictated and written passages are similar in complexity.	Pair the student with a peer buddy to transcribe his or her thoughts on paper. Have the student use speech-to-text software for first drafts of papers.
__Y __N	*Revision process.* The student revises each initial written draft before turning it in for a grade.	Create a rubric containing the elements of writing that the student should review during the editing process.
__Y __N	*Content.* The student uses brainstorming or story maps to create and organize ideas.	Provide the student with a selection of graphic organizers to use during prewriting process.
__Y __N	*Content.* Each written piece has an introduction (beginning), body (middle), and conclusion (end).	Have the student use story maps. Partner the student with a peer who will provide feedback.
__Y __N	*Content.* Ideas flow and are well connected.	Have the student complete a graphic organizer or story map.
__Y __N	*Topic selection.* The student independently selects appropriate topics for writing assignments.	Have the student generate a list of general topics that interest him or her.

Figure 5.1 Continued

2. *Analyzing individual writing samples.* There are certain characteristics that every well-developed writing product entails: a clear topic, consistency of a topic throughout the paper, correct spelling, good grammar (rules governing the use of language), accurate syntax (grammatical arrangement of words in a selection), and appropriate speed (to produce the writing product). For many teachers, finding a valid way to assess a student's writing is a difficult task. We suggest using a collection of the student's writing pieces, including such artifacts as warm-ups, brief constructed responses, and letters to authors.

3. *Holding individual prewriting conferences.* Good writers go through prewriting experiences that provide motivation and help them generate ideas and organize information. During this stage of the writing process, teachers may encourage the prewriting habit of journal keeping or journal notation. Other prewriting experiences may include linking the writing to reading or another shared experience, including sensory perception experiments, note taking, enacting creative drama, and writing free verse. Student-teacher prewriting conferences can be valuable in helping students organize their material and freeze their initial ideas into form.

4. *Using writing portfolios and journals.* A writing portfolio is a purposeful collection of student work that exhibits a student's efforts, progress, and achievements as documented by both teacher and student reflections, comments, and choices of writing samples. Similarly, a journal is a written record of usually personal experiences and observations. Journaling gives students, especially those who have great difficulty with written language, opportunities to write without being overly concerned about spelling, punctuation, and grammatical form and function. Journaling provides writing experiences without the pressures typically present when completing assignments. The use of writing portfolios and journals helps focus students, ensures ''safe'' or judgment-free writing, and develops a personal relationship between the student as the author and the audience. In addition to the benefits these activities may have for students, teachers can use journaling and portfolios to monitor and evaluate progress and identify students' areas of need in writing.

GENERAL ACCOMMODATIONS AND STRATEGIES FOR WRITERS WHO STRUGGLE

The act of writing contains its own inner rigidity. Writers must follow an inflexible set of rules that govern the mechanics and conventions of writing to ultimately formulate original, creative thought. It is no wonder that many students find writing to be a nearly impossible task, and they have little knowledge about how to chunk larger writing assignments into predictable subtasks. However, these students can develop into proficient writers. The best writing instruction places the process of written expression on a timeline—only tackling one specific skill included in the writing process at a time. This is where writing strategies come into play. Depending on their stages of development as writers, students struggling with writing will benefit from the writing strategies presented in this book, as well as from the following accommodations for difficulty with inventing, drafting, polishing, and self-regulation and self-efficacy.

For Difficulty with Inventing

What can we as teachers do when we have students who struggle with inventing topics in text? This section offers teachers suggestions for working with these students using story maps, technology, building outlines, interactive writing, and buddy writing.

Story Maps.   A story map is a visual or graphic organizer that allows a student to detail important elements of a story, including character, plot, action, and setting. Sometimes a visual story map is just the support a student needs to be successful at a writing task. Story maps allow students to filter through their complex and perhaps unclear thoughts and transfer them from mind to paper. We like to call this "taking away the thinking load." Often the process of organizing their thoughts in a graphic and visual way on paper helps students identify and pull out the valuable ideas they want to use from of a myriad of jumbled thoughts.

Technology.   There are always students who seem to have great writing ideas, but who find it nearly impossible to get these ideas on paper. Following are two examples of how technology can support students' inventing. When students digitally record themselves, they can rehearse and hear their stories. Allowing students to dictate ideas into a tape recorder and having a volunteer (such as a classmate, parent, or school staff member) transcribe them is a feasible way to provide support for these students. Further, using speech-to-text software (for example, Dragon NaturallySpeaking) to dictate first drafts of writing assignments is yet another way for these students to organize their thoughts and get information on paper.

Building Outlines by Talking Through Topics.   A student who struggles to organize his or her notes into a coherent outline can tell the teacher or a peer what he or she knows about the topic and then capture the informal logical structure of that conversation to create a working outline. After the conversation, the student jots down an outline from memory to capture the structure and main ideas of the discussion. The student can then expand and refine this outline frame into the structure for a writing sample (Writing Center, Brainstorming, n.d.).

Interactive Writing.   Interactive writing is an instruction strategy in which the teacher is a key player who shares the pen, literally, in the writing process. The teacher assists a student or group of students with collaboratively composing, constructing, and negotiating a written message. This hands-on, interactive approach provides modeling for students to become aware of and knowledgeable about all aspects of the writing process, including word analysis and phonology, how written text works, and connections between what we write and read (Swartz, Klein, & Shook, 2002).

Buddy Writing with Peers or Older Students.   Buddy writing is similar to buddy reading in that a more-able writer is paired with a less-able writer, or a younger writer is paired with an older peer. Buddy writing aims to improve the writing skills of younger children, enhancing their confidence and competence. It helps them with generating ideas, organizing texts, and deciphering the metacognitive processes involved in writing. This method works well for any student who does not have a solid grasp of the writing process. During buddy writing, pairs work together to stimulate ideas and then brainstorm together. They learn to organize their writing and to collaborate all the way through the writing process. The emphasis of buddy writing is on teaching the process of writing in a supportive peer-coaching environment to make writing enjoyable rather than stressful.

For Difficulty with Drafting

What do we as teachers do for students who have difficulty drafting? This section offers teachers suggestions of how to work with these students using cover-copy-compare, word walls and word banks, and word work.

Leveraging the Power of Memory Through Cover-Copy-Compare of the Five Hundred Most Frequently Used Words. Students increase their spelling knowledge by copying a spelling word from a correct model and then recopying the same word from memory. Give each student a list of a predetermined number of spelling words, an index card, and a blank sheet of paper. For each word on the spelling list, the student (1) copies the spelling list item onto a sheet of paper, (2) covers the newly copied word with the index card, (3) writes the spelling word again on the sheet from memory, and (4) uncovers the copied word and checks to ensure that the word copied from memory is spelled correctly. If that word is spelled incorrectly, the student repeats the sequence until the word he or she copied from memory is spelled correctly, then moves on to the next word on the spelling list (Murphy, Hern, Williams, & McLaughlin, 1990).

Word Walls and Word Banks. A word wall is a designated portion of wall space in a classroom on which words are listed alphabetically (Callella, 2001). Its purpose in all types of classrooms is to post and display words so students can read them and refer to them when they are writing. Word banks serve similar functions, but rather than using the same list for all students in the classroom, teachers can select words that individual students have learned and create a unique set of words for each student. Both of these methods provide ways for teachers to collect words that have been taught and learned so students can practice them frequently and become independent in using them in their writing.

Word Work Using Magnetic Letters, Rhyme Units, and Picture Visualization. Despite the fact that most instruction is provided in an auditory-only form, many students learn best using additional visual and hands-on approaches. Materials that have potential visual and tactile capabilities are excellent resources for students who have trouble drafting. Being able to manipulate material during the drafting portion of the writing process takes some of the cognitive load away from students who are having difficulties. For example, a first-grade student who is working on adjectives may use the magnetic letters ''C, S, S,'' which stand for color, size, and shape, to remember to add detail to his or her work while drafting.

For Difficulty with Polishing

What do we as teachers do for students who have difficulty with polishing or revising their writing? This section offers teachers suggestions for working with these students using such strategies as proofreading, peer polishing, reverse outlining, employing memory strategies, using the Author's Chair, and buddy writing.

Using Selective Proofreading. To prevent struggling writers from becoming overwhelmed by teacher proofreading corrections, focus on only one or two proof-reading areas when correcting a writing assignment. Create a student writing skills checklist (see Figure 5.1) that inventories key writing competencies (such as grammar and syntax, spelling, vocabulary, and so on). For each writing assignment, announce to students that you will grade the assignment for overall content, but will make proofreading corrections on only one or two areas chosen from the writing skills checklist. (Select different proofreading targets for each assignment according to common writing weaknesses in your classroom.) Also, to provide more organization for the editing process, underline problems in each student's text with a highlighter and number the highlighted errors sequentially on the left margin of the paper. Write teacher comments on a separate feedback sheet to explain the writing errors. With fewer proofreading comments, students can better attend to your feedback (Frus, 2006).

Peer Polishing.   Peer polishing or editing is a process in which student work is edited and reviewed by classmates or other writers. When we write, it is always good to ask for someone else's feedback. Even professional authors have qualified people edit their work and help them revise it. Using peer review in the classroom is a great way for students to practice their proofreading and revising skills. It will also teach them how to improve their own work and how to give constructive criticism. When doing peer editing in a class, it is best for the teacher to assign partners.

Reverse Outlines of Drafts.   Students can improve the internal flow of their compositions through reverse outlining. The student writes a draft of the composition. Next the student reads through the draft, sketching notes in the margins that signify the main idea of each paragraph or section. Then the student organizes the margin notes into an outline to reveal the organizational structure of the paper. This strategy is called ''reverse'' outlining because typically, in the writing process, you would outline first and then construct the narrative. This reverse outline allows the student to note whether sections of the draft are repetitive, are out of order, or do not logically connect with one another (Writing Center, ''Reorganizing Your Draft,'' n.d.).

Memory Strategies.   When students regularly use a simple, portable, easily memorized plan for proofreading, the quality of their writing can improve significantly. Create a poster summarizing SCOPE proofreading elements (Bos & Vaughn, 2002):

1. **Spelling:** Are my words spelled correctly?
2. **Capitalization:** Have I capitalized all appropriate words, including first words of sentences and proper nouns?
3. **Order of words:** Is my word order (syntax) correct?
4. **Punctuation:** Did I use end punctuation and other punctuation marks appropriately?
5. **Expression of complete thoughts:** Does each of my sentences contain a noun and verb to convey a complete thought?

One possible way to review the SCOPE proofreading steps is to copy a first-draft writing sample onto an overhead and evaluate the sample with the class using each item from the SCOPE poster. Then direct students to pair off and together evaluate their own writing samples using SCOPE. When students appear to understand the use of the SCOPE plan, you can require this type of proofreading for all submitted work.

Author's Chair.   This strategy provides a way for students to share with one another the excitement of particular moments in their own writing. Students sit in the Author's Chair to share their writing with classmates as the final step for each different stage of the writing process. When students share their drafts, they ask for feedback. When they sit in the Author's Chair with their published work, they celebrate the completion of a specific writing assignment (Tompkins, 2009). This strategy allots a special time and place to writers who wish to share their final products with an audience. Because the writing has already gone through revising and editing based on constructive criticism, sitting in the Author's Chair is typically an opportunity for writers to receive positive

DRAFTING GUIDELINES

- Skip a line between every line you write.
- Write only on ONE side of the page.
- Cross out but don't erase.
- Spell as it sounds.
- Get your ideas on paper.
- Write. Don't talk! Authors need quiet time to draft.

PRESENTING AS AN AUTHOR

(These guidelines can be developed with the children and then posted.)

- Sit up straight and tall.
- Speak in a loud voice.
- Hold your paper so the audience can see your face.

- Read slowly, clearly, and with expression.

LISTENING TO AN AUTHOR

(Students can recite these guidelines together when they gather for sharing.)

- Give your hands a clap.
- Put them in your lap.
- Eyes are on the speaker.
- Ears are listening.
- Hands and feet are still.

RESPONDING TO AN AUTHOR

- The part I liked best was...
- I'd like to know more about...
- I don't understand...

Figure 5.2 Sample Class Charts

feedback from classmates. Although we have provided an example of how the Author's Chair can be used at the end of the writing process, it is important to note that it can also be employed at different stages of the process. Figure 5.2 can be used with students to provide an example of possible guidelines for presenting as an author, and for listening and responding to the author.

Buddy Writing with Peers or Older Students.   Revising writing is a critical piece of the writing process. More and more, teachers are using the method of buddy writing to help make writing more interactive and collaborative and to teach students the importance of having support throughout this creative process. Collaborating with peer buddies in the revision process is often less intimidating than working with the teacher, especially for students who need extra support revising their written work. Buddying helps them decide more independently which suggestions they want to include in their writing.

For Difficulty with Self-Regulation and Self-Efficacy

What do we as teachers do for students who struggle with monitoring their own writing? This section offers teachers suggestions for working with these students using such strategies as graphing data, using self-evaluation checklists and rubrics, and self-monitoring with the teacher.

Self-Monitoring and Graphing Results.   Students gain motivation to write through daily monitoring and charting of their own and classwide rates of writing fluency. At least several times per week, assign your students timed periods of freewriting, during which they write in their personal journals. Freewriting periods should take up approximately the same amount of time each day. After each freewriting period, direct each student to count up their writing fluency score by tallying the number of words they have written. Chart the score on their own time-series graphs for visual feedback. Then collect the day's writing-fluency scores from all students in the class, add those scores, and chart the results on a large time-series graph posted at the front of the room. At the start of each week, calculate that week's goal for total class words written by taking last week's score and increasing it by 5 percent. At the end of each week, review the class score and praise students if they have shown good effort (Rathvon, 1999). If scores do not go up, we suggest individual writing conferences with those students who need additional support. If the class trend is static, we suggest reading a common piece of literature as a class and using the books *Strategies That Work* (Harvey & Gouvdis, 2007) and *Reading with Meaning* (Miller, 2002) to structure lively discussions that support students' writing about what they have read.

Self-Evaluation Checklists or Rubrics. A rubric is a scoring guide. It organizes criteria that describe what students need to complete for an assignment, and it measures the levels of proficiency of student work. You can use rubrics in any content area. They may be time consuming to create, but they allow students and parents to know exactly how you will grade an assignment. Rubrics and checklists can be used for student self-evaluation, peer evaluation, or teacher assessment. See Figure 5.3 for an example of a self-evaluation checklist. A student can use the self-evaluation rubric as a form of self-editing prior to submitting an assignment for a grade.

Yes	No	
☐	☐	Did I spend just enough time on the writing assignment? (This includes all rough drafting, brainstorming, writing, rewriting, and getting people to read my paper.)
☐	☐	Do I have a clear topic sentence?
☐	☐	Did I add lots of examples to support my topic?
☐	☐	Did I use a variety of words (vocabulary)?
☐	☐	Did I conclude my paper with a summary?
☐	☐	Are my periods, commas, exclamation points, and quotation marks in the right places?
☐	☐	Did I use capital letters correctly?
☐	☐	Did I check my spelling?
☐	☐	Did I reread my assignment before submitting it?
☐	☐	When I reread it, does it make sense?
☐	☐	After reading my paper over, did I change anything (revise)?
☐	☐	Did a buddy read my paper?

Figure 5.3 Self-Evaluation Writing Skills Checklist

Frequent Check-Ins with the Teacher. Although you're likely to find student-teacher conferences time consuming and exhausting, the individual conferences you hold with your students will be time well spent. Talking directly and individually with students about their writing can have a profound influence on how students interpret assignments and your comments on their work, how they approach drafts or revisions, and how motivated they are to write. You'll understand your students as writers and thinkers far better than you ever could from only seeing their written work. In addition, there is a significant amount of information you can learn about how each individual student matriculates through the writing process, and you will be able to identify both strengths and weaknesses. Remember that talking—about ideas, drafts, and revisions—is an essential part of writing. Conferences provide ideal opportunities for that talking. Table 5.1 describes the different stages of writing, highlights the potential difficulties that a student may experience at the different stages, and suggests possible strategies to support the student in overcoming those difficulties.

Table 5.1 Process Writing for the Struggling Writer

Stage	Difficulty	Suggestions for Support
Rehearsal prewriting	The student is unable to generate an initial idea, is unable to revisit text, lacks prior knowledge, is unable to link reading and writing, and is a poor risk taker.	Make a list of topics the student knows about, have the student work with a partner, engage in conversations with the student, encourage quick writing, or have the student use a semantic map (expository text) and graphic organizer.
Drafting	The student has a weak vocabulary, is unable to put thoughts on paper, is unable to "get started," lacks organization, fears failure, and writes off topic.	Pair the student with a peer, instruct the student to leave spaces between lines, have the student model and talk through his or her ideas, act as a scribe, or ask the student to revise his or her graphic organizer.
Revising	The student views the draft as a final form, lacks motivation, is uncooperative with peer revision, "reads" what he or she thinks rather than what he or she wrote, lacks sense of story structure, and is unable to vary sentence structure.	Model revision, have the student use a revision checklist, encourage peer conferencing, and act as a scribe.
Proofreading	The student is unable to use proper language mechanics, has poor handwriting and spelling difficulties, and reads what he or she thinks rather than what he or she wrote.	Develop a list of things to look for; have the student use a proofreading checklist; and make available handwriting reference charts, word walls, and spelling dictionaries.
Publishing	The student has poor motor skills, is unable to read what he or she wrote, perceives his or her work as unsuccessful, and is shy.	Use a bulletin board titled "Great Writing from Great Kids," use the Author's Chair, convene a writing circle, and guide and support.

Your Name: _____

Each time you finish a piece of writing, enter the title, date, and something you are proud of doing as a writer or something new you learned about yourself as a writer.

Title of Your Writing	Date	I Can...! and I Learned...!

Figure 5.4 Celebrate Your Writing Reflection

Students' Seeing Themselves as Writers.   Learning to write well is a process that begins early in a child's life. Although the first scribbles and pictures may seem far from what we adults think of as formal written language, they are in fact a child's first prose. Table 5.1 is a breakdown of how most children develop as writers and some of the ways teachers foster their skills in the classroom. We like to use the reflection hand-out shown in Figure 5.4, which was modified from a local school system's balanced literacy training packet to provide students with a permanent visual that allows them to see their progress as writers (Prince George's County Public Schools, 2001). We have found that this technique motivates children.

CASE STUDIES

Earlier in this chapter we discussed the idea that there is no single profile of a struggling writer. However, there are different areas into which struggling writers can be grouped based on their qualitative difficulties. In this section we present several case studies to demonstrate the kinds of struggling writers teachers may have in their classrooms.

There are many profiles of struggling writers; however, three common types of struggling writers are those who have difficulty with

• Mechanics and conventions (grammar, syntax, and spelling)
• Writing content and production (vocabulary, word choice, and the revision process)
• Physical production (speed and handwriting)

Jim is a student who struggles with the mechanics and conventions of writing. He is only able to write minimally, even about topics that interest him. He is developing as a reader. He may or may not be referred to special education. He is fidgety during the reading and writing components of the day, and he seems to not fully understand the technical components involved in writing (such as grammar and syntax).

Students like Jim who struggle with the actual mechanics and conventions of writing tend to have a difficult time composing adequate writing products in allotted time frames; are unsure of how to organize writing; produce papers that lack cohesiveness; have difficulty selecting topics, generating ideas, or adding details to compositions; and leave out critical information. Often these students are also so overwhelmed with the writing process that they are unaware of the demands of audience, purpose, and form. They forget or do not understand that writing is a means of conveying a message. Of course, there is no perfect prescription for every child who experiences this type of difficulty; however, story maps or graphic organizers are great forms to assist students with generating and organizing ideas prior to actually writing. Reteaching grammar and syntax rules using mini-lessons or providing individualized checklists of common grammar and syntax mistakes can bridge the gap for those who struggle with conventions. Having students collect lists of their own common misspellings might also help them to better identify their mistakes and make improvements.

Ethan, from our chapter opener, is a gifted student with high processing skills but low drafting ability. Remember, Ethan is the type of student who can talk about ideas, opinions, and recollections but struggles with putting his ideas on paper, formulating his ideas, or knowing what to write.

Students like Ethan seem to have great ideas when expressing them orally but never seem to demonstrate the depth of their thinking when putting their ideas on paper. They tend to write at a rate much slower than their classmates, and their writing is so illegible that it direly interferes with the quality of their writing products. Teaching keyboarding skills, or allowing these students to document ideas with tape recorders or speech-to-text software or to have peer buddies record their ideas, is a great way to support these students. Additionally, teaching keyboarding skills is a simple way to help students worry less about the written production of assignments and focus more on the content and ideas within their writing.

Finally, Jo is a student with an identified language disability. In addition to other difficulties associated with her disability, Jo struggles significantly with the physical aspects of writing. Knowing what to write about and planning for writing are also very difficult for her.

Students like Jo who struggle with the content and production of writing present challenges to teachers trying to assist them with the writing process that are very different from those of other struggling students. These students are not fluent writers, generally because they tend to have difficulty with selecting age- and grade-appropriate vocabulary, word choice, revisions, and making written work equivalent in complexity and quality to oral language. Many of these students benefit from teachers' compiling and displaying lists of vocabulary and related definitions for subject areas. They also benefit from journal writing; collaborating with peers during the revision process, especially to check for appropriate word choice; and creating and using rubrics containing the elements of writing they should focus on during the revision process.

IMPLICATIONS

Established practices in writing instruction have long focused on product-driven approaches. The implementation of these methods represents a shift in both teaching and learning strategies. Process-driven approaches allow students to be involved in writing regularly for meaningful purposes and encourage students to envision themselves as thinkers who have messages to convey to the world. Teachers using process-driven strategies focus on meaning first, and promote the accommodation of individual differences. But how do you know which approach will work for each child? Again, given the diversity of the students who struggle with writing, we cannot offer a single prescriptive approach. However, what we can do is provide a guide for selecting the most appropriate approach for each individual student who struggles with some aspect or aspects of writing.

Students need to be taught how to complete a process and how to regulate themselves through the process. More than a decade ago, Graves (1983) reminded us that writing taught once or twice a week is just frequent enough to remind students they can't write. It is important to remember, however that although teachers need to create as many opportunities as possible to teach writing, they should not overload students with a multitude of strategies. Once you have identified weak areas, teach a few strategies intensively. Coordinate the use of the same strategies across teachers, grade levels, and subjects so students have a wealth of time to practice using and perfecting a few strategies.

Struggling writers should be writing all of the time; they require extended, structured, and explicit instruction to develop skills and strategies essential for writing. Naturally, with the implementation of any new or existing systematic tool or strategy for use in the classroom that requires a lot of direct attention, there will be logistical challenges related to time. The process of developing quality writing products can be somewhat quick for some and slow for others. There is no way to predict the amount of assistance a student will need. Provide substantial support early on, and then gradually reduce support as students gain confidence and independence. For students, progressing from using single strategies to becoming strategic, independent learners may be a long-term process. The required amount of intense, systematic instruction varies from child to child. You should not only provide adequate support but also have some way to evaluate the effectiveness of the strategies being taught and used. The sooner mastery can be evaluated and achieved, the sooner the student will become an independent, confident writer. Finally, meeting the needs of struggling writers demands the attention and coordinated efforts of teachers across grade levels and content areas: students need to be able to use literacy skills across different areas to become proficient writers.

RECOMMENDATIONS

Writing competence is often measured by the ability to produce, without support, well-developed, detailed writing samples. However, for students who struggle with writing, the notion of participating in a one-hour activity may be unrealistic, inappropriate, and ineffective for writing skill development. To maintain student productivity, plan for short mini-lessons; demonstrate important aspects of the writing process with clear and plentiful examples; focus on only a few specific writing processes in one lesson; and create a relaxed, interactive environment for the lessons. We recommend the SCAMPER model presented in this book for teaching sequenced, well-planned mini-lessons.

Utilizing peer groups for writing tasks is a good strategy to reduce the attention to individual writing weaknesses. However, monitor the students during pair and group writing activities. Circulating around the classroom creates the sense that the students are being watched, and the notion of teacher proximity will help keep students on task. Don't just walk around, though; stop and observe each pair or group. Listen, provide clarification and feedback, and correct errors. Again, making students aware of your presence reinforces the purpose and objective of the assignment. Furthermore, ensure the activities don't go on too long. Using a timer, set time limits at the beginning of the activities. To wrap up, call on students to demonstrate to the class what they have practiced. This is most effective when students are informed at the onset that they will have to present their practice to their peers. Students may appreciate the mild social pressure to perform competently, and the social environment will motivate learners to concentrate on the assigned activity and put forward their best performance.

Despite the many challenges of implementing strategies to support struggling writers, teachers do not need to abandon the already established routines of the classroom. Many of the strategies and opportunities to practice writing skills fit right into the natural structure of the preexisting routines embedded in any curriculum. It could be as simple as the teacher's bringing students' attention to their work because many are unaware of their progress. The good news is, despite the fact that the strategies and programs recommended for students continue to evolve, we have made more progress in written expression for students than in any other academic area (Vaughn, Gersten, & Chard, 2000).

EVIDENCE CONNECTIONS

In this section we provide an annotated bibliography to support strategy instruction in writing and the connection between the reading and writing processes.

Cunningham, P., & Allington, R. (2007). *Classrooms that work: They can all read and write.* New York: Pearson.

This book is written for teachers, who the authors believe are the most important variable in how well children learn to read and write. The authors cite reasons that some classrooms produce children who achieve well-developed literacy skills. The book contains practical suggestions pertaining to five components of reading and writing instruction: real reading and writing, guided reading, guided writing, decoding and spelling, and word recognition and word knowledge.

Harvey, S., & Gouvdis, A. (2007). *Strategies that work: Teaching comprehension to enhance understanding* (2nd ed.). Portland, ME: Stenhouse.

The authors have designed this book to be a resource for teachers who want to explicitly teach thinking strategies that will help students become engaged, thoughtful, and independent readers. This book entails comprehension lessons that focus on exploring the central role that activating background knowledge plays in understanding. This book is a valuable resource for teachers as they work with students who struggle with both reading and writing. The reading strategies are also useful for preparing students to write about what they have read.

McCarrier, A., Pinnell, G. S., & Fountas, I. C. (2000). *Interactive writing: How language and literacy come together, K– 2*. Portsmouth, NH: Heinemann.

This book focuses on the early phases of writing, and has special relevance to prekindergarten through second-grade teachers.

Swartz, S. L., Klein, A. F., & Shook, R. E. (2002). *Interactive writing and interactive editing: Making connections between writing and reading*. Carlsbad, CA: Dominie Press.

The primary purpose of this book is to provide an introductory look at two exciting and powerful methods used to teach children to write: interactive writing and interactive editing. The book is organized into three major sections. The first two sections detail the procedures for interactive writing and interactive editing, including step-by-step descriptions of how to begin using these methods. These sections contain a collection of sample lessons with accompanying photographs. The third section focused on assessment, includes writing checklists and writing rubrics.

Tompkins, G. (2009). *50 literacy strategies*. Upper Saddle River, NJ: Pearson.

This book is a well-organized resource that provides research-based and classroom-tested instruction strategies for developing literacy abilities. Each strategy outlines the focus of instruction, grade-level appropriateness, scaffolding for English language learners, steps for implementation, why and when to use the strategy, and authentic student samples.

REFERENCES

Bos, C. S., & Vaughn, S. (2002). *Strategies for teaching students with learning and behavior problems*. Boston: Allyn & Bacon.

Callella, T. (2001). *Making your word wall interactive*. Huntington Beach, CA: Creative Teaching Press.

Frus, P. (2006). Commenting effectively on student writing. *CRLT: Center for research on learning and teaching*. Retrieved August 22, 2010, from www.crlt.umich.edu/gsis/P8_2.php.

Graham, S. (2006). Strategy instruction and the teaching of writing: A meta-analysis. In C. MacArthur, S. Graham, & J. Fitzgerald (Eds.), *Handbook of writing research* (pp. 187–207). New York: Guilford Press.

Graham, S., & Harris, K. R. (2003). Students with learning disabilities and the process of writing: A meta-analysis of SRSD studies. In H. L. Swanson, K. R. Harris, & S. Graham (Eds.), *Handbook of learning disabilities* (pp. 323–344). New York: Guilford Press.

Graham, S., & Perin, D. (2007). A meta-analysis of writing instruction for adolescent students. *Journal of Educational Psychology, 99*, 445–476.

Graves, D. (1983). *Writing: Teachers and children at work.* Portsmouth, NH: Heinemann.

Harvey, S., & Gouvdis, A. (2007). *Strategies that work: Teaching comprehension to enhance understanding* (2nd ed.). Portland, ME: Stenhouse.

Miller, D. (2002). *Reading with meaning.* Portland, ME: Stenhouse.

Murphy, J., Hern, C., Williams, R., & McLaughlin, T. (1990). The effects of the copy, cover, and compare approach in increasing spelling accuracy with learning disabled students. *Contemporary Educational Psychology, 15*, 378–386.

Prince George's County Public Schools. (2001). *Balanced literacy instruction: Training packet 2–3 classrooms.* Upper Marlboro, MD: Author.

Rathvon, N. (1999). *Effective school interventions.* New York: Guilford Press.

Santangelo, T., Harris, K. R., & Graham, S. (2007). Self-regulated strategy development: A validated model to support students who struggle with writing. *Learning Disabilities: A Contemporary Journal, 5*(1), 1–20.

Swartz, S., Klein, A., & Shook, R. (2002). *Interactive writing and interactive editing: Making connections between writing and reading.* Carlsbad, CA: Dominie Press.

Tompkins, G. (2009). *50 literacy strategies.* Upper Saddle River, NJ: Pearson.

Vaughn, S., Gersten, R., & Chard, D. (2000). The underlying message in LD intervention research. *Council for Exceptional Children, 67*, 99–114.

Vygotsky, L. (1978). The role of play in development. In *Mind in society: The development of higher psychological processes* (M. Cole, Trans.). Cambridge, MA: Harvard University Press.

Writing Center, University of North Carolina at Chapel Hill. (n.d.). Brainstorming. Retrieved October 12, 2009, from www.unc.edu/depts/wcweb/handouts/brainstorming.html.

Writing Center, University of North Carolina at Chapel Hill. (n.d.). Reorganizing your draft. Retrieved October 12, 2009, from www.unc.edu/depts/wcweb/handouts/organization.html.

Zimmerman, B. J. (2000). Attaining self-regulation: A social cognitive perspective. In M. Boekaerts, P. R. Pintrich, & M. Zeidner (Eds.), *Handbook of self-regulation* (pp. 13–39). San Diego, CA: Academic Press.

Zimmerman, B. J., & Risemberg, R. (1997). Becoming a self-regulated writer: A social cognitive perspective. *Contemporary Educational Psychology, 22*, 73–101.

Section II

Inventing Strategies

At some time, nearly every writer has experienced the problem of not being able to get started writing. This is often called writer's block. Whether you are a teacher writing reports or a graduate student composing an academic paper, the blank computer screen stares at you; the cursor is blink, blink, blinking; but your mind is blank, blank, blanking. Or maybe your mind is filled with too many ideas, and you don't know how to select the most important or appropriate one. You have no idea what to write or how to get started. Have you ever experienced these feelings? Then you probably could have benefited from some inventing strategies.

Inventing or invention is the initial part of the writing process. Effective writers invent when they brainstorm, organize, and clarify their thoughts and knowledge about a topic. Prewriting strategies, such as using graphic organizers, reading more about a topic, and employing questioning techniques, come into play during the invention phase.

HOW INVENTING STRATEGIES HELP STUDENTS

When we work with students in kindergarten through grade 3, we observe that inventing strategies help to activate students' prior knowledge about their topics as they work toward becoming independent writers. Students reflect on vocabulary related to the topics, experiences they've had around the topics, and texts they've read or viewed about the topics. Having a storehouse of inventing strategies gives students control of their writing. Mastering inventing strategies gives them the tools they need to make informed decisions as they select and write about topics of interest to them. When topics are assigned to students as part of academic tasks, inventing strategies help students think of and organize how assigned topics connect to books they have read, experiences they have had, and world events.

Inventing strategies can be particularly helpful for diverse learners and writers, such as struggling writers and students for whom English is a second language. Talking about and noting key concepts and vocabulary related to their topics before drafting are highly beneficial for these students.

STRATEGIES IN THIS SECTION

The five chapters in Section Two focus on this initial part of the writing process—inventing. Chapter Six, Noun Charts, helps students identify and generate nouns in their environment before they begin writing stories, poetry, and content text. In Chapter Seven, Growing a Poem with Interview Buddies, partners collaborate to generate ideas or "grow" a poem from a seed idea. In addition, students generate and use a few of their own questions to practice and develop the use of self-questioning as a writing strategy. The strategy presented in Chapter Eight, Let's Tell a Story, is a prerequisite to students' story writing. Students collaborate in role playing and creative drama to help them identify the four key features of stories, which they are then able to include in their writing. Chapter Nine, Writing Rockets and Other Graphic Organizers, contains a strategy that helps students use visual representations to plan and organize their nonfiction compositions. Finally, Chapter Ten, Interest Charts, helps students identify their interests and recognize their ideas are worthy as writing topics. Students add to their personal Interest Charts and use them to construct topics for writing.

Chapter 6

Noun Charts

CYNTHIA B. LEUNG

This strategy helps students identify nouns in their environment and in their writing. The Noun Charts strategy also helps students generate possible nouns they might use before they begin writing stories, poetry, and content text.

Why This Strategy Is Important

When students know and can identify parts of speech, they develop metacognitive awareness of their writing. They can talk about their writing and can understand when the teacher or peers critique what they have written. Grammar terms provide a common language to talk about revision. Also, identifying nouns is an important skill students need in order to understand subject-verb agreement. When students can identify nouns and determine if they are singular or plural, they can check to see that singular verb forms are used with singular nouns and plural verb forms are used with plural nouns. To write colorful and descriptive adjectives to modify nouns, students need to be able to identify nouns in their writing. Further, identifying nouns helps students recognize and write prepositional phrases because the objects of prepositional phrases are nouns or pronouns. Students learn that prepositional phrases can modify nouns, and that nouns that are objects of prepositional phrases cannot be subjects or objects of sentences.

As a teacher educator and literacy researcher, I receive many requests for grammar strategies from my graduate students who are elementary school teachers. Some of these teachers work with students who are learning English as a second or third language. These teachers have used grammar worksheets with their students, but their students were unable to make connections between the abstract grammar rules they learned from worksheets and their own writing (Cunningham & Cunningham, 2009). The students did not understand why it was important to learn grammar or why learning about grammar might help them improve their writing.

I developed the Noun Charts strategy to help students both identify nouns and connect their knowledge of nouns to their own writing. I found that students can more easily understand parts of speech when they use charts, rather than the traditional sentence diagramming, to analyze sentence structure. Most students are familiar with charts, so they do not need to learn a new and specialized system of diagramming to analyze their sentences. The teachers with whom I work have found Noun Charts to be useful graphic organizers for students who have not developed metacognitive awareness of their writing, or for those who need to check their subject-verb agreement.

The SCAMPER Model for Noun Charts

Survey and Assess

To identify those students who do not know what nouns are, I **survey and assess** the entire class. I give students a copy of the Noun Chart (see Figure 6.1) and a short passage of a few paragraphs from one of the books we have recently read. I ask students to find as many nouns as they can in the passage and to write the words for the nouns in the appropriate columns of the chart. I then look at their charts to see if they have correctly identified the nouns in the passage.

People	Animals	Objects	Places	Ideas

Figure 6.1 Noun Chart

Confer

To introduce the strategy, I **confer** with students in a whole-class context. I ask them to share some words that are nouns. Then I explain,

> Nouns are words that name things like people, animals, objects, places, and ideas. In fact, all these words—people, animals, objects, places, and ideas—are nouns. Nouns are important words you use in your writing. Why do you think nouns are important?

Students share their ideas. Then I add,

> If you can identify nouns, you can improve your writing. You can use more colorful nouns, and you can check to see if your verbs agree with your subjects, which are usually nouns. I will show you charts you can use to identify nouns and to tell if nouns are singular or plural, or common or proper.

Assemble Materials

Once I have surveyed, assessed, and conferred with my students, I know who needs to engage in the Noun Charts strategy mini-lesson. I next **assemble materials** we will need. I provide photocopies of the Noun Chart for each student in my small group. I use a document camera or overhead projector and transparency to project the Noun Chart onto a screen or wall so students can see more clearly. I use a pen, pencil, or overhead marker to fill in the chart. I assemble slips of paper or 3-by-5 index cards cut in half, on which students will write noun words. I also assemble small bags or boxes for students to use as they collect their nouns. Students use their Writing Strategies Journals and pencils to practice using their Noun Charts. They make charts in their journals and place appropriate nouns in the Noun Chart boxes. I photocopy passages from stories we recently read in class to practice identifying nouns from published texts. Finally, I include photocopies of both a piece of my own writing and of writing samples from several students in the class.

Model

I **model** the strategy for a small group of students by looking around the room and discovering nouns. I say, "Oh, look at the window. The word window is a noun because it is the name of an object." I then print the word *window* under the appropriate Objects column on the Noun Chart that is projected on the wall. I continue this way by saying, "We are in a classroom. The word *classroom* is a noun because it is the name of a place." I write *classroom* in a slot under Places in the Noun Chart. I then encourage students to look around the classroom for people, animals, objects, places, and ideas. I call on several students to tell me one of these nouns. For example, Carlos says that Maria, one of the students in the class, is a person, so I write *Maria* in the People column. Matt says that the desk is an object in the room, so I write *desk* in the Objects column. I give them an example of an idea that can go in the Ideas column, such as happiness or patriotism. I provide an example of a place, such as the name of their school or city, for the Places column.

Practice

When students understand how to fill in their charts, I ask them to walk around the classroom to see how many nouns they can find. I tell them to write the names of the nouns on slips of paper. I give each student a small box or bag in which to put the slips of paper. I ask second language learners to partner with native speakers. After students have ten to fifteen slips of paper in their boxes or bags, I ask them to return to their seats and look through the slips of paper they have collected. I then give them photocopies of the chart so they can **practice** the strategy. I ask them to write the names of their nouns in the appropriate columns. All the people nouns will go in the People column, the object nouns in the Objects column, and so on. After students have filled in their charts, I go over each column and ask students what noun words they put in that column. I write the words on my projected chart so all students in the small group can see them (see Figure 6.2).

We also practice using Noun Charts with a printed text. I give students a photocopied passage from a story we read in class. I ask them to circle the words that are nouns. Then I ask them to draw Noun Charts in their Writing Strategies Journals and write the noun words in the appropriate columns. After they have written the words in the columns, we go over the words, and I answer questions students may have about identifying nouns. I ask, "Did you find any nouns that you think are colorful or exciting words? Why do you think the author used those particular words?"

People	Animals	Objects	Places	Ideas
teacher Mr. Brown	hamster	desk books	classroom Happy Days School	happiness

Figure 6.2 Noun Chart with Examples

Execute

To help students **execute** the Noun Charts strategy, I work with them in small-group settings. I show students a piece of my own writing and point to several nouns. I tell students why I chose to use those particular nouns in my writing. I show them how singular nouns that are subjects of my sentences take singular verbs and plural nouns take plural verbs. I make photocopies of writing samples from several students in the class, and we hunt for nouns in the students' writing. Students draw their second Noun Charts in their Writing Strategies Journals and fill in the nouns. Then they each select one of their own writing pieces from their journals, and they hunt for nouns in their own writing. Each student draws another Noun Chart in his or her notebook and writes down the nouns.

As students begin to think of ideas for their stories, poems, and nonfiction, they continue to execute the strategy by drawing Noun Charts in their Writing Strategies Journals and filling in the slots with nouns they might use in their writing. They also use the strategy to think of synonyms and other more descriptive nouns they might employ as they write. They use a thesaurus to build their vocabulary before beginning to write, so they will not be slowed down looking for more descriptive words as they write. In addition, students independently use the strategy to identify both singular and plural nouns they might use. Once students feel confident using the Noun Charts, they can apply the strategy independently to check subject-verb agreement and to brainstorm more expressive noun words.

Reflect

As students use Noun Charts to think of nouns they might use in their writing, they begin to make connections between grammar concepts and writing. I ask students to **reflect** on their work and to share with the class or a small group their definitions of a noun. I also ask them to explain how some singular nouns can be transformed into plural nouns.

Adapting the Strategy

Adapting the Strategy for Emerging Writers

With emerging writers, I focus first on nouns that represent people, animals, and objects. I ask students to walk around the classroom with baskets of cards and markers. Each student identifies a person, animal, or object in the classroom and draws a picture of it on one of the cards taken from the basket. Students continue until they have about five cards in their baskets. When they return to their desks, students sound out the words for the nouns and write the words on the cards using invented spelling. Sometimes I ask students to write on each card the first or the last sound they hear in the word. I then give students enlarged copies of the Noun Chart with three columns for people, animals, or objects, and I ask them to place their cards in the appropriate columns. I have a small picture of a person, animal, and object at the top of the column beside the words People, Animals, and Objects. When students understand how to use the chart, I give each student a copy of a chart with cells large enough to write a word and draw a small picture in each. I then ask students to work in small groups and collect nouns from pictures in magazines. They write the words for each noun using invented spelling and draw a picture of the person, animal, or object within the same square, or they cut out the pictures from magazines and paste them in the appropriate columns. They share with the class the words they put in their Noun Charts.

Adapting the Strategy for Writers Who Struggle

Writers who struggle can practice this strategy in small groups or paired with more proficient writers. They may need additional practice with simple sentences. I make a list of simple sentences from their own writing pieces or from their peers' writing, and use these sentences for students to practice the strategy by identifying nouns and writing them in Noun Charts. Writers who struggle may prefer to use photocopied charts instead of drawing their own charts in their Writing Strategies Journals. I also have them draw pictures to represent nouns that refer to people, animals, objects, places, and sometimes ideas. I ask other students in their small group to guess what they have drawn. The cells of the chart are enlarged so students can draw pictures of each noun in the appropriate cell and copy the word from the sample sentences. I show them how to use a thesaurus to select synonyms for nouns they have placed in their Noun Charts. I ask them to add these nouns to their charts. I tell them they can use these more interesting words in their writing. The strategy is especially good for writers with limited vocabularies.

Adapting the Strategy for English Language Learners

English language learners (ELLs) who are in the preproduction stage and are not yet speaking English can draw pictures of people, animals, and objects. They can work in small groups of peers, and they can pronounce the words in English or their home languages. They can also copy the words for their nouns from index cards with words printed on them. I create a PowerPoint with pictures of various objects, one picture on each slide, with the word for the object at the bottom of the slide. I work individually with ELLs at the preproduction and early production stages to choose several objects that are nouns. I help them copy the words for those objects in their Writing

Strategies Journals and show them how to draw pictures next to the noun words to remind them of those words. I pair ELLs with English-speaking peers to complete their Noun Charts and read the words. I encourage all ELLs to draw pictures to represent the noun words they do not know and to use invented spelling to write the sounds they can identify in the words. I then ask them to use a picture dictionary to find the standard spellings of the words. They write the standard spellings in their Writing Strategies Journals with drawings of the objects. More advanced ELLs use a thesaurus to find synonyms for nouns in their charts.

Adapting the Strategy for Advanced Writers

Advanced writers can use Noun Charts to become proficient at identifying nouns. When they can identify nouns, I ask them to make two-column charts in their Writing Strategies Journals with nouns in the first column and verbs that might go with those nouns in the second column. In small groups they can review one another's charts and check for subject-verb agreement.

Extending the Strategy

When students are able to identify nouns, I introduce variations of the Noun Chart. I say, "Notice that some of the words are written with capital letters. These are names of specific people and places and are called proper nouns. The other nouns that are not capitalized are common nouns." I ask each student to take words from one of his or her charts and separate the words into proper and common nouns, as in Figure 6.3.

Common Nouns	Proper Nouns
teacher	Mr. Brown
hamster	Happy Days School
desk	
classroom	
happiness	
books	

Figure 6.3 Noun Chart for Common and Proper Nouns

Another variation to the chart is the singular and plural Noun Chart, as in Figure 6.4. I ask students first to take singular words from one of their Noun Charts and write them in the left-hand column of each new chart. Then I ask them to supply the plural forms of the words in the right-hand column. When they have filled in all their singular words, I ask them to find the plural words from their original Noun Charts and put these in the right-hand column. Then they fill in the singular forms of the nouns in the left-hand column.

When students understand the concept of a noun, they can learn other parts of speech. The Noun Charts strategy assists students who still have difficulty identifying nouns in their own writing and selecting more advanced or varied vocabulary for their

Singular Nouns	Plural Nouns
teacher	teachers
hamster	hamsters
desk	desks
classroom	classrooms
book	books

Figure 6.4 Noun Chart for Singular and Plural Nouns

writing. Using the strategy, students can independently identify nouns and use a thesaurus to find more expressive nouns before asking their teacher or peers for help.

EVIDENCE CONNECTIONS

Topping, D. H., & Hoffman, S. J. (2006). *Getting grammar: 150 new ways to teach an old subject*. Portsmouth, NH: Heinemann.
Topping and Hoffman have a playful approach to grammar instruction. At the same time, however, they stress the importance of a student's developing a vocabulary of grammar terms to aid in writing revision and metacognition related to language production. This book provides instructions for many hands-on, multimodal activities to help students understand the parts of speech and types of phrases in English. They even introduce a method of sentence diagramming that uses body movement and word strips. Photographs clearly demonstrate how to carry out some of the activities. With modifications, many of these grammar activities can become strategies to help students write independently. The authors also provide suggestions for teaching grammar terms and concepts to second language learners.

Polette, K. (2007). *Teaching grammar through writing: Activities to develop writer's craft in ALL students in grades 4–12*. Boston: Allyn & Bacon.
This book focuses on helping students understand parts of speech, phrases, and clauses through a writing approach to grammar. Polette provides activities, strategies, and examples from well-known children's books to guide students in applying what they learn about grammar to their own writing. The book is a good reference tool for teachers and students. Teachers can select activities or exercises to supplement writing lessons, or they can follow the scope and sequence of instruction the author suggests.

REFERENCE

Cunningham, P., & Cunningham, J. (2009). *What really matters in writing: Research-based practices across the elementary curriculum*. New York: Allyn & Bacon.

Chapter 7

Growing a Poem with Interview Buddies

CINDY LASSONDE

Interview buddies use a list of prompts about a feeling, concept, or object to generate ideas or "grow" a poem. In addition, each person thinks of one or two of his or her own questions in order to practice and develop the use of self-questioning as a writing strategy. The buddies draw an image representing the ideas generated from the interviews. They then record words within the image to invent ideas and build vocabulary in preparation for writing a simple poem, such as a list or shape poem.

Why This Strategy Is Important

"How do I decide what to write about?" "Where do I get ideas?" "How do I fit what I want to say into a poem?" "Do I need to use some kind of 'fancy' language?" "Does it have to rhyme?" "How do I start?" What teacher hasn't heard resistant students moan when poetry writing is mentioned? What is meant to be a creative opportunity for students is often viewed by them as a difficult, unpleasant task. Getting started with poetry—the invention part—can be intimidating for some students.

As a primary teacher, I recognized how valuable poetry writing was as a regular activity in the curriculum. I knew my students could "discover words, sound, and rhythm in unique, creative ways" and learn how to manipulate words to "capture the essence of meaning in the sparest of language" (Fountas & Pinnell, 2001, p. 410). In addition, I knew poetry allowed students to develop an appreciation of language, conceptual knowledge, empathy, self-expression, insight about themselves, and pleasure through creativity (Norton & Norton, 2010). I wanted my students to enjoy and become engaged in the experience. I didn't want them to feel it was just a meaningless, do-I-*have*-to-do-this kind of activity.

Knowing that students typically are highly motivated by working and writing with buddies, I constructed the Growing a Poem with Interview Buddies strategy to encourage interaction among my young, budding poets and to increase motivation. What resulted was amazing! I started seeing previously disengaged student writers collaborate and become immersed in the intrigue of capturing the essence of their mutual ideas within the genre of poetry. The strategy tore down their negative and almost fearful perceptions of what writing poetry involves and freed them (without their even realizing it) to enjoy the process. Through their enjoyable, shared experiences, they began to appreciate the uniqueness of poetic forms as a way to express themselves and to make words sing (Darigan, Tunnell, & Jacobs, 2002). Their partnerships ("buddieships") scaffolded them to become comfortable initiating poems independently.

The SCAMPER Model for Growing a Poem with Interview Buddies

Survey and Assess

I find it helpful to **survey and assess** students' attitudes about writing poetry before we begin writing poems ourselves. I do this by reading age-appropriate poems to them. In particular, I have found that primary students enjoy nursery rhymes and story poems. During shared reading I observe whether they jump in verbally to complete rhyming patterns or show they are caught up in the rhythm or cadence of the poem by their body movements (in other words, head-bobbing, hand movements, rocking), or if they react and respond inquisitively to the poem.

Next we write a simple group poem together so I can observe students' ability to invent ideas for poems. Here's an example of a poem I wrote interactively with a class of first graders:

> *As I was walking in the woods, I saw*
> *A tree as tall as the Statue of Liberty.*
> *As I was walking in the woods, I smelled*
> *The stuffy scent of the leaves.*
> *As I was walking in the woods, I heard*
> *My footsteps crunching down on crisp, brown leaves.*
> *As I was walking in the woods, I felt*
> *The cool October wind sweep across my cheeks.*
> *It's fall in the woods. I love fall time!*

To begin, I ask students questions that deal with writing poems, such as "Is there something special you'd like to write about?" and "How will our poem be different from a story?" Once we have a topic for our poem, I start them out with a pattern and prompt their ideas with questions. As I write their thoughts on chart paper for everyone to see, I use self-questioning to offer suggestions for how to add descriptive verbs and adjectives to make our poem interesting.

> *Hmm. As I was walking in the woods, I* saw . . . *what would I see walking in the woods? Trees. Lots of big, tall trees. How could I describe those*

trees? Well, once I went to New York City and saw this huge statue called the Statue of Liberty. She had her one arm stretched way up into the sky like the branches on trees reach upward. So let's compare the tall trees to the Statue of Liberty. What might I smell as I walked in the woods?

As we write, I note who is engaged and contributes words or ideas. This helps me determine if they understand the concept of what a poem is, and it allows me to gauge their knowledge of the challenges of writing poetry, namely line breaks, chunking ideas, inventing, and using imagery and descriptive language. I jot down anecdotal notes after I have informally observed students' responses and behaviors. Once I understand how many students are resistant to or unfamiliar with writing poems, I form small learning groups and begin our multimodal writing strategy mini-lesson.

Confer

Now that I have a small group of students who could benefit from learning the strategy together, I **confer** with them. I begin by asking, "What is a poem?" I then maintain a discussion with the group to prompt them to think about the process they will experience as they get started and their attitudes about writing poetry. I ask,

"What do you like about writing poems?"

"Is there anything you don't like about writing poems?"

"How do you get ideas for poems?"

"How do you start writing a poem?"

"Do you ever have trouble getting started?"

"Would it be helpful if you had a friend who would help you think of ideas for your poem?"

Then I explain that we will learn how to get started writing a poem with a buddy. I tell them this lesson will allow them to help each other grow ideas for their poems in a fun way—by working together and pretending they are news reporters. They will be able to apply what they learn when they want to write poems independently.

Assemble Materials

I **assemble materials,** which include some of my favorite children's poems to have on hand for inspiration and reference while working; chart paper and markers; and plenty of other writing materials to motivate young writers, such as colored pencils, crayons, scented markers, and colored paper cut into different shapes. I display the Grow a Poem poster shown in Figure 7.1 and hand out an individual copy to each student. Students should paste these copies into their journals for use when they are writing poems independently.

Model

I **model** by asking a student to be my interview buddy. I explain that we can get ideas to write poems by asking each other questions and sharing our answers. Then I show the group the poster of the seven Grow a Poem questions that I've laminated and posted on the classroom wall.

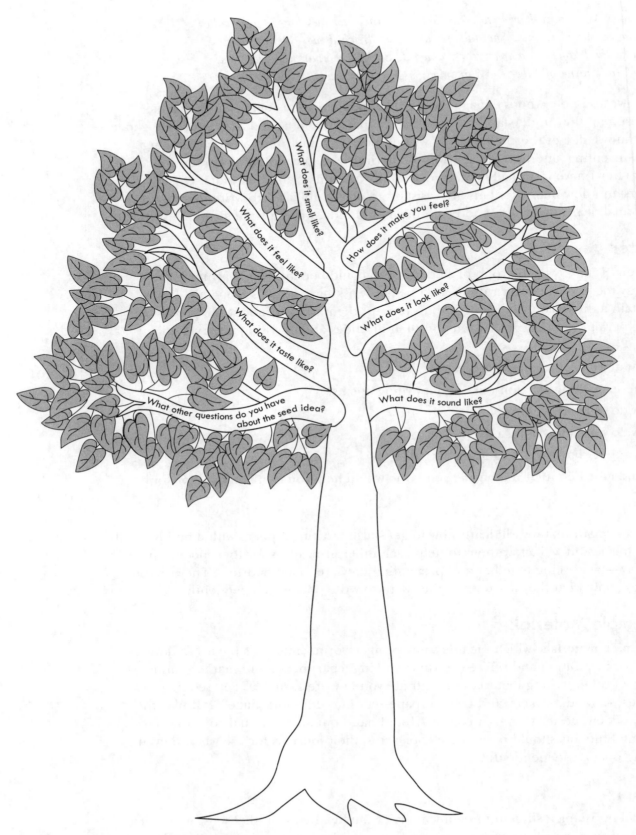

Text within the image (part of the illustration):
What does it smell like?
What does it feel like?
How does it make you feel?
What does it taste like?
What does it look like?
What other questions do you have about the seed idea?
What does it sound like?

Figure 7.1 Grow a Poem Poster

Here's a sample conversation I might have with my student buddy to model the strategy:

Cindy: Let's write a poem about our first day in second grade. That's my seed idea ...the idea that will start my brain thinking. Let's begin with the starter questions to think of some ideas. Then we can make up some of our own questions. What's the first Grow a Poem question we want to ask ourselves?

Monique: (reading from a laminated poster on the wall) How does it make you feel?

Cindy: How did you feel the first day of second grade?

Monique: I was nervous, but I was excited, too.

Cindy: Me too. I was happy, too. What's the next Grow a Poem question? Let's see. It's What does it look like?

Monique: It's a tall, brick building outside. It looks strong and big.

Cindy: But inside the classroom there were lots of colorful pictures on the walls. The desks and floors were all shiny and clean. And it was good to see some friends that I knew from last year.

In this way, we work our way through the seven Grow a Poem questions by interviewing each other. We discuss our answers to the questions. This conversation helps us generate concepts and vocabulary we may end up using in our poem. We finish our conversation by asking each other the final question: "What other questions do you have about the seed idea?" We then answer those questions.

Next we take out our paper and inspiring writing utensils and draw a picture or, if we prefer, separate pictures of the images we've just constructed through our interview. When we are done drawing, we talk about the picture or pictures and then label parts of them. This final step allows me and my buddy to generate images and vocabulary we may use in our poem.

Practice

I review the strategy with the students and ask them to **practice** buddy interviewing and self-questioning about a new topic, such as growing up or summer fun. I stand by to scaffold and support their progress, prompting them with suggestions of open-ended questions to ask about their senses and feelings.

Execute

In the next step, students **execute** the strategy and work toward independent, self-regulated writing. I support their efforts and remind them to use their copies of the Grow a Poem poster to grow their seed ideas—the main idea topics—for their poems.

Reflect

In the final step I encourage students to **reflect** and talk about their poems and their use of the strategy. We talk about how they could use this questioning and interviewing strategy when they are writing poems in the future. I ask them to talk about how this strategy made their writing better. I also find it helpful to ask students to tell each other how they think the strategy improved others' poems.

Adapting the Strategy

Adapting the Strategy for Emerging Writers

With emerging writers who may not yet be readers, I add symbols to the Grow a Poem questions. Figure 7.2 shows some examples. Or older students could be invited into the class to be interview buddies with the emerging writers. I adjust my expectations for poem length and complexity to the writing levels of the students.

Adapting the Strategy for Writers Who Struggle

Struggling writers often have very creative ideas for poems but struggle with how to put them down on paper. I provide support by posting class-generated lists on themed word walls that are relevant to the Grow a Poem questions. For example, I might post a list of words related to how something looks, tastes, feels, and so on. Struggling writers pull words from the lists for their writing, and they tell me which words we should add to expand the lists.

Adapting the Strategy for English Language Learners

English language learners benefit from the oral exchanges of this strategy. I provide multiple chances for interview buddies to work together. They repeat the questions and become familiar with them. The questions may be written in the children's first languages in their journals to reinforce the English versions. It is important that English language learners maintain control of the ideas going into their poems, so I

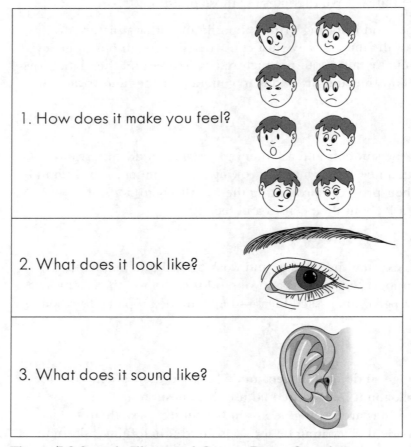

Figure 7.2 Sample Illustrated Grow a Poem Questions

scaffold the students' exchanges between their two languages to ensure that these students' ideas are not restricted by their writing and language abilities.

Adapting the Strategy for Advanced Writers

For these students, I raise my expectations for the number and depth of the questions they generate themselves after using the seven Grow a Poem questions. I expect advanced poets to be able to construct questions about the use of personification, imagery, or metaphors in a poem (such as What would it do if it were human?).

Extending the Strategy

This inventing strategy can become a useful tool that students can use for all genres of writing. I keep a basket of construction-paper leaves by the Grow a Poem poster. I tell students they can take leaves from the basket and write the questions they created on them. I add their leaves to the poster. Students use each other's self-generated questions for their own independent writing.

EVIDENCE CONNECTIONS

Vass, E., Littleton, K., Miell, D., & Jones, A. (2008). The discourse of collaborative creative writing: Peer collaboration as a context for mutual inspiration. *Thinking Skills and Creativity*, *3*, 192–202.
Drawing on sociocultural theory, Vass and colleagues undertook a study of children's classroom-based, collaborative creative writing. Their research focused on the ways in which peer collaboration can stimulate and enhance creative writing activities. The study consisted of longitudinal observations of children ages seven through nine as they were writing in small groups. Results linked students' collaboration to their engagement in the process. The research described characteristics of effective collaboration that support joint creative writing activities. Primarily, the interruptions and overlaps that occurred in the conversations between members of the groups promoted joint focus and intense sharing of ideas. Joint focus and sharing inspired members to generate content. This study supports the Growing a Poem with Interview Buddies strategy in that the Grow a Poem questions focus students and help them share their ideas through two-person dialogues.

Janssen, T. (2002). Instruction in self-questioning as a literary reading strategy: An exploration of empirical research. *Educational Studies in Language and Literature*, *2*(2), 95–120.
Janssen's summary of existing research on self-questioning reveals that several studies have found this process can play an important role in self-regulated learning (Dillon, 1988; Scardamalia & Bereiter, 1992; Weinrich, 1983). According to schema theory, students call on their experiences to build mental "scripts" that promote comprehension. Teaching students to activate relevant prior knowledge about a topic enhances questioning, restructuring the schemata and improving comprehension. Self-questioning becomes a useful comprehension tool when the student notes that he or she lacks a piece of knowledge or an experience to understand a topic or concept, and starts searching for an answer or a solution. The search initially occurs in the

mind. With guidance, questioning can become a social act among students. When we apply these findings to the Growing a Poem with Interview Buddies strategy, we see that students can be trained to ask questions that may lead to significant gains in their comprehension of a topic and, therefore, facilitate their writing about the topic.

REFERENCES

Darigan, D., Tunnell, M., & Jacobs, J. (2002). *Children's literature: Engaging teachers and children in good books.* Upper Saddle River, NJ: Prentice Hall.

Dillon, J. T. (1988). The remedial status of student questioning. *Curriculum Studies, 20,* 197–210.

Fountas, I., & Pinnell, G. (2001). *Guiding readers and writers grades 3–6: Teaching comprehension, genre, and content literacy.* Portsmouth, NH: Heinemann.

Norton, D. E. & Norton, S. (2010). *Through the eyes of a child: An introduction to children's literature* (8th ed.). Upper Saddle River, NJ: Prentice Hall.

Scardamalia, M. & Bereiter, C. (1992). Text-based and knowledge-based questioning by children. *Cognition and Instruction, 9*(3), 177–199.

Weinrich, H. (1983). Vers la constitution d'une compétence interrogative. [Towards a competence in questioning.] *Zielsprache Französisch: Zeitschrift für Französisch-Unterricht in der Welt, 2,* 57–64.

Chapter  8

Let's Tell a Story

JANET RICHARDS

The ability to identify the four key features in stories is a prerequisite to students' story writing. In this strategy, students collaboratively participate in role playing and creative drama to help them identify the four key features of stories so that they are able to include these elements in their written stories.

Why This Strategy Is Important

Many students enter school with little knowledge of narrative structures, and therefore they often fail to notice the four key features of all good stories: characters, settings, problems, and solutions. If primary students do not know basic story features, they cannot compose fully developed stories.

Jeff, one of my graduate students, told me he stresses the four main story features in quality children's literature as early as the first week of school. However, Jeff also said that by mid-December of the school year many of his students continue to have difficulty identifying the characters, settings, problems, and solutions in the stories they hear or read. Jeff explained:

> *Because many of my students have problems identifying the four key features in stories, they don't include these four major features in their own stories. For example one boy, Sam, recently wrote a story that consisted of a simple sentence that offered a personal account: "MY FRAED CRISTOBer and I play my game Boy."*

> *Other students attempt to write stories but neglect to include all of the four main story elements in their writing. Last week one of my students, Patty, wrote this story: "A buny nam was sam and he hoppt roud the yad. He ate carots."*

> *Another student, Jackson, wrote, "Mi cat, Morgan ate a lizrd and got sik."*

Jeff's three students are not atypical. As I work in primary classrooms, I meet many students like Sam, Patty, and Jackson who have difficulties coordinating the cognitive demands of writing stories that contain the four basic features of characters, settings, problems, and solutions.

I have developed a strategy entitled Let's Tell a Story, which helps primary students construct knowledge about the four key elements in stories through role playing and dramatic enactments. Role playing and creative drama scaffold students who otherwise might have difficulty recognizing characters, settings, problems, and solutions in stories and incorporating these features into their own fiction (Cline & Ingerson, 1996; Creech & Bhavnagri, 2002). In addition, meta-analysis indicates children from families of low socioeconomic status particularly benefit from dramatic enactments (Podlozny, 2000). In fact, all students learn best through the integration of different modes of learning (Bredekamp & Copple, 1997). For example, an emphasis on drama facilitates language development (Katz & Chard, 1989).

The SCAMPER Model for Let's Tell a Story

Survey and Assess

I find it helpful to **survey and assess** students' concepts of what a story is and their knowledge of the four basic story features as I read stories to them. I use a short scoring rubric I devised that helps me identify each student's ability to describe what makes a good story and to retell a story that includes characters, settings, problems, and solutions (see Figure 8.1).

Note that each story will have a set number of points possible depending upon its total number of characters, settings, problems, and solutions. For example, in "Goldilocks and the Three Bears," there are four characters. Therefore, the total number of available points is four for story characters. There are two settings: the house and the woods. Therefore, the total number of points available for settings is two. The number of problems varies according to whether you are looking at it from the three bears' perspective or Goldilocks's point of view. For example, from Goldilocks's point of view, the porridge was too hot or too cold, the chairs were too small or too big, and the beds were too hard or too soft. From the bear's perspective, Goldilocks invaded their house. She ate Baby Bear's porridge; and she broke Baby Bear's chair. In this story, children might discover solutions for Goldilocks's problems. She switched bowls of porridge, chairs, and beds until they were "just right." Therefore, the total number of points available for "Goldilocks and the Three Bears" depends on children's discussion of the fairy tale and their final conclusions.

I also ask students questions that deal with story features: "Who was in the story? Where did the story take place? What was the first problem in the story? How did (story character) solve that problem?"

Once I have a good understanding of how many students need additional help understanding the basic concept of a story and the features in stories, I form small learning groups and begin our Let's Tell a Story role-playing and creative-drama writing strategy mini-lesson.

Name: _____ Date: _____

Story Title: _____

Author: _____

Total Number of Points Available for Retelling: _____

Total Number of Points Achieved: _____

CHARACTER(S)—1 point each

1.

2.

3.

4.

SETTING(S)—1 point each

1.

2.

PROBLEM(S)—1 point each

1.

2.

3.

SOLUTION(S)—1 point each

1.

2.

3.

4.

Figure 8.1 Scoring Rubric for Retelling of a Story

Confer

I **confer** with students and say,

> *Do you like to make up stories? What is a story? Let's tell a story together. I'll tell the story, and you can help me by acting out the parts of the story. This will help you recognize the four main features of stories: characters, settings, problems, and solutions. Once you know the four main parts of stories, you can include these features in your own stories to make them interesting and fun for others to read.*

I continue to confer with students, talking about story characters, settings, problems, and solutions for approximately three to five minutes.

Assemble Materials

I **assemble materials,** including large chart paper, a variety of colored markers, and a black marker. I focus the students and organize my thoughts to present a clear, easy-to-follow demonstration.

Model

I **model** by telling a story and helping students engage in role playing.

Janet: Once upon a time there was a teacher, and her name was Janet, and she had five students. (Here I state the students' names. For example, Beth, Donald, Julie, Robert, and Gail.) The end! Was that a good story?

Beth and Donald: (with confused expressions) No.

Gail: Hmmmm.

Janet: What do you think was wrong with the story?

Julie and Robert: It was too short.

Janet: Was it boring because nothing happened?

Students: Yes.

Janet: Okay, I better tell more of the story. Once upon a time there was a teacher, and her name was Janet, and she had five students whose names were Beth, Donald, Julie, Robert, and Gail, and they were in their classroom in Bowley School. The end. How was that story?

Gail and Robert: It was still too short.

Janet: Yes, it was short. I named the characters in the story, us, and I told where the story took place, the setting, which is our classroom in Bowley School. (I write *Characters—Beth, Donald, Julie, Robert, and Gail* and *Setting—our classroom in Bowley School* on the chart.) But my story still needs two more story features, because all good stories tell about the characters, settings, problems, and solutions. So I have to retell the story and state a problem and a solution. (I repeat the beginning of the story and continue.) Well, one day, Janet called up her five students and said, ''Kids, we're going on a field trip today so I need to collect your money for the bus. Line up.'' (I then have students stand in a line. I continue to role-play with them.) Okay, please give me your money. Beth you're first. Let me check off your name. (I continue this role-play with the other students until I get to the fifth student, Gail.) Okay, Gail, please let me have your field trip money. (Then I whisper to Gail and tell her to put her hand in her pocket and say that she can't find her money.)

Gail: I can't find my money.

Janet: Oh, no! That's a terrible problem. (I write *Problem—Gail can't find her money* on the chart.) Where were you before you came to our classroom? (I whisper to Gail and tell her what to say.)

Gail: I was in the principal's office.

Janet: Maybe you dropped the money in the principal's office. Donald, go with Gail to the principal's office. (I whisper to Gail and Donald and tell them they might find the money on the floor in the principal's office. I point to a corner of the room.) Donald and Gail, go to the principal's office over there in the corner. (Gail and Donald skip over to the principal's office in the corner.) Did you find the money?

Gail and Donald: Yes, the money was on the floor.

Janet: Great! The problem is solved. (I write *Solution—money was found in the principal's office* on the chart.) Now I'm going to tell the story again. When I say the characters' names, we'll stand up and say, "Who?" When I say the setting, we'll point to the floor and say, "Where?" When I say the problem, we'll say, "Oh, no!" When I say the solution, let's all shout, "GREAT!"

Practice

The following day I review the strategy with the students. This time I ask them to **practice** telling the story with my help, and once again we engage in role playing. We practice using the cues "Who?" to identify the character or characters, "Where?" to identify the setting, "Oh, no!" to identify the problem, and "Great!" to identify the solution. I then encourage the students to plan and tell a new story. I scaffold their creative drama and help them record the characters, settings, problems, and solutions in story feature "clouds" on a chart like the one shown in Figure 8.2. Again we use the cues "Who?" "Where?" "Oh, no!" and "Great!" to identify the story features. With this assistance, I move the students to the upper levels of their zones of proximal development (Vygotsky, 1978).

Execute

In the next step students **execute** the strategy and shift from functioning in the performance-assisted zones of proximal development to functioning with minimal assistance (Bodrova & Leong, 1996; Creech & Bhavnagri, 2002). They plan and write individual stories, or they work in pairs and write collaborative stories. I support their efforts and ask them to tell or read their story plans or stories to me. I also encourage them to ask and answer these questions every time they write a story: (1) Who are the characters in my story? (2) Where does the story take place? (3) What problem or problems happen in my story? What is the "Oh, no!" feature? (4) How do the characters solve the problem or problems? What is the "Great!" feature? Gradually, I scaffold them from using the user-friendly cues to using the acronym CSPS to represent the **c**haracters, **s**ettings, **p**roblems, and **s**olutions in their stories.

Reflect

For the phase in which students **reflect,** they read or dramatize their written stories for peers in their mini-lesson group or for all members of the class. Authors ask peers for suggestions to make their stories more interesting. For example, a student might say to an author, "I don't know where the character John got the boat in your story. You did not write about that," or "What is the girl's name in your story? You did not tell us."

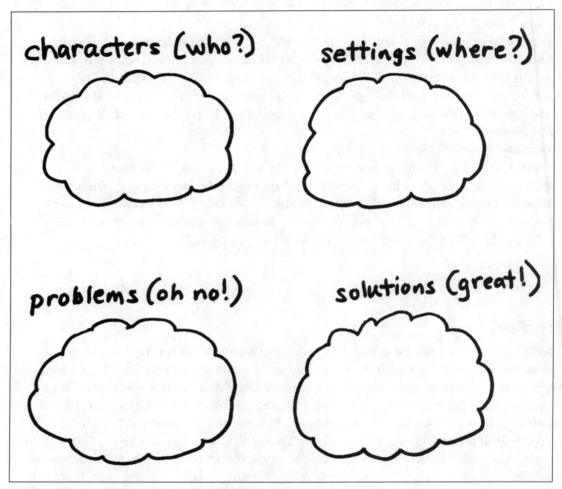

Figure 8.2 Story Feature Clouds

In this final part of the SCAMPER model I also encourage students to verbalize how they use this strategy in their independent writing.

Adapting the Strategy
Adapting the Strategy for Emerging Writers

The types of interactions used in this strategy reinforce story features for all students. My most important consideration for emerging writers is that they feel comfortable and confident as they work toward developing their writing abilities. Because emerging writers can draw their ideas, that is where I begin their mini-lesson instruction for Let's Tell a Story. I fold a large piece of paper into four parts and print the story feature *characters,* in one square. In the remaining three squares I print the story features *settings, problems,* and *solutions.* I place the paper on an easel. As we read or create a story, emerging writers come up to the easel and draw the story features pertinent to the story. I help them label the story characters' names and the settings, and I write short phrases to depict the problems and the solutions. We also draw connecting lines to show how the characters connect to the settings, problems, and solutions.

Adapting the Strategy for Writers Who Struggle

As might be expected, students who struggle with writing need considerable support learning this strategy. I use extensive dramatic enactments with these students until they feel comfortable talking about the story features of characters, settings, problems, and solutions. Often I scaffold struggling writers as they devise their own stories and share them with the class. I also take their dictation using a marker and chart paper, and then we color code the story characters, settings, problems, and solutions. (See Chapter Twenty-One, Color-Coding Editing.)

Adapting the Strategy for English Language Learners

English language learners (ELLs) also benefit from substantial practice using dramatic enactments. I scaffold ELLs' understanding of English by printing the names of the story characters and pinning these names on the students who play those parts. We also play a game I have devised called "Thumbs Up, Thumbs Down," in which we sit in a circle and name story features or fictitious story features in well-known nursery rhymes or fairy tales, such "Jack and Jill" or "Goldilocks and the Three Bears." For example, I might say, "Mama Bear is a story character in 'Goldilocks and the Three Bears,'" and we vote yes by giving a *thumbs up*. Alternately, I might say, "John Smith is a character in Goldilocks," and we vote *thumbs down* because John Smith is not a story character in Goldilocks. When ELL students master this part of the game, we move on to including story settings, problems, and solutions. For instance, I might say, "In the story 'Goldilocks and the Three Bears,' Goldilocks is the setting," and we vote *thumbs down*.

Adapting the Strategy for Advanced Writers

There are three ways to experience a story: reading the story, writing the story, and acting out the story (Creech & Bhavnagri, 2002). I encourage advanced students to experience and present their stories through all three modes of expression. I particularly encourage advanced students to collaborate and present their stories through puppet shows (see Lowe & Matthew, 2008); informal drama enactment; the visual arts; and technology. I also help students connect their stories to student-created lyrics and music, such as by playing rhythm band instruments to accompany the stories.

Extending the Strategy

We often make class books that contain students' stories. We also read or dramatize stories in other classrooms for students' enjoyment. When students are thoroughly familiar with the four key features in stories, we add other story elements to our role playing, such as story themes and foreshadowing events. Music and the visual arts work beautifully for foreshadowing events. Students also enter this strategy into their Writing Strategies Journals and describe its benefits.

EVIDENCE CONNECTIONS

Bodrova, E., & Leong, D. (1996). *Tools of the mind: The Vygotskian approach to early childhood education.* Englewood Cliffs, NJ: Merrill.

The Tools of the Mind project aims to foster the cognitive development of young children in relation to early literacy learning. The authors of the project have developed a number of tools to support early learning and a highly innovative method for training teachers in using these approaches. Piloting of the approaches has demonstrated their potential to develop children's early literacy skills, and they are being increasingly used in early childhood education programs across the United States. The project, the result of collaborative work between Russian and American education researchers, is based on the theories of Vygotsky and is applied to the cultural context of the United States.

Vygotsky, L. (1962). *Thought and language* (A. Kosulin, Ed. and Trans.). Cambridge, MA: MIT Press.

Vygotsky maintains that the child follows the adult's example and gradually develops the ability to do certain tasks without help or assistance. He called the difference between what a child can do with help and what he or she can do without guidance the zone of proximal development (ZPD). The whole-language approach to teaching reading and writing draws on this notion. As children play and interact with others at home and at school, they develop specific models of communication, expression, and explanation. Goodman and Goodman (1990) believe this social use of language forms the basis for literacy.

REFERENCES

Bodrova, E., & Leong, D. (1996). *Tools of the mind: The Vygotskian approach to early childhood education.* Englewood Cliffs, NJ: Merrill.

Bredekamp, S., & Copple, C. (1997). *Developmentally appropriate practice in early childhood programs.* Washington, DC: National Association for the Education of Young Children.

Cline, D. B., & Ingerson, D. (1996). The mystery of Humpty's fall: Primary school children as playmakers. *Young Children, 51*(6), 4–10.

Creech, N., & Bhavnagri, N. (2002). Teaching elements of story through drama to 1st graders. *Childhood Education, 7*(9), 219–224.

Goodman, K., & Goodman, Y. (1990). Managing the whole language classroom. *Instructor, 99*(6), 26–29.

Katz, L, & Chard, S (1989). *Engaging children's minds: The project approach.* Norwood, NJ: Ablex.

Lowe, J., & Matthew, K. (2008). *Puppet magic.* New York: Neal-Shulman.

Podlozny, A. (2000). Strengthening verbal skills through the use of classroom drama: A clear link. *Journal of Aesthetic Education, 34*, 239–275.

Vygotsky, L. S. (1978). *Mind in society: The development of higher psychological processes* (M. Cole, Trans.). Cambridge, MA: Harvard University Press.

Chapter

Writing Rockets and Other Graphic Organizers

TODD SUNDEEN

Writing Rockets and Other Graphic Organizers is a strategy that helps students plan and organize their nonfiction writing. Graphic organizers encourage students to access their prior knowledge about a topic and, if necessary, investigate a topic further before they compose. In this chapter I use the graphic organizer called Writing Rockets, and I show how this specific organizer helps students plan their compositions.

Why This Strategy Is Important

Primary students frequently skip the planning phase when they compose. When young writers do plan, they often spend little time thinking about what they know about a topic or developing their ideas into plans that are meaningful and useful. Thus they do not recognize ambiguities and missing information in their finished pieces. (For more on planning for nonfiction writing, see Chapter Twenty-Five, Comprehensive, Step-by-Step Composing for Nonfiction Writing.)

Prior to assuming my current role as a teacher educator, I was a teacher of young special education students in a low socioeconomic urban school in the southeast. My students often lacked the foundations of literacy necessary for academic success. Their families were from diverse backgrounds and included many from Caribbean islands whose languages did not have a written component. Parents frequently shared with me that they wanted to help their children learn, but they just did not have the ability or time to read to their children or help them with their writing assignments.

I recognized I needed to empower my students with specific writing strategies they could use independently. They needed help in understanding the steps in the process of writing, and they especially needed to learn how to organize their thoughts prior to writing drafts of nonfiction essays. Therefore, in conjunction with a unit on outer space, I devised the strategy Writing Rockets and Other Graphic Organizers to help my students plan and organize their compositions about space travel. Students named the strategy "Writing Rockets" because the Writing Rockets graphic organizer was in the shape of a rocket ship (see Figure 9.1). I found that when my students used this graphic organizer they became very enthusiastic about their writing. They experimented with their writing; they felt free to take risks and expand their thoughts. The students wrote long, complex sentences; they enjoyed sharing their writing with one another.

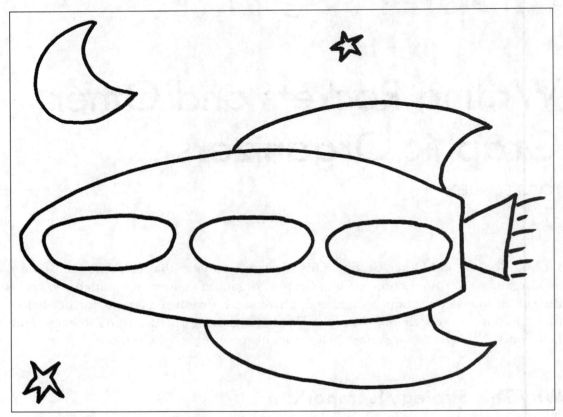

Figure 9.1 Writing Rockets Graphic Organizer

As a result, I decided to supply my students with content-specific graphic organizers for every unit of inquiry in which we engaged throughout the school year. For example, in conjunction with a unit on animals, I made graphic organizers in the shapes of various animals, and students chose the organizers that corresponded to the content of their compositions about animals. Similarly, when we studied families, I created graphic organizers in the shapes of children, parents, and grandparents. An essay about a favorite pet might entail a simple graphic organizer shaped like a fish tank with three bubbles or pudgy fish, in which students can write their main ideas; a composition about the world's greatest playground might have a swing set with three swings on which my writers can organize their thoughts. An essay about favorite vacations might include a car graphic organizer with three windows. Essentially, I devise topical graphic organizers that are easy to draw and duplicate and that relate directly to my students' writing topics (see Figure 9.2). When I teach mini-lessons about nonfiction writing to young students, I continue to use graphic organizers that connect to specific nonfiction topics.

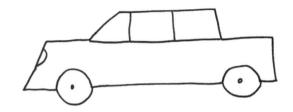

Family car: Example prompt—my favorite vacation

Swing set: Example prompt—my favorite playground equipment

Smiley face: Example prompt—what makes me laugh

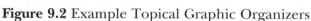

Home: Example prompt—what I like about my house

Fish bowl: Example prompt—my favorite pet

Figure 9.2 Example Topical Graphic Organizers

The SCAMPER Model for Writing Rockets and Other Graphic Organizers

Survey and Assess

I **survey and assess** my students as they write in order to understand to what degree they plan before they begin writing. In that way, I can assess who is ready to learn about and use this strategy to organize nonfiction pieces. As I observe my students, I keep several questions in mind. To what extent do they plan their writing, if at all? Do they use organizers? How do they use the organizers? Do they hurry through planning, or do they follow the steps necessary for using the organizers effectively? How much time do they spend prewriting prior to beginning their first drafts?

I formalize my student observations by keeping a checklist for each writer. Checklists do not take a significant amount of time; using checklists is a simple, convenient method of keeping accurate records for each student (see Table 9.1).

Table 9.1 Sample Checklist

Student Name	Minutes Spent Planning	Organizer Created (Y/N)	Organizer Used (Y/N)

Confer

It is critical that I discuss my students' writing with them. So I make time to share a few minutes with each student who I have determined is ready to learn the strategy. I **confer** with them about my expectations for their written products as they relate to the writing topic (in this case, outer space). I remind students of the steps of the writing process and emphasize instructions for organizing their work. Sometimes I include examples and explicitly reteach any concepts that students do not clearly understand. I balance my comments between encouragement and constructive suggestions. It is important that I listen carefully; my students provide me with a wealth of feedback about their understanding of the writing process.

Assemble Materials

I **assemble materials,** giving each student a preprinted copy of the Writing Rockets graphic organizer and a blank piece of paper. I make sure that I have markers or chalk for writing on the board, as well as extra copies of the graphic organizer. If the writing topic is about outer space, as in this example, the graphic organizer is in the shape of a rocket.

Model

I explicitly **model** each step of the graphic organizational strategy for my students. Specifically, the graphic organizer for the topic of space travel is in the shape of a rocket ship, with embedded spaces in which writers can add their main ideas as they prepare to write paragraphs that will make up short nonfiction essays. The Writing Rockets and Other Graphic Organizers mini-lesson enables students to experience prewriting within a prescribed structure. Students organize their thoughts before they begin writing in order to move their thinking from the abstract to the concrete. I have found this mini-lesson to be particularly effective in helping students develop sequencing in their writing.

I model each of the following steps for my writers:

1. I display the graphic organizer of a space ship shown in Figure 9.1.

2. As a lead-in, I might extend a science lesson on planets or the solar system. Another starting point could be a picture related to space travel or planets. Sometimes I present the nonfiction writing topic by expanding on a story students have just read about space travel. Or I may introduce the topic by simply writing on the board a sentence about a fantasy experience, such as traveling through space. We may talk about what it would be like to travel to another planet, sharing ideas and conceptions with one another. The lesson is an excellent choice for students from diverse backgrounds because the whole lesson is based on an imaginary trip rather than individuals' past experiences.

3. As I guide students through the process, I frequently think aloud while I model the steps. We begin by developing a sequence of events that starts on Earth and ends on Mars or another planet, perhaps choosing to create a list of items we would need on a trip to outer space. Students contribute their ideas about issues we might encounter as we plan for the trip, and I guide their thinking with facts about space while encouraging them to vividly imagine space travel. What might we need to get ready for the trip through space? What would be most important to pack on our trip? We also talk about the emotions that they might feel just before liftoff and how they would feel about leaving their friends at home on Earth. I encourage my students to also consider their senses during the trip. What would it feel like to be weightless? Would the stars look different? How would special food from plastic containers taste?

4. After we narrow our topic, we look at the Writing Rockets graphic organizers. Embedded in the rockets are three ovals into which the students write the main ideas of their paragraphs. Sometimes we add additional ovals for subtopics. I find that portraying the rocket ship horizontally in space allows me to create ovals large enough for students to write inside them. A horizontal ship also allows each main idea to receive equal weight. A vertical ship is appropriate if students want to write a sequential or chronological story.

5. I explicitly teach my students how to use their graphic organizers. To facilitate the planning process, I model my thoughts as I write on the board. I say, "If I were getting ready to travel to Mars, what would be the most important things I would need?" I write the items we choose during brainstorming in the "outer space" area surrounding the rocket ship. Only the most important choices will be transferred to the drawing of the rocket ship itself.

6. After writing five or six items on the board to model the brainstorming process, I think out loud, "Now I need to decide which three of these items are the very *most* important for my trip." I encourage students to share their thoughts and opinions with their peers as I support their discussion with examples. Students must justify why they think an item should be included on the list. We often have spirited discussions as the group collaborates on deciding which items are most important for the trip to outer space. When we have arrived at a consensus, I write the three items on my rocket ship.

7. I again think aloud as I formulate sentences based on our three main ideas. We expand the sentences together using additional words to help describe our items for the journey.

Practice

Now the **practice** begins. Students draft their essays using preprinted versions of the Writing Rockets graphic organizer. After practicing writing at least one essay using the preprinted Writing Rockets graphic organizer, each student makes a simple line drawing of the rocket at the top of his or her paper. I help students practice writing by asking them such questions as

"What will you need to pack for your trip to outer space? Why?"
"What toys will you bring on your trip to outer space? Why?"
"Which friends will get to go on your trip to Mars? Why?"

Execute

1. Students next **execute** the Writing Rockets and Other Graphic Organizers strategy independently or with partners. I circulate throughout the group and encourage students to use the Writing Rockets graphic organizer as they prioritize their lists (see the sample completed organizer in Figure 9.3). I give students each an additional copy of the graphic organizer to keep in their Writing Strategies Journals for future use.

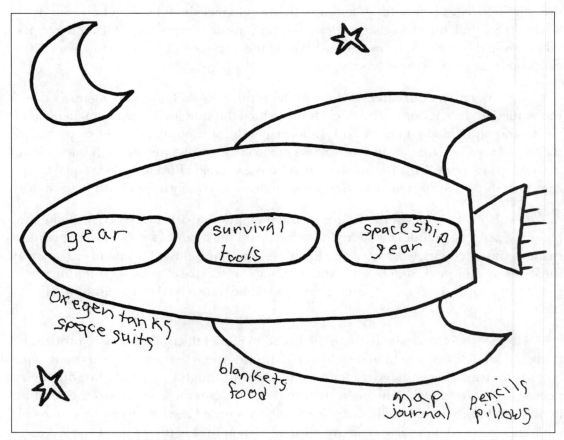

Figure 9.3 Sample Writing Rockets Graphic Organizer as Completed by a Student

Reflect

I always bring the group together to **reflect** after completing this mini-lesson. We discuss students' ideas and record them on the blackboard to facilitate further discussion. Students from diverse backgrounds may be reluctant to read their work out loud. So I provide opportunities for them to share their work through pictures they have either drawn or cut out of magazines. Finally, I reinforce my writers' progress by reviewing the steps of the writing process that I have incorporated into my mini-lesson for nonfiction writing. I often find it necessary to reflect with individual students. We discuss their success and concerns with the organizational process.

Adapting the Strategy

Adapting the Strategy for Emerging Writers

I work directly with emerging writers so that they move through the mini-lesson and achieve success. I often take their dictation. Sometimes I ask them to draw pictures of their ideas on the graphic organizers, and then we write the essays together.

Adapting the Strategy for Writers Who Struggle

I find that writers who struggle enjoy working with simple graphic organizers that connect to the topic. As with emerging writers, I work individually with writers who struggle so they achieve success.

Adapting the Strategy for English Language Learners

Teaching prewriting with graphic organizers makes what is abstract tangible. For students with limited English vocabulary, I develop graphic organizers with a single word for each main idea, and I encourage students to create their own drawings. As they develop their own graphic organizers, students from diverse backgrounds often surprise me with their wonderful choices for their main ideas for their essays. Supporting their ideas, no matter how unique, is important, because their vocabulary may not sustain the concepts that they are trying to share with me. My role is to help them connect their ideas for each essay to their unique cultures, languages, and experiences. They may have an abundance of ideas to share once they begin organizing their thoughts. I dismiss no idea, but continue to inquire further as I help them support their reasoning. I find that as my diverse writers improve their organizational skills, the complexity of their language skills increases.

Adapting the Strategy for Advanced Writers

Advanced writers usually learn to use graphic organizers quickly. Once they have mastered graphic organizers, I teach them more sophisticated organizing strategies, such as extending the complexity of their graphic organizers by adding details.

Extending the Strategy

To extend the strategy I ask for student volunteers to teach the use of graphic organizers to students in other classes. This provides opportunities for all students, regardless of developmental stages or writing abilities, to show what they know. In this way, all of my students enhance their feelings of self-efficacy as writers. In addition, as students explain the use of graphic organizers to others, they reinforce their own understanding of these tools.

EVIDENCE CONNECTIONS

Houston, G. (2004). *How writing works: Imposing organizational structure within the writing process.* Boston: Pearson.

How Writing Works provides a scaffolded and strategic approach to teaching the organizational structures of writing. The author provides numerous examples of graphic organizers for use in developing cohesive compositions. Houston encourages educators to teach planning for writing using visual organizers to make abstract concepts more concrete.

Bereiter, C., & Scardamalia, M. (1987). *The psychology of written composition.* Hillsdale, NJ: Erlbaum.

The authors describe cognitive processes of writing based on models of knowledge telling and knowledge transforming. They differentiate between the writing habits of inexperienced and struggling writers and those of experienced writers. Beginning writers simply tell the knowledge that is foremost in their minds at the very moment they begin writing rather than transforming knowledge into more meaningful essays. The authors also provide evidence of the power of planning during the writing process.

Chapter 10

Interest Charts

SUSAN DAVIS LENSKI AND FRANCES RAMOS VERBRUGGEN

This strategy helps students identify their interests and recognize that their ideas are worthy writing topics. Students fill out Interest Charts and use them to construct topics for writing.

Why This Strategy Is Important

"I don't know what to write about!" We have heard this complaint numerous times over our careers as teachers. Many teachers think giving students the opportunity to write is all they need; and students will begin to write. But that's not the case. Students raise an important point when they say they don't know what to write about. It's extremely difficult to think of a compelling topic without prewriting activities, so Lenski and Johns (2004) developed a strategy titled Interest Charts to help students explore their interests before they begin to write.

The Interest Charts strategy capitalizes on the notion that students' lives are filled with stories and that one of the roles of the teacher is to help students recognize their stories and write about them (Furr, 2003). These stories can help students develop their identities through positioning themselves in relation to their families, their friends, and their communities (Wortham, 2001). When students have opportunities to write about their personal lives, they share interests and events with their teachers and their classmates. In turn, this sharing promotes a sense of community in the classroom (Buss & Karnowski, 2000).

There are three areas from which students can choose topics for writing: personal experiences, imagination, and outside knowledge. Graves (2003) suggests that students should write primarily from their experiences, but he adds that students can find rich topics for writing by exploring their interests as well. Stotsky (1995) notes that students should use their imaginations when they are thinking of writing topics. Students who write from their imaginations move beyond a focus on themselves and look at the world from a wider perspective.

We have used Interest Charts in many writing classrooms to encourage students to identify their interests for use as writing topics. The first time we used Interest Charts, each chart had four boxes, and we just asked students to respond to Things I Like, Things I Don't Like, Hobbies, and Family. We found it helpful to encourage students to think of concrete examples, such as books, sports, and television. Over the years we have expanded the Interest Charts to include more items, as in Figure 10.1. Last year we added the boxes Good Things About Me and Things About Me That Aren't So Good. We would say these two boxes are optional, depending on your students. In the following sections, we'll share how we go about teaching this strategy using the SCAMPER model.

Things I Like	Things I Don't Like	Hobbies I Enjoy
Books I've Read	Sports I Like	TV and Games I Like
Things My Family Does	Good Things About Me	Things About Me That Aren't So Good

Figure 10.1 Blank Interest Chart

The SCAMPER Model for Interest Charts

Survey and Assess

Although this strategy is usually helpful to all young writers because it stirs their imagination and prompts them to think about personal feelings, topics, and experiences, we look for the students who struggle with generating ideas on a regular basis. We pull them into a small group to help them learn this effective strategy. To determine who could benefit from the Interest Charts strategy, we **survey and assess** all of the students during writing time when we don't assign a topic. We look for students who do not start to write right away or who seem disinterested in their writing. We look at what they write and how much they have written. We talk with them about their topics to determine their levels of motivation and interest in writing about the topics they have chosen. We also analyze their writing over time. Do they write about the same topics frequently? This might indicate that they can't think of other ideas about which to write.

Confer

Next we **confer** with the students that we suspect have trouble generating new ideas for their writing. We might tell them,

> *I like to write stories and poems, but sometimes I have trouble coming up with an idea of what to write about. Or sometimes I keep writing about the same thing because I can't think of anything else. Do you ever have that problem? What do you do when you can't think of anything new or interesting to write?*

We listen to their ideas. We have students make note of them in their Writing Strategies Journals for future reference. Then we tell them that there are ways to think of additional ideas for writing.

Assemble Materials

We **assemble materials,** making enough handouts of the Interest Charts to give one to each student. We also display a completed chart to show students as an example and have pencils on hand. Students bring their Writing Strategies Journals with them. We also assemble a variety of graphic organizers that might be useful for struggling writers.

Model

Using an Interest Chart is quite easy. We simply tell students we want them to record things that interest them so they will have a list of topics to explore when they write. We have students keep the Interest Charts in their Writing Strategies Journals so they can add ideas when they think of them.

In order to **model** the strategy, Mrs. Verbruggen introduces Interest Charts to the group for the first time:

> *I love to write. Yesterday I had some free time, and I wanted to write a story. But I couldn't think of anything to write about. I wanted to write about something that I was interested in because I knew it would be more fun to write about something I knew about. So I took out my Interest Chart (showing a completed chart). I read through the boxes, looking for an idea that struck me as something I'd like to write about that day. First, I looked at Things I Like. In that box I had already recorded that I like my dogs, my family, school, pizza, and chocolate. Under Things I Don't Like, I had already listed shoveling snow and doing housework. I didn't feel like writing about any of those things, so I looked at another box, Books I've Read. I had* Charlotte's Web *in that box. That got me thinking about other books in which animals talk, like the Clifford books and* Stuart Little. *So I decided I wanted to write a story about a chicken named Chica that lived on a farm and didn't like the snow. See how I used my Interest Chart to search out ideas for writing? It was easy.*

Practice

Now that our students have an idea of how to use an Interest Chart to find ideas for writing, we help them **practice** doing it themselves. We walk them through the process.

Mrs. Verbruggen: Today I'd like you to think about topics for writing by filling out an Interest Chart of your very own. You will be doing this individually, and we'll also develop a group Interest Chart with some ideas from each of you.

Tiffany: I love dogs. Can I write that down?

Mrs. Verbruggen: That's exactly the kind of thing you will record on your Interest Chart. Let me go over the areas I'd like you to think about before you begin writing. (Mrs. Verbruggen takes out her sample Interest Chart.) We're going to fill out the first three boxes today. Another day we'll add more ideas to the Interest Chart. Let's look at the three categories: Things I Like, Things I Don't Like, and Hobbies. Think about the things you really like. Tiffany has said she really likes dogs. She could put that on her Interest Chart. What ideas do others have? (Mrs. Verbruggen helps them think about things they like to eat, to do, to hear, to touch, to sing, and so on.)

Adam: I like video games.

Keenan: I like soccer.

Renee: I like trees.

Mrs. Verbruggen: All of these topics can be listed on your Interest Charts. You can fill out the three boxes on the top for today, and use these ideas when we have writing time. Some of the categories seem to be nearly the same, but don't worry about that. Just record whatever you think of first, whatever comes to mind, in each of the boxes. Try to put at least three things in each box.

Over the next few weeks we'll continue to add to our charts. Before you begin, I want to show you an Interest Chart my son, Sean, filled out (see Figure 10.2). Sean's chart will give you an idea of what the entire thing will look like once it's completed. It might give you some ideas of what to put into your boxes, too! It's okay to share ideas. Look for ideas everywhere you go!

After showing the class Sean's Interest Chart, Mrs. Verbruggen then says, "Let's practice how to use an Interest Chart to find ideas for writing. Let's say Sean wants to write a story. How would he use this chart to help him?"

We talk about how he would read through the boxes and think about how some of the ideas could be turned into stories. We have students tell us what they would write about if this were their chart. We expand on their suggestions and clarify as needed.

Students then begin to fill in the boxes in their Interest Charts. We stand by to support them. We encourage them to use spelling strategies and resources, but we also accept invented spelling.

Things I Like	Things I Don't Like	Hobbies I Enjoy
Watching football games My friends Raking leaves Running	Cooking Doing homework Washing the car Video games	My pets Reading Collecting rocks Bicycling
Books I've Read	**Sports I Like**	**TV and Games I Like**
Aliens for Breakfast *Adventures of Taxi Dog* *Frog and Toad* books	Watching baseball Playing tag, soccer, T-ball	Go Fish! *The Transformers* *The Lion King*
Things My Family Does	**Good Things About Me**	**Things About Me That Aren't So Good**
Bicycling Going to the park Watching TV	I like to laugh. I'm a good friend. I do my work in school.	I can be a pest. I don't help my mom.

Figure 10.2 Sean's Sample Interest Chart

Execute

Now it's time for students to **execute** the strategy independently. They use their Interest Charts to find ideas about which to write.

Mrs. Verbruggen: Take your Interest Charts out and read all of the ideas you have written down so far. Choose one or two that you think you'd like to write a story about, and talk about them with a partner. Then decide what you'll write about today. If that idea doesn't work once you start writing, what could you do?

Cindy: Look at the Interest Chart again and find another idea.

Mrs. Verbruggen: Sure! Or ask a friend if you can look at her chart or if she could share an idea from her chart with you.

Once students start reading their charts and writing, we circulate around the group to make sure students have all found ideas they like. If not, we help them add more ideas to their Interest Charts by prompting them with different ways to think about each category. For example, we might ask them to think about not only sports they play themselves but also sports they like to watch on television.

Reflect

To encourage students to **reflect,** we talk with them about how the strategy worked for them. We ask them to share how they came up with ideas to add to their Interest

Charts and how they selected ideas for writing from the charts. We ask them how they will use this strategy in the future to generate ideas for writing.

Adapting the Strategy

Adapting the Strategy for Emerging Writers

We help emerging writers generate topics for writing using the principles of the Interest Chart. Young writers are often brimming with ideas for writing; they just need help in channeling their enthusiasm. We adapt headings of the Interest Chart to match the needs of our emerging writers by using such topics as Family, Animals I Like, and Things I Do at Home. Then we model the thinking process of topic generation by completing a group Interest Chart. We draw pictures and label them in each of the grid sections. Then we ask students to draw pictures and each write about one of the topics. This acknowledges students' varied interests and helps them recognize that they have ideas worth exploring by writing.

Adapting the Strategy for Writers Who Struggle

According to Gunning (2010), struggling writers may have fewer experiences than do other students with selecting topics for writing. One reason is that teachers tend to give struggling writers shorter writing assignments and more pattern writing. When students are given pattern writing, the topic is already developed, and the students do not have opportunities to think of their own topics. Struggling writers, therefore, may be less likely than other writers to have written pieces from their own personal experiences and imagination. We convince them they have ideas for writing, which is an important step in helping struggling writers.

Even when they have identified a topic to write about, some of our struggling writers may not know what to say. They need help thinking through the details of why certain topics interest them, and what they would like others to know about their topics. So we provide students with a list of questions that help them think about the *who, what, when, where, why,* and *how* of their topics in order to help them reflect on specific aspects that they want to include in their writing pieces. When they are writing about personal experiences or imaginary events, we encourage struggling writers to add details so that the writing "paints a picture" in the mind of the reader.

Some struggling writers are also frustrated when they organize the different aspects of their chosen topics in their writing. So we supply these students with graphic organizers. There are numerous graphic organizers available commercially and on the Internet that students find helpful to further explore topics of interest and organize their thoughts into coherent sentences and paragraphs.

Adapting the Strategy for English Language Learners

English language learners are a diverse group of students, and no one set of strategies will fit all of them. Yet there are many ways you can adapt Interest Charts for the English language learners in your classroom.

For newcomers and students whose English language skills are not strong, we encourage them to write in their home languages when necessary. Encouraging them to use their native languages when they have difficulty finding the right English words allows students to write with fluency, and affirms their cultural and linguistic backgrounds (Lenski & Verbruggen, 2010). As they develop proficiency in English, they can do more of their writing in English.

Our English language learners also benefit from partnering with native English speakers who have similar interests. By writing collaboratively or by writing in interest groups with native English speakers, our English language learners have opportunities to discuss their interests and learn the vocabulary specific to their chosen topics. Native English speakers also model such writing features as syntax and spelling for their classmates who are learning English.

Immigrant students and those whose parents immigrated to the United States have many experiences from their home cultures that they can share with their classmates, thereby enriching the learning environment of every member of the class. We encourage students to write about what life was like for them before moving to the United States, or to share stories that their parents have told about the countries from which they emigrated, as a way of incorporating their cultures into the classroom.

Adapting the Strategy for Advanced Writers

Keeping advanced students engaged in the writing process sometimes presents a challenge. Because advanced writers often see so many possible topics, asking them to write about "anything you want" can sometimes be overwhelming. However, many advanced writers dislike writing to prompts. So we provide a balance between too broad and too narrow of a topic by helping advanced writers choose what they want to write about.

Our advanced writers are often also advanced readers. We challenge advanced writers by having them copy the style of one of their favorite authors in their writing or blend styles to make their own styles. We help them expand the options on the Interest Chart by suggesting that they might elaborate on an idea that was alluded to in their readings but not fully explored in the text.

Extending the Strategy

We construct a classroom composite Interest Chart to prompt all students to think of things that interest them. This is posted in the writing center so that students can contribute ideas and use those ideas. For example, Jamie was interested in whales and wrote that on her Interest Chart. She decided that the topic of whales was a good one to put on the composite Interest Chart. When Adam saw the topic of whales, he was reminded of the time he went to the ocean and saw dolphins. Adam wrote *dolphins* on his individual Interest Chart.

Another way we extend this strategy is to expand the Interest Chart by adding topic boxes. Many of our student writers enjoy writing about their wishes, dreams, and values or beliefs. Some students have vivid imaginations, whereas others like to analyze and interpret the world around them.

EVIDENCE CONNECTIONS

Graham, S., & Perin, D. (2007). A meta-analysis of writing instruction for adolescent students. *Journal of Educational Psychology, 99,* 445–476.

For this investigation, Graham and Perin conducted a meta-analysis of studies that involved students in grades 4 to 12 who were learning to write or writing to learn. Each of the studies they selected used an experimental or quasi-experimental design and included a reliable outcome measure of writing quality. The authors found 142 studies that met these criteria. Among the findings, Graham and Perin determined that using a process approach to writing in which students are engaged in prewriting activities, such as topic selection, is effective for writing instruction.

Meichenbaum, D., & Biemiller, A. (1992). In search of student expertise in the classroom: A metacognitive analysis. In M. Pressley, K. Harris, & J. Guthrie (Eds.), *Promoting academic competence and literacy in school* (pp. 3–56). San Diego, CA: Academic Press.

Meichenbaum and Biemiller conducted a metacognitive analysis of students' self-regulating behaviors. The authors found that students who have the ability to work independently and select topics for writing tend to write more. According to Graves (2003), topic selection in writing should be based on students' interests, whether these are personal experiences or areas of curiosity. Teachers, therefore, need to help students identify areas of interest to use as topics for writing assignments.

REFERENCES

Buss, K., & Karnowski, L. (2000). *Reading and writing literary genres*. Newark, DE: International Reading Association.

Furr, D. (2003). Struggling readers get hooked on writing. *Reading Teacher, 56,* 518–525.

Graves, D. (2003). *Writing: Teachers and children at work* (2nd ed.). Portsmouth, NH: Heinemann.

Gunning, T. (2010). *Assessing and correcting reading and writing difficulties* (4th ed.). Boston: Allyn & Bacon.

Lenski, S., & Johns, J. (2004). *Improving writing: Strategies, assessments, resources* (2nd ed.). Dubuque, IA: Kendall/Hunt.

Lenski, S., & Verbruggen, F. (2010). *Writing and assessment instruction for English language learners*. New York: Guilford Press.

Stotsky, S. (1995). The uses and limitations of personal or personalized writing in writing theory, research, and instruction. *Reading Research Quarterly, 30,* 758–776.

Wortham, S. (2001). *Narratives in action: A strategy for research and analysis*. New York: Teachers College Press.

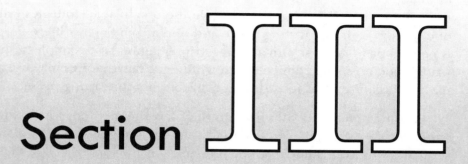

Section III

Drafting Strategies

When writers have many great ideas about what they will write, they start to compose drafts or write down ideas in semi-organized ways or sequences. At this stage in the writing process, students think about the ideas they want to include and the ones they will exclude, how they will organize their thoughts, and how their ideas will fit the genre formats or styles they want to use. That can be a tall order for young writers!

We have found in our work with primary students that all writers compose differently. Some move back and forth between drafting and editing. Others forge ahead and complete their first drafts. Once writers have initial drafts, they reread what they have composed. If possible, they should also get a chance to have others read or listen to their drafted ideas. Multiple perspectives help writers extend their thinking, focus them, and help make the organization of their writing pieces coherent. Writers' personal reflections and feedback from others may cause writers to add parts, revise others, move sections from one place to another, and leave some areas exactly as they are.

Drafting is a complex process in which writers must give thoughtful consideration to their intentions and readers' needs. One can see how this stage of the writing process can intimidate writers, especially those new to the process or those who struggle.

HOW DRAFTING STRATEGIES HELP STUDENTS

We have observed from our work with young writers that there are different styles of drafting. Some students need to just sit and "spill" their ideas out onto paper in streams of thought. First they get them out; then they sort and organize them. Other students like to outline or visually organize what they're going to write about (in other words, using graphic organizers) before they begin writing sentences. Some students like to isolate themselves at this stage, whereas others like to talk their way through the process with others.

We have learned to be flexible with students as they work on their drafts. We model and teach them various strategies to add to their writing repertoires, scaffold their use of multiple strategies, then help them decide what strategies are most productive for them. Often a student who has a storehouse of available strategies will select and use one strategy with one writing genre and find a completely different drafting strategy is needed or works best with another writing genre. For example, a student who finds writing poetry is more difficult than writing narrative stories may use a graphic organizer to organize ideas for writing poems but not for writing prose.

We encourage teachers to reflect on their favorite methods for drafting. When you write your first draft, do you like to just start writing, or are you a planner? Share your strategies with your students to help them reflect on and regulate their needs.

Drafting strategies are particularly helpful to diverse learners and writers, such as struggling writers and students for whom English is a second language. Talking about, modeling, and noting key strategies and approaches to drafting can be highly beneficial to these students.

STRATEGIES IN THIS SECTION

The six chapters in Section Three focus on helping students get their ideas down on paper in draft form. Chapter Eleven, Reread So You Know What to Write Next, shares a drafting strategy in which teachers explicitly model how writers reread as they are writing, a strategy students use to produce coherent text independently. In Chapter Twelve, Where Have I Seen That Word Before? students learn how to improve their writing fluency by easily accessing the spelling of words. Chapter Thirteen, Storyteller Blocks, shares a strategy that gives students visual clues to help them write stories that incorporate the story elements of characters, settings, problems, and solutions. Chapter Fourteen, Adding Information, encourages writers to provide information that clarifies their "big points." Chapter Fifteen, To Rhyme or Not to Rhyme? helps students evaluate the poems they and others write to decide if each poem sounds better and makes more sense when it rhymes or when it does not. Finally, Chapter Sixteen, Think, Draw, Write, and Share (TDWS), provides a format that allows K–3 students to convert their oral stories into written productions by drawing their ideas and then labeling their drawings.

Chapter 11

Reread So You Know What to Write Next

DEBORAH G. LITT

Students use this sentence-composing strategy to produce coherent text independently. Teachers explicitly model how writers reread as they are writing, a routine that ensures sentences make sense and faithfully represent the writer's intent.

Why This Strategy Is Important

As they write, experienced writers recursively reread what they have already written so they keep their writing in order. However, beginning and struggling writers often do not reread what they have already composed. Therefore, they may omit important words in sentences, abandon their original thoughts, or veer off in new directions.

When I first began teaching, I was puzzled and frustrated by my beginning students who left out important words in sentences, or who suddenly strayed from their topics. In Writers' Workshop, I taught my students to reread what they wrote to determine the revisions they needed to make as they polished their drafts. However, many of my students continued to turn in stories and poems with missing words or that changed topics mid-sentence.

During the 1994–95 academic year I trained as a Reading Recovery teacher and learned how to scaffold emergent writers who were beginning to write. I learned the importance of having a student repeat multiple times a sentence he or she wanted to write and commit it to memory. For beginners who know how to write very few words automatically, this oral rehearsal is a necessary step. Beginning writers use up so much working memory figuring out the spelling of each word they write that they frequently forget the larger message. By committing their sentences to memory, they are able to write what they intended despite having to temporarily devote full attention to figuring out spelling. I also learned to teach students the routine of rereading what they have written after every second or third word so they know what word comes next. I discovered that using these two simple steps, beginning students can write coherent sentences that represent what they wish to communicate. (For the full instructions on how to scaffold sentence writing, see Clay, 2005.)

The SCAMPER Model for Reread So You Know What to Write Next

Survey and Assess

I **survey and assess** my students as they draw and attempt to write. I notice which students are able to produce short narratives, which students draw but don't attempt to compose text, and which students produce one- to four-word labels for their drawings. I also notice students who attempt to write sentence-length compositions, but whose sentences don't make sense because they omit words, or their topics change direction.

Confer

Students who draw but cannot yet write, those who label their drawings, and those who produce long messages that contain missing words or confusing text benefit from this strategy. I gather a small group of these students with me on the floor in front of the easel to **confer** with them. I explain that I've noticed that when they tell me stories, they are able to convey a lot more than when they write stories. I also tell them that when I read aloud the stories they write, many are surprised because their stories don't say what they intended. Next I read some of these anonymous examples aloud. My students can often quickly discover what words are missing or when the stories veer off course. Then I tell them I'm going to teach them a strategy that will help them write exactly what it is they want to say.

Assemble Materials

I **assemble materials** that include markers and a piece of chart paper on which I have drawn a picture of a cat and a person at a computer keyboard at the top. I also have small whiteboards, dry-erase markers, and mini-whiteboard erasers for the children. Sometimes I'll use paper on clipboards with pencils for the children.

Model

I **model** the strategy through these steps:

1. I show them the drawing I have made, and I tell them the story that goes with the drawing. I say,

   I was trying to write using my computer last night, but my cat, Cassie, kept nibbling my fingers and pushing at them, making it very hard to get my work done. Yet every time I put her on the floor, she just jumped right back up.

2. I think aloud about choosing one idea from that whole story to write down. I explain that before I start writing I have to think and decide exactly what I am going to write about in my story. I pause and then say, "I know. I'll say, 'Cassie pushes my fingers when I try to type.'"

3. I explain to the students that once I've thought of my sentence, I say it over a few times to myself so I can remember it. I demonstrate by repeating it aloud three times,

asking the students to join in to help me. Then I say to them, "Now I won't forget what I'm going to write," and repeat the sentence one more time. Modeling how I generate and repeat my sentence is a critical step for students who are either labeling or drawing without labels. Some of these children need guidance in generating sentences, particularly children who do not yet use many complete sentences longer than three or four words in their oral language. By modeling a more elaborate sentence and having children repeat it, I support their overall language development.

4. With the sentence established, I think aloud as I model how to go from speech to print. I pick up a marker while saying, "*Cassie* is my first word, so I'll write *Cassie* here," and bring the marker to the left side of the page below my drawing. Then I write *Cassie* slowly as I stretch the word out orally. I point to *Cassie* as I read "Cassie," and then say, "pushes." I then write *pushes* while orally stretching out the word.

5. After I write the first two words, I demonstrate how writers reread as they are writing. I say, "Now what I need to do is reread what I've already written so I know what to write next." I then point under the word *Cassie* and read "Cassie," and point under *pushes* and read "pushes." "Oh, Cassie pushes," I read quickly. After a slight pause, I say somewhat slowly, "my fingers," and I write *my* and *fingers* while stretching out those words.

"Now, you know what I need to do? I need to reread what I've written so far, so I know what to write next." I go back to the beginning, pointing under each word as I read, and I invite the students to join me in reading the sentence back. I ask them what I need to write next. A student usually tells me the next word I need to write is "when." I write *when* while stretching out the word. By this time the students have usually caught on to the pattern of rereading. When I ask them what I need to do next, they chime in, "Reread so you know what to write next." We continue to read together up to the last word written as I point under each word. I pause, and they tell me the next word or two I need to write. I write in the words, and then ask what we need to do, repeating the sequence until the sentence is complete.

When the sentence is complete, we read the entire sentence together. I comment that it says exactly what I want it to say. I tell them, "Whenever you write, you need to reread what you have written so you know what to write next. What's the strategy we learned?" We all chant, "Reread so you know what to write next."

Practice

Once students have seen me model the sequence, it is time for them to **practice** with my help. I tell them that together we're going to come up with another sentence to practice rereading so we know what to write next, but that this time they will all get a chance to write. I give them time to talk with partners to come up with sentences to add to our story. I listen in while the students talk to each another. I ask a few of the student pairs to share their ideas and then select a short, manageable sentence from among their suggestions. For example, one student pair creates this sentence: "Cassie is a funny cat." I ask them to repeat the sentence several times. Because students must be able to follow these steps independently, I also ask them to tell me why they needed to repeat the sentence.

Following this phase of the strategy, I hand out the whiteboards, markers, and erasers or clipboards and pencils. (The students have had previous experience with using these materials and already understand the ground rules.) Once they have their materials, I ask them to say their sentences one more time. Then I guide them through writing the sentences a few words at a time, with rereading in between to make sure they point to the words as they read them and use the rereading strategy.

Before sending them back to their seats, I close with this reminder:

> *Remember, whenever you are writing, it is very important to do just what we did today. When you write, reread what you have already written. That way you will know what to write next, and your writing will always make sense. What do we say to check what we've written?*

We all chant, "Reread so you know what to write next."

Execute

In a final small-group session, I monitor these students as they attempt to **execute** the strategy independently. Before they begin, I ask them to describe how they will repeat their sentences orally several times and reread the words as they write their sentences. I circulate around the room to see if they reread as they write.

I help students execute this strategy from this point on whenever they write. I continue to monitor students as they reread when they write independently. I work one-on-one with the few students who need more support to make the routine theirs.

Reflect

At the end of the day, when as a whole class we pause for a few minutes to recount what we have learned and **reflect** on it, I guide students to tell me something that they learned in each part of the day and make sure someone from the small group reports, "Reread so you know what to write next." Because this routine is so basic and essential to the composing of written text, we repeat this phrase throughout the school year. Eventually, rereading as they write will become automatic for all of the students.

Adapting the Strategy

Adapting the Strategy for Emerging Writers

Students who draw as a precursor to writing, and students who have begun to label drawings but have not attempted to write sentences, are emerging writers. I help these students orally rehearse sentences of their choice and encourage them to dictate their sentences to me as I write the sentences and model the strategy by repeating the words I have written. This modeling helps emerging writers because the actions of generating a sentence and rereading it as it is written down are normally hidden, and emerging writers need to develop an awareness of the procedure in order to eventually control it for themselves.

Adapting the Strategy for Writers Who Struggle

I typically teach this strategy in kindergarten or first grade, but I find that older students who struggle with writing often need explicit instruction in rereading as they write. These students may omit essential words, or produce rambling collections of sentence fragments rather than complete sentences, rendering their prose confusing or incoherent. Often the reason for this jumbled writing is that these students do not reread as they write. With struggling writers, I usually teach this strategy in one-on-one conferences. For example, in a conference with a typical struggling writer I'll call Oscar, I first explain that I have a writing trick I use to keep my own writing on track that I think will be helpful to him. Then I model a few sentences of my own, showing how I reread after every few words. I ask Oscar to come up with a sentence and repeat it. I then observe while he writes the sentence, and I praise the rereading I observe. We then extend this procedure for a longer composition. I ask Oscar to talk to me about a topic in which he's interested. Once he has generated several ideas orally, I ask him to write down some of his ideas into a paragraph. I observe him while he's writing. When I notice him rereading, I praise him for it. I make sure to praise him for any errors and omissions he notices, pointing out that everyone makes mistakes, but that what makes someone a good writer is noticing and fixing those mistakes. If I notice he is not rereading, I model again and remind him to make sure to stop and reread after every few words. I have found that writers who struggle sometimes need more than one practice session, and often need several weeks of reminders before rereading becomes habitual. However, I have seen the quality of their writing improve dramatically once they implement this simple strategy.

Adapting the Strategy for English Language Learners

Before I teach, I want to make sure the strategy I model is one that will be helpful to my students. I recognize that there are many reasons, aside from a failure to reread while writing, why the writing of an English language learner (ELL) might lack coherence. ELL students sometimes mix English word order with the word order of their home languages or don't know when to use "the" in English. So I take special care to observe my ELL students while they write to see if they reread as they write. Only those students who are composing without rereading while they write will benefit from the lesson.

Those ELLs who do not reread while composing will benefit from an explicit demonstration. To ensure that ELLs understand what I mean when I model, I take care to make my gestures clear and to make my actions match my words. I have a tendency to speak fast, so I make a conscious effort to slow down and watch their faces to ensure that they are following me. I also encourage the more advanced ELLs who speak the same languages as newcomers to explain what I've said in their home languages.

Adapting the Strategy for Advanced Writers

I usually find that advanced writers already reread as they write. So I do not use my limited instruction time for these students by teaching them to reread, something they already know. However, I challenge advanced writers to think about the overall structure of their texts, including the sequence of their paragraphs and sentences. They will reread larger sections of text with an eye and ear to overall sequence and flow. Advanced writers can also tutor their classmates who need more support. I show the advanced writers how to model the Reread So You Know What to Write Next strategy, and then each advanced writer works with one student, modeling the strategy and supporting the student as he or she uses the strategy.

Extending the Strategy

Once beyond the beginning stages, writers typically reread at the sentence level without conscious awareness of doing so. Once young writers have incorporated rereading as they write into their writing process, the teacher no longer needs to draw their attention to it. However, as writers develop and write longer texts, they will need to reread in larger chunks to check the flow and organization of their writing pieces. With a longer text, one rereads to determine the best order of sentences within paragraphs, and of paragraphs within sections or chapters. During lessons on revision or on organization, the teacher can demonstrate rereading with an ear toward flow, sequence, and organization. Without rereading, revision is not possible.

EVIDENCE CONNECTIONS

Clay, M., & Cazden, C. (1990). A Vygotskian interpretation of Reading Recovery. In L. C. Moll (Ed.), *Vygotsky and education: Instructional implications and applications of socio-historical psychology* (pp. 206–222). Cambridge, England: Cambridge University Press. Using examples from actual Reading Recovery lessons, the authors show not only what mediated or scaffolded instruction in writing and reading looks like but also how the teacher adjusts the difficulty of the tasks and the amount of support provided to ensure that children are always working at the cutting edge of learning. Reread So You Know What to Write Next employs teacher modeling to provide a needed scaffold.

Lyons C., Pinnell G. S., & Deford D. E. (1993). *Partners in learning: Teachers and children in Reading Recovery.* New York: Teachers College Press.
Chapter Six of *Partners in Learning* provides a theoretical justification for the inclusion of writing in an early intervention program for struggling literacy learners. In Chapter Seven the authors summarize a study on the relationship between scaffolded writing and growth in reading proficiency. Children who had teachers who "fostered independent actions" (p. 138) in writing made better progress in literacy acquisition. Rereading while composing is one of the independent self-monitoring actions a young writer can take.

REFERENCE

Clay, M., (2005). *Literacy lessons designed for individuals: Part 2, Teaching procedures.* Portsmouth, NH: Heinemann.

Chapter 12

Where Have I Seen That Word Before?

ILENE CHRISTIAN

This strategy supports students' writing fluency. Students who use this strategy can easily access the spelling of words, which in turn facilitates continuous writing.

Why This Strategy Is Important

Some writers can easily represent their thoughts on paper. Many take risks with invented spelling to sound out words as best they can. However, many young writers often become frustrated, and the writing process stops when they come to a word they do not know how to spell. When writers stop writing and labor over the spelling of a word, they often lose their train of thought and become discouraged with their writing.

For the primary grades, Where Have I Seen That Word Before? is the first strategy I teach or review with my students each year because it fulfills two purposes. First, it is an easy strategy to learn, and it quickly enables students to become authors as they develop pages for their own color books. Second, early success with writing positively affects each student's emerging identity as a writer.

It is important that young students begin to develop identities as authors and writers. As young writers compose, they are "developing a sense of what it feels like to be that sort of person" (Johnston, 2004, p. 23). Young students enter school with a wide variety of writing experiences. Some can write sentences, whereas others have barely used a pen or pencil. However, regardless of my students' backgrounds, beginning with the first day of school, I want them to identify themselves as authors who can convey their thoughts in written language that can be understood and appreciated by others. As their teacher, I want to remove obstacles that prevent young writers from being successful in these attempts. This strategy allows students to move beyond the stage at which they focus intently on how to represent words to the more important state at which they concentrate on the messages they wish to communicate. Success in creating writing pieces encourages students to see themselves as authors who can communicate messages through written language.

The SCAMPER Model for Where Have I Seen That Word Before?

Survey and Assess

It is important for me to know what resources students use as they attempt to write words they do not know how to spell. When I **survey and assess** what resources students employ, I determine which resources I need to introduce, review, or further explain. These assessments usually take the form of teacher observations during student writing time. During the observations, I take deliberate note of what students do when they come to words they do not know how to spell. I record which of the following resources students use: wall charts, class dictionaries, personal dictionaries, word walls, trade books, previous writing pieces, and class books. Using the observation data as a foundation for instruction decisions, I design mini-lesson sessions that focus on using resources in the classroom to facilitate writing fluency. These sessions could be conducted with either a small group or the whole class.

Confer

At the beginning of the school year, I **confer** with my primary students about how we can help ourselves when we are authors. I share with my students that sometimes we do not know how to spell the words we need when we are writing. I explain, "Today we will talk about one of the ways we can help ourselves when we don't know how to spell a word. One of the things we can do is think, "Where have I seen that word before?" I confer with small groups of students or work with individual students to talk about the usefulness of the strategy.

Assemble Materials

For the first introduction of the Where Have I Seen that Word Before? strategy, I **assemble materials** grouped into two sets—a wall chart that lists all the color words and a variety of trade books. I write the color words on the wall chart with a marker that corresponds to each color word. For example, large red letters spell the word *red*, and large purple letters spell the word *purple*. The trade books focus on the concept of color. Some of the trade books I use are board books published for very young children. These books have one color word per page. In addition, each illustration features an object or objects associated with the color, such as a red apple on the red page. These books provide strong support for students who are searching for the spelling of a color word. Other trade books feature simple story lines with supportive illustrations. For example, on one page of the book *Brown Bear, Brown Bear* by Eric Carle (1967) the author states, "Green frog, green frog, What do you see?" To reinforce the use of the color word, a bright green frog fills the two-page spread. The close connection between the use of the color word and the illustration provides assistance for emerging writers.

To begin the strategy instruction, I gather students around the teaching easel. I attach paper to my teaching easel that is identical to the paper the students will use when they write their own individual books. Using the same size and shape of paper helps new writers visualize how their book pages might look. To make the print visible for all students, I write in large letters with a marker.

Model

Before I **model** the Where Have I Seen That Word Before? strategy, I read several board books and trade books to the class. These books all focus on the concept of color. As we read the books, we discuss the role of an author. Important points we discuss are that authors write words in books, that authors decide which words to write, and that sometimes authors create the illustrations. The students and I then use these books as touchstone texts and reference materials.

To model the Where Have I Seen That Word Before? strategy with kindergarten students at the beginning of the year, I use the following steps.

1. I explain that I am an author because I write books. I share with students that when I read the color books earlier today, the books gave me an idea for a book I would like to write. To explain and reinforce the actions of an author, I use a think-aloud to share my insights on the authoring process (Baumann, Jones, & Swifert-Kessell, 1993). I say,

> *I want to write a book like the color books we read earlier. But I want my book to be all about the color red because I like the color red. And I want my book to be like this book (I show a board book) because I want just one word on each page. But I want all my pages to say "red," because I like red.*

Although red is one of my favorite colors, I deliberately chose it for this lesson at the beginning of the year for several reasons. First, most children are familiar with the color red. Second, most children can name several items that are red, such as hearts, balloons, apples, crayons, shirts, or balls. Third, the word *red* is a short word, so it works well for initial writing attempts. Fewer letters shorten the time spent writing the word on each page. At this point in the year, writing stamina may be a concern for several students. Using a short word supports their successful completion of their own books without frustration.

Next I display three pieces of paper on the easel. Continuing the think-aloud about an author's role, I explain,

> *I will use three pieces of paper to make the pages of my book, because that is how many pages I want in my book. On each page I will write the word* red *and then draw a picture of something red, just like the authors do in the books we read.*

2. Then I share my writing dilemma with the students by saying,

> *If I want to write the word* red, *I need to think about where I can find that word so I can write it down. Hmmmm, I know! I have seen it on the wall chart with all the other color words. I will look at the chart of color words and write it down.*

I walk over to the color chart, point to the word *red,* and then go back to the easel. I deliberately look back at the chart for each letter. I say the letter names as I write them down: "r . . . e . . . d."

3. After I have written *red* on the first page, the students and I talk about things that are red that I could draw on my page. Common suggestions from the students are apple, strawberry, fire truck, balloon, crayon, heart, or wagon. Again, I use a think-aloud to model my choice for an illustration. "I like hearts and fire trucks, but I think I will draw a balloon. I'm choosing the balloon because I want to draw the string that ties the balloon." As the students watch, I draw the balloon picture on the first page.

4. To expand the number of resources students could use to write the word *red*, I share an additional resource:

> *I thought of something else I could do to help me spell* red. *I could think about where else I have seen the word* red. *I can look at this book we read with all the colors in it. (I hold up a board book as an example.) I will turn to the* red *page and look at the word. There it is, right there. I will write that down on the second page of my book.*

I intentionally shift my eyes back and forth between the book and the paper for each letter, writing the letters one at a time on the page. We review our ideas for red items to draw on the page, I choose one, and I add it to the page.

5. To complete the final page, I review the strategy with the students.

> *When I want to write a word, I think about where I have seen it before so I can look at the word and copy it onto my paper. I want to write the word* red *on this page, too. I'm thinking about where I have seen the word* red. *Hmmmm, I could find it in this book. I know where else I could find it. It is on the color chart on the wall. Hey, I could look at the pages I have already written. That's what I'm going to do. I'm going to look at the pages I have already written to help me write the word* red.

I touch each letter on one of the pages I have already written and again say the letters out loud as I write them on my final page, "r . . . e . . . d." I review pictures I could draw on the page, choose one, and complete the page.

◆◆◆◆◆◆

Practice

Before students write their own books, they practice the strategy with their peers. First, I model the practice session with a student volunteer. I select a volunteer I think can successfully participate, because I want the modeling to be a positive example of what the students should do. I ask the volunteer, "I wonder how to write the word *red*?" The volunteer student responds, "Where have you seen the word before?" I respond, "I know where I have seen that word. It is in this book (I show a book), right on this page."

Next I divide the group into pairs. Following the example modeled for the class, the first student asks, "I wonder how to write the word *red*?" The first student's partner responds, "Where have you seen the word before?" The first student points out where he or she saw the word. For example, the student might walk over to the word wall and point to the word *red*. Then the students reverse roles and I challenge them to find the word *red* using different resources. This time the second student asks, "I wonder how to write the word *red?*" After his or her partner asks, "Where have

I seen that word before?" the second student might locate the word *red* in a familiar book.

Execute

After students practice the strategy with their partners, I again review how to use the Where Have I Seen That Word Before? strategy. Additional review of the strategy provides students with further support to ensure successful implementation. I explain,

> *The paper for your books is on the red table. Today we will make our pages, and tomorrow we will put them together in our books. At the end of our writing time, we will talk about how you knew how to spell* red *in your own books. I wonder what you will do to spell the word* red. *I wonder if you will look at the wall chart, if you will look in the color books, if you will look at my pages, or if you will do something else. I can't wait to hear how you figured out how to spell* red.

As the students pick up their pages and begin to write, I circulate throughout the group and provide assistance as needed. Most often I offer assistance in the form of a question, "Hmmmm, I'm thinking back to what I did that helped me figure out how to write the word *red*. Let's look at the easel. What did I do?" This prompt provides students with enough support to independently recall the strategy.

On the first day, we make the pages for the books. The following day we make the cover and put the books together with staples or spiral bindings. This makes it a short-term project so the students and I can quickly refer to each other as authors.

Reflect

As we near the end of our writing period, I again gather the students around the teaching easel to share their writing experiences and their use of the strategy. I encourage students to **reflect** and articulate what helped them write the word *red*. As students report back, I notice and name the use of the Where Have I Seen That Word Before? strategy and reinforce the students' identities as authors (Johnston, 2004). For example, after a student shares how she found the word *red* on the wall chart, I respond, "That's what authors do! They think about where they have seen the word before. They find the word in a book or on wall charts and use it in their own writing."

Adapting the Strategy

Adapting the Strategy for Emerging Writers

The mini-lesson described in this chapter is primarily for emerging writers; however, this strategy may be easily adapted to students in the scribble, prephonemic, and semiphonemic stages of writing development (Cecil, 2007). Instead of expecting students to write the word *red* in their own books, I provide pages with the word *red* already written on them. Together, we identify the letters and read the word as we trace the letters "r," "e," and "d." Then students find pictures in magazines or draw their own pictures to match the word on the page.

Adapting the Strategy for Writers Who Struggle

Some students may need additional support for their first authoring efforts to be successful. Although students may know how to use the Where Have I Seen That Word

Before? strategy, they may not have the fine-motor control or the experience with handwriting to successfully print the letters. For these students, I provide printed copies of the word *red*. I have drawn a box around each of the words. The defined lines of the boxes provide students with cutting guides.

For each page of their books, the students cut out the word *red* and glue it to the page. They finish each page with a simple illustration, such as an apple or a heart. By using preprinted words, each student can complete his or her own Red Book. Then we can refer to ourselves and one another as authors.

Adapting the Strategy for English Language Learners

In the primary grades I work with English language learners (ELLs) on developing English oral language and celebrating their bilingualism (or multilingualism). The Where Have I Seen That Word Before? strategy supports ELLs' oral language development because it provides multiple supports for English language learning. As we read the collection of trade books about colors together as a class, the ELL students make connections between the colors and the English color words. The students and I later reread the books aloud together. These shared, repeated readings of board books and repetitive-pattern trade books support ELLs' expressive language as they vocalize English color words and English language structural patterns. Reviewing the color words on the wall chart provides all students with another chance to make connections between the colors and the color words. The modeling of the Where Have I Seen That Word Before? strategy also provides ELLs with opportunities to move beyond receptive language to expressive language development in both oral and written forms. In return, ELLs also provide native English speakers with opportunities to learn words and phrases in additional languages.

Adapting the Strategy for Advanced Writers

As I noted previously, students come to school with a broad range of experiences. Some students in the beginning writer stage see themselves as writer-authors. As students begin to work on their color books, I quickly observe that a few already use the Where Have I Seen That Word Before? strategy to create their first pages. Through individual conferences, I encourage these more advanced students to create books similar to the board books and trade books we read at the beginning of the mini-lesson. Using these books as mentor texts, students develop books with different color words on each page (*red, green, yellow*); write sentences about their pictures ("I like green balloons"); and extend the length of the books (Dorfman & Cappelli, 2007).

Extending the Strategy

The Where Have I Seen That Word Before? strategy can be used throughout the content areas. Word walls or other classroom charts provide students with access to words currently used in the classroom. Having these words readily available facilitates students' writing fluency on different topics.

EVIDENCE CONNECTIONS

Clay, M. (1991). *Becoming literate: The construction of inner control*. Portsmouth, NH: Heinemann.

Teaching children the Where Have I Seen That Word Before? strategy helps them develop control over their reading and writing processes. Clay's research-based argument suggests that children gain control over these processes by developing a generative problem-solving stance that becomes self-extending.

Johnston, P. H. (2004). *Choice words.* Portland, ME: Stenhouse
The language that teachers use in teaching the Where Have I Seen That Word Before? strategy supports students as they develop identities as writers. In his book *Choice Words*, Johnston discusses how children develop personal and social identities in the classroom, how this development affects their learning, and the role the teacher plays in this process.

REFERENCES

Baumann, J. F., Jones, L., & Swifert-Kessell, N. (1993). Using think-alouds to enhance children's comprehension monitoring abilities. *Reading Teacher, 47*, 184–193.

Carle, E. (1967). *Brown bear, brown bear.* New York: Holt, Rinehart and Winston.

Cecil, N. L. (2007). *Striking a balance: Best practices for early literacy* (3rd ed.). Scottsdale, AZ: Holcomb Hathaway.

Dorfman, L. R., & Cappelli, R. (2007). *Mentor texts: Teaching writing through children's literature, K–6.* Portland, ME: Stenhouse.

Johnston, P. H. (2004). *Choice words.* Portland, ME: Stenhouse.

Chapter 13

Storyteller Blocks

JOYCE C. FINE

This strategy provides students with visual clues to help them write stories that contain and connect the story elements of characters, settings, problems, and solutions.

Why This Strategy Is Important

Although primary students are often familiar with stories, they may not recognize the relationships among the four essential story features critical for writing a good story (Bruner, 1986). Often students miss important parts of a story that help them empathize with a character or recognize the ingenuity of the solutions characters devise. With drawings and discussion, students learn to appreciate the deeper meanings and connections of each story part.

After years of working with primary students, I know firsthand that many students need explicit lessons to learn how to write stories that contain the four basic features—characters, settings, problems, and solutions. In addition, students need to understand how these four story features connect to one another. Therefore, I decided to devise a strategy to help primary students see a pattern of relationships among these story parts. My inspiration came from Native American storyteller dolls I saw in Albuquerque, New Mexico. These beautifully painted pottery dolls represent elders of the tribe, with children sitting on their laps, arms, and legs as they listen to stories. I thought of all the students who have never had the chance to enter the world of imagination by sitting on the laps of their loved ones to hear stories and to build a sense of story. Students who have not heard stories in rich learning contexts often think stories are just compilations of disconnected events.

The SCAMPER Model for Storyteller Blocks

Survey and Assess

I **survey and assess** students' ability to understand story features by first reading a story to them. Then I ask students to retell the story in a whole-class setting before I ask them to retell stories on their own. In general, the younger the students, the more I need to model the process of retelling. I ask them, "Who would like to help retell the story?" I may ask, "Who was in the story? Where were the story characters?"

I often use props or pictures to help students retell the story. When an individual student offers to begin the story, I encourage him or her. Then, after a few minutes, I stop the student and ask other volunteers to continue where the first student left off.

When I sense students are ready to retell a story independently, one of the best ways for me to monitor their understanding of story elements is to ask them each to retell a narrative while I evaluate their individual knowledge of story structure using the rubric in Figure 13.1. This rubric may be used to evaluate oral or written retellings of narrative features or elements. If the retelling is oral, consider recording it to capture what the student says to be able to listen closely again or to keep a record of the student's progress in retelling. You might begin with an unaided recall, without any prompts. If the student hesitates, offer a general prompt, such as, "What happened in the beginning?" to aid students' thinking. Besides noting what students remember, I listen to learn if they mention the relationships among the different parts of their stories. I keep a state-of-the-class chart with students' names listed down the left side of the chart and, across the top, a column for each of the elements of story and one to indicate if the student makes any connections between the elements (see Figure 13.2). This gives me a record sheet with details of which students know which story elements. It is a good idea to audio-tape the retellings so you can listen to them again or keep them for student portfolios.

Confer

After I analyze the class chart according to how many story features students recognize and remember, I begin to plan the step-by-step process of introducing each of the new elements by modeling from stories I read aloud. I create flexible groups to differentiate instruction for those who understand the concepts of character, setting, problem, and solution to different degrees. This allows me to focus on students' zones of proximal development with respect to their readiness to learn how to recognize and connect story elements (Vygotsky, 1978). The small-group setting allows me to **confer** with students in multiple instructional sessions if they need to hear the explanations again.

Assemble Materials

I **assemble materials,** including some real objects as examples of important nouns from stories, magazine pictures, and culturally relevant books. I also collect large sheets of brown paper, or rolls of wrapping paper with a blank side, or desk blotter paper, taped to a wall or put on a hard surface on the floor. The Storyteller Blocks strategy's name comes from the Native American storyteller dolls and the blocks of a folded piece of paper. I have water-soluble or flip-chart colored markers to draw the blocks, pictures, and words. I like being close to students who are sitting near me on the floor to keep their attention and to create social interaction and community. The proximity creates a rich, natural learning environment. When complete, the example

Directions: For each quality, give one point for full credit. Give one-half of a point for partial credit. Give zero points if the quality is not evident.

Category	Qualities	Examples from Student Retelling	Score
Character	States the main character and other characters if present		_____
Setting	Mentions time and place		_____
Problem	Mentions the gist of the problem		_____
	Has action attempt or attempts related to the problem		_____
Resolution	Relates to the problem		_____
Organization	Describes the flow or sequencing of ideas		_____
Word Choice	Uses appropriate levels of vocabulary for grade and age		_____
Voice	Shows own personality through the retelling		_____
Sentence Structure	Uses complete sentences		_____
	Uses some variety of sentences		_____
Conventions	Uses standard grammar in retelling		_____
Ideas	Shows creativity and insight into the situation		_____
Total			_____ / 12

Figure 13.1 Retelling Rubric for Narrative Text
Source: Adapted from Morrow, 2009.

of the Storyteller Blocks graphic organizer will hang in the room so students can view it and recall their experience with the Storyteller Blocks strategy. Once students' concept of each element is developed through the use of the folded paper blocks, I print out copies of the graphic organizer (see the blank copy that appears in Figure 13.3) for students to add to their Writing Strategies Journals for use in their independent writing. I recommend the following narrative books for use with this strategy:

Carle, E. (1969). *The Very Hungry Caterpillar*. New York: Philomel.

Clement, R. (1997). *Grandpa's Teeth*. Sidney: HarperCollins.

Freeman, D. (1968). *Corduroy*. New York: Viking.

Galdone, P. (1975). *The Gingerbread Boy*. New York: Clarion Books.

Silverstein, S. (1964). *The Giving Tree*. New York: Harper & Row.

Student's Name	Who/ Characters?	Where/ Setting?	What/ Problem or Goal?	Solution?	Connections Between Elements?

Figure 13.2 Storyteller Blocks State-of-the-Class Chart

Directions: Students draw in the top blocks and write in the bottom blocks.

Characters in Setting Draw	Problem / Goal Draw	Action/ Attempt Draw	End/ Outcome Draw
Write	Write	Write	Write

Figure 13.3 Blank Storyteller Blocks Graphic Organizer

Model

I tell students the title of the strategy, and then I read a story and ask the students to use materials to retell the story with pictures and words. I **model** with explicit instruction about each of the features of the story. I start with story characters in the setting. When students recognize story characters and describe the setting, I draw in the first top square of the Storyteller Blocks what the students describe (visualize); then I write a sentence (verbalize) about the characters in the setting, and ask students to think about the sensations the characters feel where they are (attaching physical sensations), and how they feel (attaching emotions), writing these as I model the process.

In this modeling phase, students first listen to the story and then interact as I create the Storyteller Blocks. When I am beginning with just developing characters and settings, I often use whole pieces of paper as single blocks. As I work with developing more elements, I tape and label a paper for each element side-by-side. I hang the model in the room so that students can see it and we can review it as we continue on subsequent days to construct the story. When students are ready to try to create their Storyteller Blocks following along with me, I give them each one sheet of $8\frac{1}{2}$-by-11 paper. I ask each student to fold the paper down the middle so it is long and looks like a hot dog. Then I have each fold his or her paper in half the other way so it looks like a hamburger. Each student then folds the paper in half again so that, when the paper is open, there are eight blocks, four on top and four on the bottom, when held in landscape position. This folded paper is like the graphic organizer shown in Figure 13.3.

After reading a story to the group, I work through the blocks as I discuss the elements of the story. Figure 13.4 suggests questions to guide the completion of the Storyteller Blocks graphic organizer. The first block on the top row on the left is the block in which I ask students to draw who is in the story. I explain that people, animals, or inanimate objects are the characters in the story. The bottom block is where students write the names of the characters. I ask students to draw what the characters look like and discuss what it would be like to be those characters. I ask students what they think might matter most to those characters: "What are the characters' feelings at the beginning?" Next I ask students to draw where the characters are and to add the scenery around the characters. In the bottom left block, we write a description of where the characters are, and when and why the characters are in that place. We put in details that are important to the characters about the place. I ask, "What do you think the characters would see or notice? What do you think you would smell if you were in this place? How hot or cold would it be? What are the characters wearing?"

In the second block, I want to build the concept of the problem or goal. This includes both the conflict and complications. I ask students to think about what the main character or characters want, need, or hope to do. I ask why the character wants this and what makes it difficult for the character to obtain what he or she wants. Also, I ask students to draw the character with other characters, and I ask what the characters might be saying to one another. I ask, "What are they doing?" Often I ask students to act out what the character wants. (Please refer to Chapter Seventeen, Act It Out to Discover the Details, in this book.)

In the bottom block in the second column, I have students write what the characters are saying to one another. I query, "What kinds of words would the characters use?" and I ask them to tell what the characters are doing and why they are doing it.

In the third block on top, I ask a student to draw what the main character did to attempt to get what he or she wants. For some stories, I divide the block into parts horizontally to show that the character might make different attempts to try to get what he or she desires. I emphasize that what the character tries must be related directly to what the problem or goal is in the second block, or the story will not make sense. Sometimes I ask students to act out what the character tries to do to solve the problem. Dramatizing the action helps the students think about and visualize what this action would look like. If the action is in the character's head, the dramatization is more difficult. Discussion about the character's attempts to solve the problem helps make the character's thinking visible in the minds of the students. We write a sentence under that block to tell about the attempts. The complications of the story become developed in this block. I point out the character's feelings about each situation and relate them to what the problem or goal is. This linking back to the character's problem in the second block is critical for comprehending the motivations of the character. We keep making sure that the story is cohesive.

Characters in Setting	Problem / Goal	Action/ Attempt	Resolution/ Outcome
Draw who is in the story. It can be one or more people or characters in the story. Draw where the character or characters are. Put in the scenery around the characters.	Draw what the character or characters want or need or hope to do? Draw the character or characters with other characters. What are they doing? (Can first have children act out what the characters are doing.)	Draw what the character or characters do to try to solve the problem or get what he or she or they want to happen. Emphasize that what was done had to be related to the problem or goal. (Children can act out attempts before they draw.)	Draw the character (or characters) where he or she is at the end. What are the character or characters feeling at the end when the problem is solved?
Write who the character or characters are. What do the characters look like? What is the character wearing? What are the characters' feelings? Where are the characters? Why are the characters there? What do you think the characters would see there? What do you smell there? How hot or cold is it?	Write what the characters are saying. What words would the characters use? Tell what the characters are doing and why they are doing it. What are the character's feelings about the problem?	Write what the attempts were to solve the problem. If different actions were tried, why did each work or not work? What did work? Emphasize relating the attempts back to the problem.	Write what the resolution or outcome is. What do you think the character would say he or she learned? How does the character or characters feel now?

Figure 13.4 Instructions for the Storyteller Blocks Graphic Organizer

The fourth block on the top is for visualizing the ending of the story. I ask a student to draw a picture of the character at the end of the story in a setting or scene. I ask students, "Where is the character? What is the character feeling now? How has the character changed? What do you think the character might say he or she has gained or learned?" I write the answers to these questions in the block below. Then I ask students what they gained or learned from reading about the story. What they say usually corresponds to the author's purpose in writing the story. We look back to see if all the ideas fit or hang together from one block to the next in order to see how the author created the story to serve that purpose.

Practice

Once the format of Storyteller Blocks is a familiar routine and students understand how the elements of story must relate to each other to work together coherently, I tell them they can be authors and use this same strategy to plan drafts of their stories. Students then **practice** using the Storyteller Blocks strategy. They work individually or in pairs or triads to plan stories. I travel around the room, offering suggestions and assistance when needed. I ask each student, pair, or triad to draw colored arrows from the characters to the setting, problem, and solution. Once we agree the story elements are interconnected, the student or students are ready to write a story draft.

Execute

Next I encourage students to **execute** the entire strategy individually by planning their stories using Storyteller Blocks graphic organizers and then drafting complete stories by following their planning. When the story is complete, each student shares his or her Storyteller Blocks planning sheet with a friend. Students then read the stories aloud to their friends and ask their friends to follow along with the Storyteller Blocks planning sheets. Friends offer opinions and suggestions, and tell the story authors whether all of the story connections have been made. If all connections have not been accomplished, the story author changes the Storyteller Blocks draft and story so there are direct connections.

Reflect

After they have written their stories, I ask students to reflect on their accomplishments in their Writing Strategies Journals. Every time they use the Storyteller Bocks strategy, they first read their reflections to determine what they must remember to do and what they might have missed in their last story-writing attempts. They return to their Writing Strategies Journals and write their reflections every time they use Storyteller Blocks to draft stories. They thus have a record of their improvements, which gives them a strong sense of accomplishment.

The time spent drawing, verbalizing, dramatizing, and sharing emotional and physical responses draws students into the world of storytelling, much as I imagine the Native American storytellers of the southwestern tribes welcomed children into their world of story. Only by having students experience a sense of story on a physical, mental, and emotional level can we hope to totally engage students in a life of appreciation and enjoyment of narrative literature.

Adapting the Strategy

Adapting the Strategy for Emerging Writers

As emerging writers and I write several stories together, I draw the Storyteller Blocks on the SMART Board using four different-colored fonts for the various story elements. I also sometimes use an overhead projector and markers. When I write the story text, I use the same colored fonts or markers that I used in the Storyteller Blocks planning sheet for the characters, settings, problems, and solutions.

Adapting the Strategy for Writers Who Struggle

When I work with writers who struggle, I have students complete an additional step between filling out their Storyteller Blocks and composing their stories. I include the Who, Where, Problem, Solution (WWPS) strategy designed by Richards and Lassonde (2010). This strategy helps students identify a main character, locate the character in a place, devise a character's problem, and work out the character's solution to the problem. As Richards and Lassonde suggest, I make two rows of four blocks, labeling them as follows:

Who	Where	Problem	Solution

I sit by the students to scaffold them with guiding questions as I did for the larger group, such as "Who is your character?" and "Where is your character?" This extra step helps writers who struggle make the transition from concrete pictures to abstract words.

Adapting the Strategy for English Language Learners

The multisensory nature of this strategy is excellent for English language learners. You can enhance visualization by using real objects, magazine pictures, or clip art. Using stories that are linguistically and culturally relevant, or that include cognate words (for example, elephant and *elefante;* music and *musica*), provides familiar content and vocabulary. I usually pair students with buddies who are also bilingual learners, but who are at a more advanced stage of English language competence. In this way, the pairs of students help each other create successful stories.

Adapting the Strategy for Advanced Writers

Students who are more advanced writers are often more advanced readers. They comprehend stories with events that are not told in a direct sequence. Writing a story that has such features as flashbacks can be difficult. If advanced writers examine a text that has these time twists, they can use the Storyteller Blocks strategy to draw the story and tape note cards as extra blocks on top of the paper in the right sequence. Then each advanced writer can create a similar extra note card for his or her planned story and write about the event as a flashback at a later point in the story.

Extending the Strategy

Students can apply this strategy with stories they have viewed on television or the computer. Also, older students might like to use Inspiration software, which allows them to select colorful shapes, pictures, and text to create their Storyteller Blocks on the computer.

EVIDENCE CONNECTIONS

Fine, J. (1991). The effect of direct instruction in story grammar using deep processing on the reading and writing achievement of second graders. *Dissertation Abstracts International, 52*(12), 204A. (UMI No. 9210706)

When students actively participate in literacy experiences, their knowledge of text structure and their comprehension increases, and their writing improves (Morrow, 1985). This dissertation offers the research base for teaching story elements to improve writing through the senses. It is built on a theory of deep processing (visualization, verbalization, and attaching physical sensations and emotions), a concept-development procedure (Marzano & Arredondo, 1986).

Morrow, L. M. (2009). *Literacy development in the early years: Helping children read and write* (6th ed.). Boston: Allyn & Bacon.

Morrow suggests how to use retellings of stories for evaluation. She shares an example of transcripts of a student's retellings over time and compares them to show growth in comprehension. She also gives caveats, such as not to ask leading questions while a student is retelling.

REFERENCES

Bruner, J. S. (1986). Play, thought, and language. *Prospects, 16*(1), 77–83.

Marzano, R. J., & Arredondo, D. E. (1986). *Tactics for thinking*. Alexandria, VA: Association for Supervision and Curriculum Development.

Morrow, L. M. (1985). Retelling stories: A strategy for improving children's comprehension, concept of story structures and oral language complexity. *Elementary School Journal, 85*, 647–661.

Morrow, L. M. (2009). *Literacy development in the early years: Helping children read and write* (6th ed.). Boston: Allyn & Bacon.

Richards, J. C., & Lassonde, C. A. (2010). *The who, where, problem, solution strategy*. Manuscript in preparation.

Vygotsky, L. (1978). Interaction between learning and development. In *Mind in society: The development of higher psychological processes* (M. Cole, Trans., pp. 79–91). Cambridge, MA: Harvard University Press.

Chapter 14

Adding Information

JANE HANSEN

In general, the first form of revision writers use is adding information, and this chapter shows how children can determine which information is useful and which will clutter the text. This strategy encourages writers to add information to their writing to help them clarify their central ideas.

Why This Strategy Is Important

Primary students love to add information to their illustrations and texts; the strategy Adding Information mirrors their natural tendency to add new shapes, figures, letters, words, and ideas. As they do this over time, and as teachers help students hone their skills, young writers internalize this strategy and the reasons behind it. Expanding on their information is fun for young writers who love to write long texts. They also start to realize that it helps them understand their ideas (Heard, 2002). By reflecting on this strategy, students develop metacognitive awareness of how it facilitates their progress as writers.

As a veteran researcher and teacher educator, I integrate the addition of information into my courses so that future and in-service teachers engage in this strategy. Later they teach their primary students to use it to enhance their writing. I show examples and tell the teachers about students I have studied in several primary classrooms, and I also share what I have learned from members of my research team (Hansen, 2005, 2007; Kissel, 2008; Lawrence, 2006). The students' work I share in this chapter is from a classroom in which I served as a researcher for two years, and the examples are some that the teachers in my university classes appreciate.

The SCAMPER Model for Adding Information
Survey and Assess

Before she teaches this strategy, Ms. O'Connor, the teacher I write about in this chapter, takes time to **survey and assess** her students' writing, and talks with students while they write. In preparation for a focus on adding information, she keeps that aspect of writing in mind for approximately five days as she listens, observes, and interacts with her young writers while they share, respond, write, and reflect. These assessments help Ms. O'Connor decide what mini-lesson sessions to create for the upcoming Adding Information strategy.

Surveying students' writing has been a sanctioned practice for many years (Harste, Woodward, & Burke, 1984; Temple & Nathan, 2006). In particular, when teachers survey, they note what their students can do, are on the verge of being able to do, and have not yet learned. In one of the two examples for this chapter, I focus on a girl who writes about an incident while she was fishing with her dad. On the day when Jessica initially writes about fishing, Ms. O'Connor doesn't happen to stop beside her as she circulates, conferring with several other students as they write. Later, however, when Ms. O'Connor studies the students' drafts, this is what she sees:

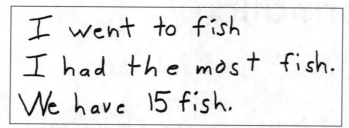

Figure 14.1

As she studies this draft, Ms. O'Connor thinks, "Jessica can write more than this. I imagine her central idea is that she caught the most fish. If so, I wonder what else she can say about them. I'll ask her tomorrow."

As Ms. O'Connor continues to peruse the drafts she collected that day, she sees the following draft authored by a boy named Charles who frequently writes about his dad and himself as policemen. He wrote: "My dad is a police. My mom is nice. I'm a police. My sister is talking."

Figure 14.2

Ms. O'Connor thinks,

In various ways, Charles is always writing about his dad being a policeman, and I know, from what Charles tells us, that he wants to be a policeman when he grows up. He can write more than he did here, which is only, in effect, a caption under a drawing. Maybe the next time he writes on his policeman theme, he can say more. I'll ask him some questions to find out about his own police car, or about his dad. Maybe I can hear a central idea.

Surveying her students' writing helps Ms. O'Connor think about the various ways to approach the Adding Information strategy. Jessica's writing is short and may be somewhat easy to address. Charles's repetitive writing about his dad and himself as policemen may take a bit more probing to find out a central idea, such as their relationship, the details of what his dad does, or what Charles does when he plays police. In order for Charles to focus this, he may also have to delete mom and sister, which may be difficult. Regardless, this is a topic about which Charles loves to talk, write, and draw, so he will be willing to elaborate in a conference.

Confer

When writing teachers **confer** as they circulate among their students, they engage in a highly regarded instruction and evaluation process (Calkins, Hartman, & White, 2005). The value of conferring leads us to realize how little we learn when we survey students' pieces of writing without their oral explanations (Shagoury, 2009). We hear and learn a great deal when our young writers talk about their topics.

When Ms. O'Connor asks Jessica about her fifteen fish, Jessica quickly moves past her catch and says, in one breath,

My fishing pole got stuck in a tree because I don't know how to cast too good, and when my dad got it down a little branch hit my hand and I started to cry, and he said fishermen don't cry, so I stopped.

The two of them talk about this, and Ms. O'Connor, noticing that Jessica is in the midst of a new draft about her best friend, closes their conference by saying, "Maybe some day you'll decide to write some more about your fishing experience."

They exchange smiles, and Ms. O'Connor thinks, "This is a good example that I can use, somehow, when I present the Adding Information strategy next week."

When Ms. O'Connor stops beside Charles, she opens his writing folder to his draft from the previous day. He smiles but continues to work on a new draft about something unrelated to his recurring police topic. Ms. O'Connor tries to engage him in a conversation about his police interests, but the moment has been lost. Charles is writing—and wants to talk—about volcanoes today. They do, and as Ms. O'Connor walks to another child, she thinks, "There are quite a few students who sort of write captions for their drawings, without really saying anything. Maybe I can use that general tendency in next week's study about adding information."

Throughout this week of conferring, Ms. O'Connor continues to notice what her young writers are doing, and collects samples of their work that she might use in her upcoming instruction—a few of which you will see in the following sections.

Assemble Materials

When the time comes to **assemble materials** in preparation for the Adding Information strategy, Ms. O'Connor collects examples of students' writing from the class, children's literature, and chart pads and markers on which to create her own writing for demonstrations within the mini-lesson sessions. Using students' writing as an object of study within a mini-lesson is a way to be sure they see the relevance of the mini-lesson to their work (Ray, 2001). Instruction in writing is meant to be authentic, and one way to ensure this is to start by showcasing the work of students in the classroom.

Of the various materials assembled, the chart pads and markers for the teacher's demonstration with her own writing are of particular significance. The importance of teachers as writers is one of the foundations of writing instruction (Murray, 2003; Painter, 2006). When teachers engage in writing in their classrooms, the students not only see teachers as insiders but also trust teachers' knowledge. And the teachers trust their own knowledge. Given that many teachers do not consider themselves to be good writers, using their own work as part of demonstration lessons helps them understand the hesitation their students may experience.

Model

While students are gathered around Ms. O'Connor for their writing strategy mini-lesson, we see her **model** the use of the materials she has assembled. On this first day of their study of adding information, Ms. O'Connor sits with a child's draft on her lap. All of the students stretch their necks, waiting to see whose it is, as Ms. O'Connor smiles a secretive smile. Now she reads the model of the day:

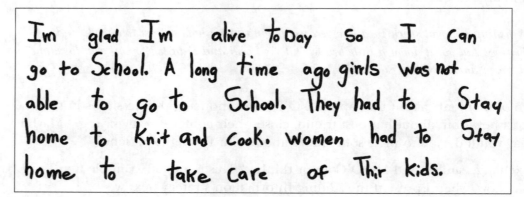

Im glad Im alive toDay so I can go to School. A long time ago girls was not able to go to School. They had to Stay home to Knit and Cook. Women had to Stay home to take care of Thir kids.

Figure 14.3

As soon as she finishes, someone says, "That's Shorena's!" So true. The students share their writing when they are working at their tables, and someone could recognize any draft Ms. O'Connor chooses to read aloud. Then Ms. O'Connor says, "What is so important about this draft?"

"We studied about women's rights."

"This is about girls' rights."

"Long time ago girls didn't go to school."

"Boys always did."

Ms. O'Connor says,

> Yes, this is mostly about girls. Shorena starts with "I'm glad I'm alive today so I can go to school," and she ends with, "Women had to stay home to take care of their kids." Shorena and I conferred about this, and she would like three ideas for a thought she can add to the end about why she is glad she can go to school.

"We get PE."

"We hear you read about Clifford."

Ms. O'Connor confirms,

> Yes, he is my favorite character, isn't he? One idea for Shorena is to say she likes PE; another is to say she likes to hear Clifford books. Shorena, what is your own best reason to be glad you can go to school?

Shorena sits, the students wait, and Shorena says, "Ms. O'Connor, I think I like the book about the elephant the best."

Ms. O'Connor smiles, nods, and confirms, "Excellent, Shorena. When you add your information, you can add whatever it is that makes you glad to be here."

Ms. O'Connor knows that in the long run, just adding information wherever they want may not help students focus each draft on a central idea. But this is their first lesson on adding information, and she starts with a simple invitation. To the class, Ms. O'Connor says, "When you go to write today, I invite you to look at your old drafts to see if you can find a draft you would like to add information to. How many of you think you will practice this today?"

Practice

Ms. O'Connor decides to let the students start writing immediately after modeling the strategy for the first time. She schedules ten days of the **practice** component of SCAMPER into her weekly plans so students will have many opportunities to use the Adding Information strategy, with her assistance, on various pieces of writing. Here you will see how Ms. O'Connor scaffolds students' practice.

Ms. O'Connor watches students settle in. She sees a table where two students huddle, looking through their folders. She walks toward them and confers with them as they look for drafts to which they can add information. Throughout the students' writing time, students can talk among themselves if they wish, and Ms. O'Connor moves from student to student, conferring with them about adding information when appropriate (Read, 2005). She makes sure to stop beside Shorena, who is, of course, adding information about the elephant book. Some students, as is expected, are not engaged in adding information. In those cases, Ms. O'Connor confers with them about the drafts in which they are immersed. She realizes that there are many drafts to which students will never add information; they are pleased with their initial creations, and she supports their decisions (Boldt, 2009).

◆◆◆◆◆◆

Now we join the class on the second day. On the chair Ms. O'Connor usually occupies we see Shorena reading today's model—her draft from yesterday plus her new sentence. When she is finished, the students applaud, and Shorena bows and sits among them.

Ms. O'Connor reclaims her chair and asks, "So, what did Shorena add?"

The students know, and Ms. O'Connor asks, "Why did she add something?"

Their comments lead Ms. O'Connor to summarize by saying that Shorena ended with her most important idea—what is most important to her in school.

Then Ms. O'Connor asks a student who has been sitting on his writing folder to come forward—today's second model. She has chosen him because he added information about his most important idea, and the class sees and hears what he added to a draft after their lesson on day one. They talk about that addition, and Ms. O'Connor ends the session with, "I invite you to look through your folders for a draft to which you can add information about your most important idea. How many of you think you will practice this today?" This is how Ms. O'Connor ended her modeling on the previous day, and, for the sake of consistency, she ends this lesson the same way.

Several of the students raise their hands, and all go off to write, talking among themselves as they compose. As Ms. O'Connor confers with some of them, she notices that a few more writers than yesterday are intent on adding information. Her task is to help them figure out their central ideas and possible information to add.

They end their writing block with one student on the Author's Chair to read aloud a draft to which she added information—an additional model for this day (Mermelstein, 2007).

◆◆◆◆◆

It is now day three of their study, and as the students gather, they sit carefully on their writing folders, each folder with a pencil tucked inside it. One student quickly shares an addition of central information—today's model—and Ms. O'Connor says, "Now all of you are going to open your folders and look for one draft that you think you can add information to, so your central idea is clearer."

They chatter as they look, and Ms. O'Connor scoots around the edges, highlighting a student who finds a possibility for adding to a draft.

The students go to their tables, and all of them practice adding information. Some of them become engaged in their old drafts, and not only add a single piece of information to fulfill Ms. O'Connor's request but also find several places where they can add something. Other children find old drafts, add a bit, and quickly start new drafts from scratch. All work on their own drafts, conferring with one another as they write, as they will continue to do every day throughout this focus on adding information.

◆◆◆◆◆

It is now day four, and Jessica is in the chair, wiggly with excitement. As the class quiets down she reads today's first model in a careful, loud voice.

> I went to fish. I had the most fish. We have fifteen fish. I went too far for
> a second. But who I went fishing with is my dad and two brothers. My
> fishing pole got stuck in a tree. But my dad got it down. When he got it
> down a little branch hit my hand. It didn't really hurt. That's the big point.

Jessica understands this entire adding information concept! In fact, she overtly tells us so. First, she notes how she "went too far for a second," meaning that she ended her narrative way too soon. Now she tells about her complete experience and, to be sure we get it, she ends with, "That's the big point." We understand, Jessica.

I went to fish
I had the most fish.
We have 15 fish. I went
too far for a sacint.
But who I whent fishing
with is my Dad and 2 Brouthers.
My fishing pole got stuck in
a tree. But my Dad got it
down. When he got it
down a little branch hit
my hand. It diti't rily hert
Thats the big point.

Daddy Help

Figure 14.4

The students, Jessica, and Ms. O'Connor talk about what Jessica did. Many are impressed by how much she added. Inspired, they go to their tables to engage in their writing for the day, and several practice in ways that show Jessica's influence.

They end their day with two students' sharing drafts from the Author's Chair. One has added information to a former draft (today's second model), and the other is excited about a new draft.

❖❖❖❖❖❖

On days five, six, and seven, the students and Ms. O'Connor share portions of children's literature to model what an author does when providing information that clarifies his or her "big point." As always, after their mini-lesson session, the students go to their tables to write on their various topics, some related to the science and math topics in which their class is currently engaged and others about various events in their lives. Some write fiction, others poetry. Every day, Ms. O'Connor emphasizes the need to practice adding information so the "big points" of their favorite drafts are clear. Each day they close their work time with someone on the Author's Chair.

❖❖❖❖❖

On days eight, nine, and ten, Ms. O'Connor works on one piece of writing as a model, adding information each day to show how one extended piece of writing can focus on one central idea rather than becoming an elaborated list, which had become common as the students gained fluency. Now she is trying to direct their fluency, and many students show some understanding of her invitations to practice. On day nine, and again on day ten, Charles writes for the entire day about what he does when he practices being a policeman in his own model of a police car.

Ten days of lessons, conferences, and Author's Chair sessions influence many of the students, and provide Ms. O'Connor with occasions to remind them about the Adding Information strategy during the next week as they continue with this focus.

Execute

Students **execute** the Adding Information strategy for a week after the ten days during which they studied models and practiced. This extra week is crucial so the young writers have multiple opportunities to experience the usefulness of this strategy.

In this phase, Ms. O'Connor works closely with individual students, or small groups, and reminds them, after they have written drafts, to think about their central ideas. If a student sounds interested in pursuing a particular draft, Ms. O'Connor invites him or her to brainstorm possible additions. She makes sure to confer with students who need extra support.

Reflect

During the week in which students execute the strategy, Ms. O'Connor asks them to **reflect** on how the strategy helped them better understand their topics and ideas. She engages students in reflection when conferring with them and when some of the students share from the Author's Chair. In any of these situations, she uses prompts like the following to help guide their thoughts:

- When you added information, what did you add that was important?
- How did that important information help show your central idea?
- Find two pieces of your writing that show you are becoming a better writer.
- Read to us from the better of these two pieces, and tell us what is good about it.

In responding to these prompts, the students' reflections vary. Many can answer the first question, and a few can answer the second question. The variation is to be expected, as adding information to strengthen a central idea is a difficult concept (Cappello, 2006; Sumida & Meyer, 2006).

At the same time, it is important for excited young writers to begin to think about their central ideas as they intentionally strive to improve their work. Gradually, as the students start to value certain parts of events over others and become fluent with putting ideas on paper, they begin to emphasize particular aspects of incidents over others in their writing (Graves, 2003). As Jessica did, they transition from seeing all happenings in a day equally to each highlighting one of them.

This is difficult, however, for many young writers. All of them can complete the task in the third prompt—finding two pieces of their writing that show they are becoming better writers. However, when responding to the fourth prompt, not all of them will choose as their better draft the one that provides evidence of adding information to clarify a central idea.

Adapting the Strategy

Adapting the Strategy for Emerging Writers

When emerging writers engage in writing, they add details to their drawings, and it is necessary for them to realize the significance of what they are doing. When they start to add fingers to hands and use letters and words to label objects within their drawings, they need to understand the importance of these additions. In these cases, Ms. O'Conner helps students talk about their additions in mini-lesson sessions, conferences, and from the Author's Chair.

Adapting the Strategy for Writers Who Struggle

Writers do not necessarily struggle with using the Adding Information strategy, but some will do so at earlier and later dates than others. For some students, the task of writing is a difficult motor skill and adding information is tiring. For others, their oral language patterns may not be elaborative, so their texts are expectedly sparse. As these students gain in oral fluency, their writing shows similar growth. In any case, Ms. O'Connor encourages students to add information when they talk, draw, and write—always being sensitive to the students' interests. Ms. O'Connor knows when a young writer's engagement in a task has waned; it may not be productive to encourage the writer to add information at that stage.

Adapting the Strategy for English Language Learners

Sometimes more than half of the students in the classrooms in my own research projects are English language learners (ELLs). These students learn to write with native English speakers in writing workshops, as is the case in many schools (Fay & Whaley, 2004). These students, like native English speakers, naturally add information to their drawings (Gallas, 2003). Young artists see their work as changeable. They can use this assumption to transition into the addition of labels and words. Before long, most young ELLs start to speak English, and their writing reflects their oral usage. The students, excited by the new information and vocabulary they learn, tend to add information to their texts. However, whether an ELL will intentionally add information to foster the clarity of his or her central idea will depend on the child.

Adapting the Strategy for Advanced Writers

An advanced writer is sometimes difficult to define among young writers. Some are advanced because they write in strong voices—their writing sounds like their delightful, little selves. Some are advanced because they know how invented spelling works, and others are advanced because they always know what they want to write about—choosing a topic never poses a concern.

Regardless, the Adding Information strategy is designed to provide opportunities for advanced writers and all others to intentionally add information to their creations, which requires adaptations throughout the process to ensure everyone's success. The main difference is that the more advanced young writers understand the notion of creating a central idea for a draft and adding information that ensures the clarity of their focus. Other writers may tend to add information in various places, not necessarily using this new material to further a central idea.

When Ms. O'Connor confers with advanced writers, she asks questions to extend their perception of what they know and helps them make decisions about what information to add and where to put it in their writing—as she does with all the students. Finally, when advanced students share from the Author's Chair, they may set the bar high, which is good. Ms. O'Connor makes sure their intention with adding information—to clarify their central point—is included in the discussion.

Extending the Strategy

Ms. O'Connor encourages students to use this strategy when they build with blocks, build in the sandbox, and create with straws; they add turrets to castles, annexes to buildings, and reinforcements to jungle gyms. They also use this strategy when they form structures with pipe cleaners, clay, and colored paper. Ms. O'Connor uses versions of the phrase "adding information" when she enriches what students know in social studies and science. The students will be adding information to their storehouses of knowledge for the rest of their lives.

EVIDENCE CONNECTIONS

Avery, C. (2002) *... And with a light touch: Learning about reading, writing, and teaching with first graders*. Portsmouth, NH: Heinemann.
In this book we learn about individual students who add information to their pictures and texts over a period of days as they gradually remember more information, think of additional details, and share their writing. Questions from others help the students think of their ideas in more depth, and that thinking often leads them to revision, usually by adding information.

Horn, M., & Giacobbe, M. E. (2007). *Talking, drawing, writing: Lessons for our youngest writers*. Portland, ME: Stenhouse.
For young writers the idea of adding information seems logical, so to focus on it in writing is consistent with what the children do as they gain expertise in talking and drawing. When Horn and Giacobbe teach kindergarten writers, their first lesson (after students have devoted one work period to drawing stories) ends with words similar to these (p. 40):

> When you go back to your table to work, the first thing you do is open your book to the page you worked on yesterday, take a good look at your drawing, and then ask yourself a very important question: What else do I need to put in so readers will understand my story?

REFERENCES

Boldt, G. M. (2009). Kyle and the Basilisk: Understanding children's writing as play. *Language Arts, 87*, 9–17.

Calkins, L., Hartman, A., & White, Z. (2005). *One to one: The art of conferring with young writers*. Portsmouth, NH: Heinemann.

Cappello, M. (2006). Under construction: Voice and identity development in writing workshop. *Language Arts, 83*, 482–491.

Fay, K., & Whaley, S. (2004). *Becoming one community: Reading and writing with English language learners*. Portland, ME: Stenhouse.

Gallas, K. (2003). *Imagination and literacy: A teacher's search for the heart of learning.* New York: Teachers College Press.

Graves, D. H. (2003). *Writing: Teachers and children at work: 20th anniversary edition.* Portsmouth, NH: Heinemann.

Hansen, J. (2005). Young children's versions of curriculum: "How do you turn a square into a grown-up?" *Language Arts, 82,* 269–277.

Hansen, J. (2007). First-grade writers revisit their work. *Young Children, 62*(1), 28–33.

Harste, J., Woodward, V., & Burke, C. (1984). *Language stories and literacy lessons.* Portsmouth, NH: Heinemann.

Heard, G. (2002). *The revision toolbox: Teaching techniques that work.* Portsmouth, NH: Heinemann.

Kissel, B. (2008, March). Apples on train tracks: Observing young children reenvision their thinking. *Young Children,* pp. 26–32.

Lawrence, J. (2006). Revoicing: How one teacher's language creates active learners in a constructivist classroom. *Constructivist* [online journal], *17*(1). Retrieved September 24, 2010, from http://www.odu.edu/educ/act/journal/vol17no1/.

Mermelstein, L. (2007). *Don't forget to share: The crucial last step in the writing workshop.* Portsmouth, NH: Heinemann.

Murray, D. M. (2003). *A writer teaches writing: Revised.* Florence, KY: Cengage Learning.

Painter, K. (2006). *Living and teaching the writing workshop.* Portsmouth, NH: Heinemann.

Ray, K. W. (with Laminack, L.). (2001). *The writing workshop: Working through the hard parts (And they're all hard parts).* Urbana, IL: National Council of Teachers of English.

Read, S. (2005). First and second graders writing informational text. *Reading Teacher, 59,* 36–44.

Shagoury, R. E. (2009). *Raising writers: Understanding and nurturing young children's writing development.* Boston: Pearson.

Sumida, A., & Meyer, M. (2006). Teaching to the fourth power: Transformative inquiry and the stirring of cultural waters. *Language Arts, 83,* 437–449.

Temple, C. A. & Nathan, R. (2006). *The beginnings of writing* (4th ed.). Boston: Allyn & Bacon.

Chapter 15

To Rhyme or Not to Rhyme?

CINDY LASSONDE

Some poems rhyme, and others do not. The poet makes the decision. How do we decide whether or not we want a poem to rhyme? To Rhyme or Not to Rhyme helps students evaluate the poems they write to determine if a given poem sounds better and makes more sense when it rhymes or when it does not. This strategy involves writing a poem two ways to determine what structure or form better conveys the poet's message.

Why This Strategy Is Important

When primary students try to compose poetry, they frequently are more concerned with creating a rhyming pattern than they are with conveying a message in poetic form (Graves, 1992). They tend to force the poem into the rhymes rather than focusing on the sound and the sense of the potential poem. Here's an example:

My dog's name is Jake.
He is not a fake.
Barks he makes.
In the morning he wakes.

The To Rhyme or Not to Rhyme strategy teaches young poets to draft their poems in two forms, one that rhymes and one that does not. Then, peers help the poet use a checklist to evaluate both forms and choose the one they think sounds better, makes sense, and sounds more like a poem.

The SCAMPER Model for To Rhyme or Not to Rhyme

Survey and Assess

I **survey and assess** students' poetry writing. Through informal observations, I note their participation in the class's interactive poem writing. I listen to how they talk about poetry and composing poems while they work with partners or write independently. I jot down questions they ask each other and me during writing conferences. These observations and notes help me understand with which strategies and skills they are comfortable and which could be helpful to them to learn. Over time, I look at the types of poems they create. In particular, I determine if To Rhyme or Not to Rhyme would be a helpful strategy to teach them by observing and listening to their remarks as they write and by studying their poems. I use the list of questions shown in Table 15.1 to prompt my observations as I record anecdotal notes and comments about students' poetry in my Writing Strategies Notebook.

Table 15.1 List of Questions to Prompt Observations About Poetry Writing

What kinds of poems does the student write?

Does he or she use rhyming? How frequently—in all poems, some poems, no poems?

Do the rhyming poems he or she writes make sense?

Do his or her non-rhyming poems make sense?

Do the rhyming poems he or she writes flow smoothly and have a strong voice?

Do his or her non-rhyming poems flow smoothly and have a strong voice?

Which poem style or styles are generally more comprehendible and poetic?

Once I have determined which students might benefit from learning this strategy, I form a small learning group and begin our To Rhyme or Not to Rhyme multimodal writing strategy mini-lesson.

Confer

Now that I have a small group of students who could benefit from learning the strategy together, I **confer** with them. I begin by asking, "What do you know about writing poems?" I prompt discussion with the group about deciding what style of poem to write. I ask, "Do all poems have to rhyme? When you write a poem, how do you decide if you are going to make it rhyme or not?"

Then I explain that we will learn a new strategy to help us decide whether the poem we write today would sound better and make better sense if it rhymed or if it didn't. I tell them we'll do this by writing the same poem two ways and helping each other decide which one is better. I explain that they will want to use this strategy when they write poems independently.

Assemble Materials

I **assemble materials** that include some of my favorite children's poetry collections, such as those by Jack Prelutsky and Shel Silverstein, and classics, such as works by Robert Louis Stevenson and Christina Rossetti, to have on hand for inspiration and reference while working. I find examples of many styles of poems, including those that rhyme and those that do not. I have on hand chart paper and markers, and a wide array of materials to motivate young writers, such as colored pencils, crayons, scented markers, and colored paper cut into different shapes. I collect the To Rhyme or Not to Rhyme poster shown in Figure 15.1 and a journal-size copy of the poster for each student. After I use the poems on the poster to model using the strategy, students will paste their copies into their journals for use when they are writing poems independently. I will also need copies of the You Be the Judge Checklist shown in Figure 15.2.

Step 1. *Maybe it should rhyme? Try it!*

My dog's name is Jake.
He is not a fake.
Barks he makes.
In the morning he wakes
For goodness' sake!
Sometimes he shakes.
I love Jake.

Step 2. *Maybe it should not rhyme? Try it!*

My dog's name is Jake.
He's my good friend
Even if he wakes me
In the morning,
Early in the morning,
With his bark,
Bark,
Bark!
Even on Saturdays!
Ah well, . . . I still love him.

Step 3. *Now, you be the judge. Ask*

	Rhyming	Not Rhyming
Which tells a better story?	_____	_____
Which makes more sense?	_____	_____
Which sounds better or more like a poem?	_____	_____
Which says what I want to say?	_____	_____
Which will make people feel the way I do?	_____	_____
Which would I rather read?	_____	_____
Which do I like better?	_____	_____
Totals	_____	_____

Figure 15.1 To Rhyme or Not to Rhyme Poster

	Rhyming	Not Rhyming
Which tells a better story?	_____	_____
Which makes more sense?	_____	_____
Which sounds better or more like a poem?	_____	_____
Which says what I want to say?	_____	_____
Which will make people feel the way I do?	_____	_____
Which would I rather read?	_____	_____
Which do I like better?	_____	_____
Totals	_____	_____

Figure 15.2 You Be the Judge Checklist

Model

I model by telling students I am going to write a poem about my little dog named Jake. I love Jake very much, and he is a loyal, true-blue, very good friend. I show them a picture of Jake and tell them some of the things we like to do together. Then I say,

> *But Jake has one bad habit: he likes to bark. Sometimes he wakes me up early in the morning by barking to go outside. Yikes! I wish he would sleep in, especially when I don't have to get up early, like on Saturdays. I want to write a poem about my dog. I want to say that I love him even though he wakes me up early in the morning. Should I make it rhyme or not? There are lots of words that rhyme with Jake if I make it rhyme. There's Jake, fake, wake. I'll try rhyming.*

I bring out the poster with only Step 1 revealed. I have paper taped over Steps 2 and 3. I read them the poem I wrote that rhymes (Step 1), pointing out that I made it rhyme. Then I tell them I want to see what happens if I don't make the poem rhyme. What might it sound like? I reveal Step 2 and read that poem.

Now I have two poems about Jake. I read them both again. Then I ask the questions in Step 3 to see which poem I think my readers, Jake, and I like better. I count the tally marks and make a final decision as to which draft is the better poem. I finish by saying,

> *By writing my ideas and feelings about Jake down in two different kinds of poems—one that rhymes and one that does not rhyme—I can see that even though the first poem rhymes, I like the second poem better. It tells the story I want to tell about Jake; it sounds more like a poem. I can hear Jake barking, and I can hear how annoyed I feel when he wakes me up early. The second poem has more feelings in it and sounds like I'm telling you how Jake makes me feel inside. I'm glad I didn't just write the first poem. Looking at my ideas two different ways was a good way to decide which way was better.*

Practice

I review the strategy with students and ask them to **practice** writing two drafts of a poem—one that rhymes and one that does not rhyme—about a new topic. I stand by to scaffold and support their progress. I ask them to describe their senses and feelings. I help them construct rhyming and non-rhyming drafts of their poems by referring them to the questions on their Grow a Poem guides in their journals (see Chapter Seven, Growing a Poem with Interview Buddies). Once two students have drafted their two poems, I pair them up to read each other's poems. With a copy of the You Be the Judge checklist shown in Figure 15.2, partners collaborate to choose the better poem based on the criteria. Students should add copies of this checklist and the To Rhyme or Not to Rhyme poster (see Figure 15.1) to their Writing Strategies Journals.

Execute

In the next step, students **execute** the strategy and work toward independent, self-regulated writing. I support their efforts and remind them to write each poem with rhymes and without rhymes, then to use the You Be the Judge checklist to decide which of their poems they prefer.

Reflect

In the final step, in which students **reflect,** I encourage them to talk about their poems and their use of the strategy. We talk about how they could use the steps in the checklist to evaluate two versions of the same writing piece as they draft poems in the future. I ask them to talk about how this strategy made their writing better. Then we talk about poem structures and forms:

- What is a poem?
- How do we write poems?
- Do all poems have to rhyme?
- What do we have to remember when we do want to use rhyming in a poem?

I want them to reflect on the importance of integrating their voices into their poems rather than forcing their poems into rhyming schemes just because they think that's what poetry is.

Adapting the Strategy

Adapting the Strategy for Emerging Writers

With emerging writers who may not yet be confident readers, I simplify the questions by breaking them down into key phrases (in other words, Tell a story? Sound better?). Also, they read their poems to the partners who help evaluate them rather than relying on the partners' being able to read their invented spelling. For some groups of emerging writers, I help them practice and execute components of the SCAMPER model for this strategy to support their eventual transfer to independent writing as their writing skills develop.

Adapting the Strategy for Writers Who Struggle

Students who struggle with writing may be resistant to writing two drafts of the same poem if they find it difficult to write just one poem. For these writers, I first present the strategy as one that will help them compose poems of which they will be very proud. Then I tell them each to write two to four lines of a rhyming poem, then two to four lines of the same poem without rhyming, rather than expecting them to write whole poems twice. Limiting the number of lines I expect students to write alleviates anxiety and resistance yet still allows students to experience the benefits of the strategy.

Adapting the Strategy for English Language Learners

I bring in rhyming and non-rhyming poems in the children's first languages so they have models of various structures. The You Be the Judge questions may be written in the children's first languages in their journals to reinforce the English versions. Also, English language learners benefit from the partner work and oral exchanges of this strategy. I provide multiple opportunities for partners to talk about their writing together. They repeat the questions and become familiar with them. It is important for English language learners to maintain control of the ideas going into their poems, so I scaffold each student's exchanges between the two languages to ensure the student's ideas are not restricted by his or her writing and language abilities. Finally, I introduce students to a rhyming dictionary so they have a list of possible rhymes.

Adapting the Strategy for Advanced Writers

Advanced writers may be resistant to rewriting their poems in a different format. They may think they do not need to write both versions of their poems because they "like it the way it is" or because they don't think they will learn anything from the experience. I encourage them to do so at least once and to reflect on the strategy's value. After going through the process once, they may be able to internalize the thinking process as they write their first drafts. To check this, I ask students, "Did you think about writing this using or not using rhymes? What made you decide to do it this way?"

Extending the Strategy

This strategy leads nicely into a lesson on what makes a poem interesting. To extend the strategy, I have students bring in poems to share with the class. They tell why they found their poems engaging. I encourage them to describe reasons besides those simply related to finding the topic interesting, such as "It has a strong beat," "It makes me feel a certain way," or "I can make pictures in my head when I read it." I start a list of characteristics of what makes a poem interesting and display it in the poetry center for students to use when they write independently.

EVIDENCE CONNECTIONS

Wilson, A. (2007). Finding a voice: Do literary forms work creatively in teaching poetry writing? *Cambridge Journal of Education, 37,* 441–457.
The linguistic demands of writing poetry— chunking meaning, breaking lines, and managing imagery— make it perhaps the most challenging genre that young students encounter. However, there are many benefits to integrating a variety of poetic forms— rhyming and non-rhyming— into the curriculum. This article looks at how poetry allows each student to find and develop his or her writing voice by reading poems in various formats, structures, and styles and learning from model poems (Heaney, 1980). Wilson describes the "reverberative power" (p. 442) of poetry. How do we encourage students to write so their voices echo throughout their poems as they reveal their beliefs, values, and experiences? When they read others' poems, they build on their knowledge of how to express a concept or event in a personal voice so they aren't just telling what they want to say but also are transforming what they know. Through the To Rhyme or Not to Rhyme strategy, each student compares two forms of a poem to determine which draft has more reverberative power— more of the student's voice— and learns how to evaluate whether or not the poem conveys his or her intended message and emotions.

Andrade, H., & Valtcheva, A. (2009). Promoting learning and achievement through self-assessment. *Theory into Practice, 48,* 12–19.
Research tells us that students can be useful sources of feedback through their self-assessment of their work (Andrade & Boulay, 2003; Andrade, Du, & Wang, 2008). Self-assessment involves students in thinking about the quality of their own writing. They don't only rely on the teacher to tell them what might benefit from revision.

Students should self-assess drafts of their writing as they proceed through the writing process to confirm if their work reflects their intent. Self-assessment is not a matter of students' determining their own grades but rather of improving their work. In this strategy, when students rewrite their poems another way and then judge their two drafts, they are self-assessing and improving their work.

REFERENCES

Andrade, H., & Boulay, B. (2003). Gender and the role of rubric-referenced self-assessment in learning to write. *Journal of Educational Research, 97,* 21–34.

Andrade, H., Du, Y., & Wang, X. (2008). Putting rubrics to the test: The effect of a model, criteria generation, and rubric-referenced self-assessment on elementary school students' writing. *Educational Measurement: Issues and Practices, 27*(2), 3–13.

Graves, D. H. (1992). *Explore poetry.* Portsmouth, NH: Heinemann.

Heaney, S. (1980). *Preoccupations: Selected prose 1968–1978.* London: Faber & Faber.

Chapter 16

Think, Draw, Write, and Share (TDWS)

CYNTHIA B. LEUNG

This multimodal strategy provides a format K–3 writers can follow to turn their oral stories into written productions by drawing their ideas and then labeling their drawings.

Why This Strategy Is Important

Young children use multimodal forms of expression—oral language, drawings, body movements, and print-like shapes or alphabet letters—as they explore ways to put their stories on paper. Oral language is the foundation of writing, and children's stories originate in oral language (Dyson, 1981, 1983). Emergent literacy research has also shown that children's drawings and scribbles are early forms of writing. Vygotsky (1978) observed in studies of children drawing and scribbling that they frequently switched to using gestures and dramatization as they expressed actions on paper with visual marks. From these observations he concluded that gesture is "the initial visual sign that contains the child's future writing" (p. 107). Therefore, it is important to recognize the connections between students' drawings and their writing pieces. Students who express their thoughts in pictures and words become more proficient, productive writers. In addition, creating stories using print, drawings, gestures, and dramatization helps students develop confidence in their ability to express themselves through multimodal forms of communication.

As a teacher educator and literacy researcher doing classroom ethnography, I observe, record, and analyze different types of classroom literacy events that help students develop writing skills. I then share what I learn with my pre-service and in-service teachers. I am particularly interested in strategies that lead to writing development. For eighteen months I worked with a kindergarten teacher named Lori in her morning and afternoon classes. Over the course of the school year, I observed the students' love of writing and saw their writing abilities grow. The kindergartners started the year with a strong interest in drawing. Thus Lori set up a drawing table for students to use during free choice, a time when students could select from different learning activities. The students always gravitated toward the drawing table.

As students drew their pictures with colorful markers, they talked about what they were drawing. They were eager to share their drawings and oral stories with Lori and me. By October, most of the students in Lori's class preferred drawing to the other activities offered during free choice. To make connections between their oral stories and drawings, we developed the Think, Draw, Write, and Share (TDWS) strategy. The four steps to the strategy are

1. **Think** of a story.
2. **Draw** a picture about your story.
3. **Write** a word (words) about your story.
4. **Share** your story with another person.

First we ask each student to think of a story and then draw a picture to represent the story. Next we ask each to think of a word that goes with or represents his or her story. Lori and I write each student's word on an index card and ask students to copy the words onto their pages. Then students individually tell the stories to Lori or to me. Every time a student writes a story, we ask him or her to follow this strategy. We find the Think, Draw, Write, and Share strategy is a natural way to help students transition from drawing pictures to creating multimodal writing.

As students learn more about the English alphabet and understand that letters represent sounds, their written words become more elaborate. They begin to write alphabet letters more clearly, and they use invented spelling to write words and then sentences. As the year progresses, their writing productions become more like conventional texts. Students work in a social atmosphere and share their work with peers. In this positive learning environment, writing becomes students' favorite activity. Later in the year, Lori and I introduce content journals—a Plant Journal and an Insect Journal. Students extend their oral stories to informational texts as they write facts about plants and insects.

Having the opportunity to observe and participate in the literacy learning of these students has taught me the importance of building on students' drawings, visualizations, and oral language to develop their written stories and nonfiction texts. During the school year, students authentically develop their writing skills and creativity, providing a strong foundation for future writing development. The TDWS strategy helps them understand the connection between their oral stories and written texts, and provides a framework they can follow independently to create their own stories.

I now teach this strategy to pre-service and in-service teachers. They tell me the strategy helps their emerging writers become more independent in the writing process. The strategy particularly helps students who have had few storybook reading experiences to make connections between print and oral language.

The SCAMPER Model for Think, Draw, Write, and Share (TDWS)

Survey and Assess

The TDWS strategy is appropriate for students at various stages of literacy development, including writers who struggle and learners of English as a second language. It is especially appropriate for beginning writers in kindergarten and first grade, who benefit from visualizing what they plan to write. At the beginning of the school year, I **survey and assess** students' emerging writing skills by asking them each to draw a picture and write something about the picture on the same page. When they finish their "writings," I ask the students to tell me about their drawings. As students tell me about their drawings, I take their dictations. I save these writing pieces to use as a benchmark to keep track of each student's writing development during the school year. From the first writing assessment, I learn if individual students know how to hold their markers or writing implements, can write any alphabet letters, are comfortable drawing pictures, have a concept of story, and feel comfortable orally sharing in front of the class.

Because the TDWS strategy involves drawing pictures, writing, and using oral language, I assess the students' multimodal productions to see if specific students have difficulty with one or all of these modes of expression. Once students begin using the strategy in their writing, I assess their writing development once a month by analyzing their multimodal productions. When students share their stories, they orally tell the stories they put on paper. I assess their understanding of story elements through their oral stories. I use story sharing as a method of continuous, authentic assessment. Students who are more advanced will write using conventional spelling, and will write longer, more sophisticated texts. Students who are not proficient in writing alphabet letters will practice letters by looking at their word cards and imitating the letters. As students' writing skills develop, they use these new skills in their multimodal journal productions.

Confer

I **confer** with students about their stories. I encourage them to tell stories about incidents that happened at home or on the playground, or to use their imaginations to make up stories. I explain they can also retell stories I read aloud to them in class. I encourage students to draw and talk about their drawings, so they will be able to make connections between their drawings and oral stories. I set up a drawing table for students to work on their drawings. When they finish their drawings, I ask them to tell me about their pictures or tell me the stories that go with their pictures. I sit by them at the table, and they "read" to me individually. I also show students how to retell stories during read-alouds. I use the Language Experience Approach (see Dorr, 2006) to write individual and group stories on a large notepad mounted on an easel. I use all of these types of experiences to show students how oral language connects to print.

Assemble Materials

I **assemble materials** to include Writing Strategies Journals for each student, and for myself, pencils, markers, 3-by-5 index cards, masking tape, and envelopes to hold students' collection of index (word) cards. Before modeling the strategy, I write *dog* on one of the index cards and tape an envelope inside the front cover of my model Writing Strategies Journal. I do not tape down the flap of the envelope so I will be able to slip index cards into it. I also place the TDWS poster near our meeting area and photocopy enough 8½-by-11 copies of the poster for each student to add one copy to his or her journal for future use in independent writing (see Figure 16.1).

Figure 16.1 TDWS Poster and Handout

Model

I tell students we will practice a strategy called Think, Draw, Write, and Share, which they can use when they write independently. To **model** the strategy, I point to "Think" on the TDWS poster and say, "First we *think* of a story. I think I will write a story about my dog." I then tell students a funny short story about my dog. Next I point to "Draw" on the poster and say, "The next step of the strategy is to *draw* a picture of our story." I open my Writing Strategies Journal to a blank page and begin to draw my dog. I say, "My drawing is a picture of my dog and shows the story I just told you." When I finish drawing, I take the 3-by-5 index card with "dog" printed on it and tell students that the word on the card says "dog." I call the index card my word card. I tell students the third step in the strategy is to *write*, and I point to "Write" on the poster. Then I copy the word *dog* onto the page under my drawing of the dog. I tell students that the picture and the word "dog" tell the story of my dog. I tell students,

We will use the index cards later for reading and spelling. When you write independently and don't know how to spell a word you wrote in your previous stories, you can look in your envelope for the card with that word. You can copy the word on your word card into your new story.

I show how to slip the index card into the envelope inside the front cover of my journal. Finally, I explain to students that the last step in the strategy is to *share* the story. I say,

When I was thinking about my story, I already shared it with you. But when you write your own story, you will share it with me or with other students after you finish it. Do you remember the four steps of this writing strategy?

I point to the poster. "What are the four steps?" As I point to the words on the TDWS poster, students call out, "Think, draw, write, and share." I reinforce the strategy name by saying, "Yes, this writing strategy is called Think, Draw, Write, and Share because those are the four steps to the strategy. We can also call it 'TDWS': 'T' for think, 'D' for draw, 'W' for write, and 'S' for share."

Practice

Students get their Writing Strategies Journals, and I tell them they will **practice** using the Think, Draw, Write, and Share strategy to write stories in their journals. We tape a small clasp envelope onto the inside of the front cover of each journal. I give students copies of the TDWS poster on $8\frac{1}{2}$-by-11 paper and ask them to add them to their journals. I tell them they can refer to the poster to remind themselves of the steps to the strategy. First I ask students to *think* of their own stories and a word that goes with each of their stories. For a story about a cat, the word might be "cat" or "meow." I write students' words on index cards and ask them to take their word cards. At this point I do not make explicit connections between their drawings and conventional writing. Next I ask each student to *draw* a picture about his or her story on a blank page of the Writing Strategies Journal. When students finish drawing, I ask them to *write* the words from their word cards onto the same pages as their drawings. I suggest they write each word underneath the corresponding drawing. After students complete their drawing and writing, I ask them to read the words on their index cards and to *share* their stories with me. I ask those students who finish their journal pages first to tell me their stories individually. I make sure all students have a chance to share their stories, either individually or with the group. I ask students to be sure to put their word cards in the envelopes in their journals when they finish writing. I remind them they can use the word cards when writing new stories independently. If a student doesn't remember how to spell the word on the card and wants to use that word in a new story, the student can copy the word from the card already in his or her envelope. I tell students they can practice reading the cards in their envelopes by matching the cards to their drawings and reading the words they wrote on their journal pages. We discuss other ways they can use the TDWS strategy in the future. I tell them, "The TDWS strategy is a good strategy for those times when you can't think of what to write about. Drawing a picture of a story often helps you think of words you can use to tell that story."

Execute

To help students remember the four steps to the Think, Draw, Write, and Share strategy, I place the poster of the strategy in the writing center. Students can use either the poster or the handouts of the poster to refresh their memories when they use the strategy independently. After students have created several pages in their Writing Strategies Journals using the TDWS strategy, I ask them to take the index cards from their envelopes and match the words on the cards with the same words on their journal pages. These pages have drawings students can use to aid their recall of the words. I then ask students to read the words they matched. I reinforce how they can use the word cards in the future to write any of those words in their new writing pieces. As students work on their stories, I encourage them to spread their paper, markers, and other materials over classroom tables and the carpet. This promotes collaborative work with peers and provides time for me to work with students who need additional assistance. As students **execute** the Think, Draw, Write, and Share strategy and become more accustomed to using the strategy, they learn how to add settings and characters to their stories.

Reflect

Students **reflect** as they share their stories with peers. I select several students' writing pieces and ask those students to tell the stories they represented. For each student, I point out features of the drawing and read the word the student copied on the page. I revoice students' talk, adding more technical or advanced vocabulary. I also highlight examples of students' work that exemplify writing concepts. As students learn about sound–alphabet letter correspondence, I encourage them to sound out words they want to write on their pages. I show the class examples of invented spelling on pages of their classmates' Writing Strategies Journals, and I encourage others to use invented spelling. If students' invented spelling is difficult to understand, I write their dictated stories in conventional spelling under their writing, so they have their stories preserved to refer back to later. I also remind students to use their word cards to write those same words on other story pages. As a finale to this strategy, I ask students to share how they might use Think, Draw, Write, and Share in their independent writing. We conclude that they can look through their envelopes to find words they need for their stories, and they can draw pictures to help them think about story ideas. Figure 16.2 is an example of a page from a student's journal.

Figure 16.2 Journal Page Created Using the Think, Draw, Write, and Share Strategy
[*The butterfly is flying to its nest. She had babies. A butterfly is beautiful. It has a lot of colors.*]

Adapting the Strategy

Adapting the Strategy for Emerging Writers

This strategy involves multimodal forms of expression familiar to emerging writers. I do not need to adapt the strategy for these writers. Students who have difficulty writing alphabet letters can copy the letters from the word cards I prepare for them. They can tell their stories to their peers as they draw and write. Also, I am available to work individually with students who have difficulty during any stage of the strategy.

Adapting the Strategy for Writers Who Struggle

The Think, Draw, Write, and Share strategy works well with struggling writers, without modifications, because it involves telling oral stories and drawing, as well as writing. Students who like to draw but have difficulty writing alphabet letters can still "write" through their drawings and oral stories. The strategy gives students opportunities to develop oral stories, which will eventually become written stories. Struggling writers can use their word cards to copy words onto their pages and refer back later to the cards in the envelopes when they want to write those words again. I can adapt the strategy in several ways. For students who have difficulty thinking of stories, I work individually with them and ask them to tell me their stories first. I can also change the time when I give students the word cards, either before or after they draw their pictures. Students can refer to the TDWS strategy poster or handout to remind themselves of the steps to the strategy.

Adapting the Strategy for English Language Learners

This strategy works well with English language learners (ELLs) at different stages of English language fluency. Students who are at the preproduction stage and are not yet speaking or using English words can focus on their drawings. They can share their stories in their primary languages. I ask ELLs at all stages of fluency to draw small pictures that represent the words on the backs of their word cards to aid their recall. I pair ELLs with fluent English-speaking peers to work together as they talk about their story ideas, draw their pictures, and write their words. I work with individuals and with small groups of students, showing them picture cards and saying words that go with the cards. Students repeat the words and can choose from these pictures to make their own stories. When ELLs share their stories, I ask each student to tell a word or sentence from his or her story. I ask their fluent English-speaking partners to elaborate on the ELLs' stories.

Adapting the Strategy for Advanced Writers

The multimodal nature of the Think, Draw, Write, and Share strategy makes it fun for advanced writers who want to write with more details, descriptions, and colorful words. Having drawings to refer to while writing stories helps advanced writers visualize what they are writing. Instead of choosing one word to write on each word card, advanced writers can choose several words that relate to their stories and use a thesaurus to find synonyms for those words. When they write, they can use the more advanced vocabulary. Sharing their drawings and stories builds confidence and provides peers with examples to use as models in their future writing. The strategy also provides a way for advanced writers to organize their work. At times, advanced writers have difficulty thinking of stories or writing topics. This strategy helps those writers use different modes of expression to come up with exciting topics. I have found that some advanced writers create more elaborate stories if they first draw pictures of their stories before writing them down in words.

Extending the Strategy

As students' skills mature, the nature of their writing changes, with more invented and conventional spelling occurring in their work. I extend the strategy by tying phonics and alphabet lessons to the students' multimodal written productions. I select words from their journals for the word wall. Students can have individual word lists on which they write words from their word cards. They can write informational texts as well as stories. Finally, the classroom atmosphere that develops when students apply the Think, Draw, Write, and Share strategy sets the stage for writing workshops and authentic writing.

EVIDENCE CONNECTIONS

Dyson, A. H. (1982). The emergence of visible language: Interrelationships between drawing and early writing. *Visible Language, 6*, 360–381.

Anne Haas Dyson's research on emergent literacy, especially emergent writing, uncovered relationships among children's oral stories, drawings, and writing. Her work in this area changed the way literacy researchers and teachers of young children approach children's writing. This article focuses on connections between drawing and early writing, and highlights the multimodal nature of early literacy development.

Berghoff, B., Egawa, K. A., Harste, J. C., & Hoonan, B. T. (2000). *Beyond reading and writing: Inquiry, curriculum, and multiple ways of knowing.* Urbana, IL: National Council of Teachers of English.

This book provides classroom examples of teachers using multiple sign systems, including art, music, print, and movement, to develop students' critical thinking skills. The authors focus on ways that different sign systems influence curriculum development. In literacy activities, such as Sketch to Stretch, discussed in this book, students use drawing in conjunction with their writing to go beyond simple presentations of plot. Several chapters are case studies of students whose literacy development benefited from multi-modal teaching approaches.

REFERENCES

Dorr, R. (2006). Something old is new again: Revisiting language experience. *Reading Teacher, 60*, 138–146

Dyson, A. H. (1981). Oral language: The rooting system for learning to write. *Language Arts, 58*, 776–784.

Dyson, A. H. (1983). The role of oral language in early writing processes. *Research in the Teaching of English, 17*, 1–30.

Vygotsky, L. (1978). *Mind in society: The development of higher psychological processes.* (M. Cole, Trans.). Cambridge, MA: Harvard University Press.

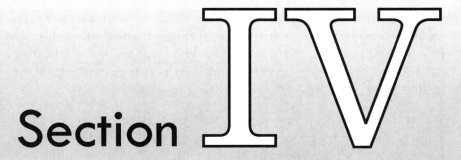

Section IV

Polishing Strategies

Writers polish their work when they have finished coherent drafts that sound pretty good. A good writer knows there are some rough edges to smooth over before a piece of writing is finished. At this stage in the writing process, a writer needs to revise and edit to make it the best work possible.

To polish a piece of writing, one has to be skilled and knowledgeable about how to evaluate writing. Polishing doesn't involve just correcting spelling and grammatical errors and reworking according to other conventions of print, although these are important parts of polishing. When a writer gets to the stage of having a sound draft, he or she needs to be able to look at it with a critical eye to determine its strengths and needs. There are many things for writers to consider when polishing their work. They might ask themselves:

- Will readers understand my message? If not, what have I left out, or what do I need to explain in more detail to be clear?
- Can I express myself in a more engaging, clear, or precise way?
- Do I stay on topic or do I stray and ramble? Do I confuse readers, or is my writing easy to follow?
- Will using dialogue improve my voice or the voice of my characters?
- Have I correctly used written language conventions?

Evaluating one's own work and knowing how to remedy it when necessary can be difficult. Even experienced writers find it difficult to put themselves in readers' shoes to determine what is needed, and, understandably, developing writers still need to work on the skills and knowledge needed to accurately and easily use the conventions of print. Polishing is multifaceted and can be tricky and frustrating for young writers.

HOW POLISHING STRATEGIES HELP STUDENTS

Polishing strategies should be creative, because the revision of a piece of writing is a creative process. Often a writer goes through many drafts before getting to a draft at which he or she says, "This is exactly what I wanted to say and how I wanted to say it." All good writers polish, repolish, and then polish some more. (Janet tells her graduate students to revise and edit one hundred times!)

When we work with young writers, we find they are often resistant to the polishing stage of the writing process. Once they get their thoughts on paper, they frequently say, "But this is how I want it. I don't want to change anything."

As teachers we must model the polishing strategies we use ourselves. We must demonstrate how we take drafts, ones that are good, and make them better by changing words, adding information, fixing up grammar, and altering sentence structures when necessary. Teachers know that showing pride in their own final writing products helps ensure that writers learn to enjoy the benefits of polishing their work. They learn by our good examples. Gradually, their resistance to polishing is rubbed away by the pride they feel in their final pieces. They see and experience the reward of their efforts.

STRATEGIES IN THIS SECTION

Chapter Seventeen, Act It Out to Discover the Details, teaches a strategy that helps students develop details in their writing. Through the use of creative dramatics and oral language, they act out and describe an event. Then, in Chapter Eighteen, Personal Editing Checklists, students, with the teacher's assistance, design and use Personal Editing Checklists to help them proofread and edit their writing on their own. Students learn to maintain their checklists for use over time. Chapter Nineteen, Adding Dialogue to Fiction and Nonfiction, helps students understand how dialogue can bring out a character's feelings and intentions and bring life to writing. Students learn how to insert dialogue into their independent writing of fiction and nonfiction texts. Chapter Twenty, Following Conventions for Writing Dialogue, provides a format students can follow to help them adhere to the conventions of written language when they are writing dialogue. Chapter Twenty-One, Color-Coding Editing, encourages students to review their drafts in order to identify and resolve their editing needs. Chapter Twenty-Two, Turning Up the Volume of Voice in Poetry, guides students to detect action words (verbs) and describers (adverbs and adjectives) within poems of their creation. The strategy also helps students look for action and describing words they might revise to express their feelings in stronger language to "turn up the volume" and strengthen their voices in the poems. Finally, Chapter Twenty-Three, STEP into the Shoes of a Reader, details a strategy for helping students revise their descriptive writing. STEP stands for **S**witch roles, **T**hink, **E**valuate, and **P**lan.

Chapter 17

Act It Out to Discover the Details

JOANNE DURHAM

This strategy helps students develop details in their writing by using creative dramatics to act out and describe events.

Why This Strategy Is Important

Students need multiple ways to help them expand their writing. A kinesthetic approach is a useful and motivating tool for bolstering students' writing repertoires. English language learners especially will benefit from being able to act out their stories and then finding vocabulary to fit their actions.

As an elementary classroom teacher engaging students in Writers' Workshop, I always looked for ways to help my students expand their writing. I quickly learned the futility of simply exhorting, ''Add details.'' I studied the experts and learned many time-honored teaching strategies. For example, I learned to share great mentor texts with students to demonstrate how authors show rather than tell; to revise my own writing from drab summaries of events into detail-filled explosions of the moment; and to teach students to hold peer conferences in which they ask the questions that motivate their classmates to expand. All of these ideas were useful in building students' understanding of how much more interesting it is to read the specifics than the general—to witness the filled cheeks of the birthday boy as he snuffs out the six candles on his cake in one huge breath, rather than being told, ''He blew out the candles.'' But once students know their writing needs to be developed, they require strategies they can use on their own to accomplish that sometimes daunting feat of providing details.

Once again, the experts came to my rescue. Susan Griss (1998), who uses kinesthetic learning to reach students in every content area, explores movement to aid writing.

I found that teaching students to physically act out their stories supports them to find the details, and then the language, that will bring the reader into the experience. It is a strategy they can learn to use—on their own (OTO)—leading them toward growing independence as writers. Lucy Calkins and colleagues (2005), in describing how to confer with a primary student to "mentally reenact her vignette in order to add significant details" (p. 1), writes, "Writing and drama have a lot to do with each other. We reenact and chronicle" (p. 5). Acting out their thoughts is also a strategy that helps students view revision in a positive light, moving revision away from how it is sometimes taught, "like being sent back to clean your room again because you didn't do a good job the first time" (Ray, 1999, pp. 60–61). Act It Out to Discover the Details turns revision into something enjoyable that students want to do.

The SCAMPER Model for Act It Out to Discover the Details

Survey and Assess

When I **survey and assess** students' drafts of their personal narratives, I find students at various stages of bringing their pieces alive for the reader. I look for those who need more support to develop their writing. For example, does a student have only a line or two on the page? ("I went with my family to the park.") Or does the student have a bed-to-bed story that needs focus and development of appropriate details? ("We woke up. We ate breakfast. We went to the park. We played on the swings. We went home.") I also analyze whether students' stories include actions that they would be able to pantomime to help them discover language to enhance the reader's understanding. Finally, I look to see if there are students writing about similar topics who might benefit from partnering to dramatize their activities. For example, in one class several students chose to write about their soccer games; another group described birthdays.

Almost any primary student is developmentally ready for this strategy, because it taps into the kinesthetic knowledge that students have regardless of their reading or writing proficiency. It therefore can be taught to students with a variety of writing competencies and can be easily differentiated—one student might add a more precise action verb whereas another might add several sentences; all can participate in acting out their own stories.

Confer

Once I decide on a group of students who will benefit from the strategy and who might work well as partners or individually, I bring them together to **confer.** I explain that they have such interesting topics, and that as a reader I want to be able to picture just what happened in my mind from their words. I tell them that I will teach them a fun way to figure out on their own what they might add to their stories that would bring them alive for their readers.

Assemble Materials

Before teaching the lesson, I **assemble materials.** I am ready with two versions of my own narrative draft, an idea for the topic the class will work on together, and chart paper and markers or technology to make my writing visible to the class.

Model

I **model** the strategy for my students.

1. I display and read the students a draft of my writing that lacks in specific details. I make sure to use a piece with physical actions and a topic that will be familiar to students. Here's a first-grade example:

> I got on my bike to ride to my friend's house. I went up and down the hill. Then I saw Edie, waving at me.

2. I explain that I want my readers to know what it was really like for me to ride my bike to my friend's house. I say something like,

> *Let me see if acting it out for myself can help me describe it better. As I act out riding my bike to my friend's house, I will notice what I am doing and see if I can put it into words.*

3. Next I pantomime riding the bike. I talk through the language that comes to me as I show the motions, for example, "When I went up the hill, I had to push down hard on the pedals, like this. Pretty soon my legs got tired. I started sweating."

4. After pantomiming the actions and talking through what is happening with the students, I tell them I will now try to write down what I learned about my story as I was acting it out. I write it on chart paper or another visual display. When I finish, I reread it slowly from beginning to end.

> I got on my bike to ride to my friend's house. When I went up the hill, I had to push down hard on the pedals. Pretty soon my legs got tired and I started sweating. Finally, I got to the top. I loved feeling the wind blow through my hair as I rolled down the hill fast. I knew I was close when I smelled the lilacs in Edie's yard. Then I saw Edie, waving at me.

5. Finally, I ask students for thumbs up or down as to whether they know more about my bike ride from the revised version and if they enjoyed it more. I ask each student to turn and talk with a partner about a part he or she learned more about from the second version. I circulate, listen, prompt, and then share a few examples from students who have articulated the differences between the first and second drafts. By seeking simultaneous student feedback and having children turn and talk with partners, I not only keep the students involved but also am better able to assess whether they understand how to use the strategy.

Practice

I provide an opportunity for all students to **practice** acting out another story with me for about two minutes. The story is usually based on a common experience, like blowing out birthday candles or a shared classroom activity. I write one sentence, such as "I blew out the candles on my cake." I have the students stand up and spread out so that each one can use his or her individual space for his or her own actions. I explain that they are their own audience; the idea is to notice what they are doing so they will be able to bring this event alive for the reader. I guide them to recognize what their bodies are doing—how they are feeling, and how they are showing their emotions on their faces and with their bodies, like I did when I modeled. As I see students engage in actions that express the topic, I give language for what they are doing and ask them to show the others their motions. Then they sit down and we work together to write the experience on a chart as I did with my story. Here's an example developed with a first-grade classroom:

> The birthday cake looked yummy. I closed my eyes and thought my wish in my mind. I took a big breath. The air was all puffy in my cheeks like a chipmunk. Then I let all the air go at once, and all six candles went out.

I praise how they have made their experience so much more interesting for the reader by paying such close attention to what their bodies and minds were actually doing.

The last part of the practice phase is rehearsal for students to use this strategy in their own writing. I give them a minute to review their current writing and see if there are pieces they could develop by acting them out. I ask them to share possibilities, and guide them. This rehearsal serves as a helpful transition to their working alone. If there are students who have similar topics, such as riding scooters or playing soccer, I may pair them up to work together.

Execute

We now move into the student writing portion of the strategy, during which students independently or with partners **execute** what they have learned. I encourage them to act out their stories and then work to revise them with the language they have discovered through their movements. I might work with a small group who need additional support, and of course I confer with students as necessary. For example, I have a student read his writing to me (or a specific part of a longer piece), and I say, "I want to know more about this. Try acting it out and see if you can tell more about what is happening."

Reflect

After the individual writing portion of the strategy, it's time for students to **reflect** on how this strategy has helped and can continue to improve their writing. We gather together again on the rug, and I choose some students to share in the Author's Chair how they expanded their writing and show us what they acted out to help them describe their experiences. I pick students with whom I have conferred or who I know have positive examples of implementing the strategy to share.

Adapting the Strategy

Adapting the Strategy for Emerging Writers

The Act It Out to Discover the Details strategy is adaptable to every learner. Emerging writers need to know that writing is about expressing their ideas through the forms they are currently capable of using. They are encouraged to capture the details that emerge from ''acting it out'' through whatever stage of beginning writing they can negotiate OTO (for example, first letters, beginning and ending letters, the vowel sounds they hear, and so on). Children who are not yet matching letters to sounds can be encouraged to add the details they acted out to their drawings.

Adapting the Strategy for Writers Who Struggle

As noted earlier, during conferences or with small groups I am able to teach new vocabulary to students, including English language learners, who lack the precise words to describe their actions. Having students work with partners can also be effective, helping struggling writers stay focused and hear peers' use of language to describe the actions they are pantomiming. The writing community is further developed through these interactions, and students become more willing to take risks in expressing themselves through their motions and their words.

Adapting the Strategy for English Language Learners

This strategy also plays a useful role with English language learners (ELLs) and in helping all students expand their vocabulary. They are able to express their ideas in another modality, and receive support in translating that into English words. They learn that acting something out is a legitimate way to demonstrate a concept for which a word is needed, and that it provides an opportunity for the teacher to teach vocabulary that will stick because it is derived from students' authentic needs. A student who pantomimes moving her scooter to avoid an oncoming rider might learn the word ''swerve.'' A student who shows being out of breath might learn ''panting.'' The strategy echoes total physical response (TPR), which has been successfully used with English language learners (Drucker, 2003). TPR is ''built around the coordination of speech and action; it attempts to teach language through physical (motor) activity'' (Richards & Rodgers, 1998, p. 87).

Adapting the Strategy for Advanced Writers

As when I am conferring with all students, what I choose to emphasize with advanced writers will depend greatly on what the students could most benefit from learning next. Some advanced writers may need encouragement to act out their stories if they have not done this before, whereas others might better be left alone to use other strategies with which they are already successful to develop their ideas. In general, students are able to choose more precise words to express actions, construct more complex sentences, expand descriptions of short episodes, and sometimes create figurative language as an outgrowth of working with this strategy.

Extending the Strategy

I often keep a chart of revision strategies and examples in the classroom, with an illustration of a wise old owl and the title ''Be Wise. Revise!'' After a group of students uses the strategy, we add it to our revision chart, with an example or two from students' writing and pictures of the children making the motions. These examples jog their memory of the strategy while simultaneously celebrating their achievements. Making revision visible helps students understand that I am not just judging final products; I am teaching them strategies to use to become more capable writers.

Acting out also can be very useful in procedural writing. A student who forgot about rinsing off her toothbrush remembered to add this step when she pantomimed the process of brushing her teeth. A child explaining how to build a sandcastle connected the words "flip over the bucket" and "plant a flag on top" with her procedure through acting it out.

I also reinforce the strategy in reading workshops by having students act out a snippet of a story I am reading to them whenever there is an action that they could further understand by doing it. It becomes apparent which students do not understand specific words when they try to act them out, and we can therefore develop more language by determining through students' actions what they do and don't understand.

Throughout the process, I emphasize that this is a personal strategy: the idea is not to "perform" for others, but to notice one's own movements and learn more about one's own actions and thoughts in the process. It is therefore essentially a very metacognitive strategy, and yet less intimidating for young students because it involves movement, which is one of their most familiar and loved forms of expression.

EVIDENCE CONNECTIONS

Calkins, L., Hartman, A., & White, Z. (2005). *Conferring with primary writers* [CD-ROM]. Portsmouth, NH: Heinemann Firsthand.
Conferring is a key component in supporting children in using any strategy. This CD-ROM includes annotated transcripts of sixty-one individual conferences with primary students, illustrating the conferring structure, types of conferences, and conferences for different writing purposes. It is invaluable in that it not only allows the reader to watch a master at work but also includes Calkins's commentary on her own thinking as each conference develops.

Griss, S. (1998). *Minds in motion: A kinesthetic approach to teaching elementary curriculum.* Portsmouth, NH: Heinemann.
Susan Griss's work was the inspiration for the strategy described in this chapter. I had the good fortune many years ago to attend her professional development workshops at the Kennedy Center in Washington, DC, in which she taught teachers how movement can support everything from learning how molecules interact to using punctuation correctly. This book captures basic concepts of movement and includes many ideas for incorporating kinesthetic learning in the classroom.

REFERENCES

Calkins, L., Hartman, A., & White, Z. (2005). *Conferring with primary writers* [CD-ROM]. Portsmouth, NH: Heinemann Firsthand.

Drucker, M. J. (2003). What reading teachers should know about ESL learners. *Reading Teacher*, *57*, 22–29.

Griss, S. (1998). *Minds in motion: A kinesthetic approach to teaching elementary curriculum.* Portsmouth, NH: Heinemann.

Ray, K. W. (1999). *Wondrous words: Writers and writing in the elementary classroom.* Urbana, IL: National Council of Teachers of English.

Richards, J., & Rodgers, T. (1998). *Approaches and methods in language teaching.* New York: Cambridge University Press.

Chapter 18

Personal Editing Checklists

JANET RICHARDS

Students create and consult Personal Editing Checklists to help them proofread and independently edit their writing. Teachers assist students to construct their checklists and apply them to their writing. As students learn to write complex compositions and mature over the course of an academic year, their editing knowledge evolves. Students learn to update and adjust their checklists for continued use.

Why This Strategy Is Important

Teachers spend considerable amounts of time helping students edit their compositions. This strategy provides a way for students to become skilled at and responsible for carrying out their own editing processes, thus increasing their self-confidence in their ability to complete successful writing projects. Students who learn to take responsibility for their immediate editing requirements become more motivated about editing and more independent in producing grammatically accurate papers (Cunningham & Cunningham, 2010).

One of my graduate students, Addie, is a literacy tutor in a high-poverty elementary school. She works with kindergarten through third-grade students who have particular difficulties with conventions of written language that include unconventional spelling; run-on sentences; lack of spaces between words; and incorrect uses of capitalization, apostrophes, and punctuation. Addie told me she spends a considerable amount of time helping her students edit their writing. She explained,

> *I often use an entire one-hour writing tutoring session assisting students with their editing difficulties. As I work one-on-one with students to help them edit their writing, the other five or six students in my group become bored and restless. They do not receive their full hour of writing instruction. I definitely do not use my teaching time wisely because of my students' lack of editing knowledge and my own shortfall in teaching students to edit. What editing assistance a student*

needs on any given day might be what another student needs on another day. Even worse, no matter how I attempt to teach students to edit, they compose a composition, poem, or letter; quickly read through it; and barely make any corrections. They do not seem to notice what they need to rewrite, delete, or insert.

Clearly, Addie's students needed to develop awareness and understanding about how to edit their writing, which would give her time to model and teach writing. They also needed to become aware of the importance of editing. I mused over this dilemma for a while. Then I asked myself, "What if I devised a generic checklist students could follow to help them independently improve what they write?"

However, as I reflected more about a general editing checklist, I realized that the length of such a list would confuse students who were not ready to learn and did not need to learn everything at once about editing. For example, I knew that a comprehensive editing checklist for a third-grade student was too complex and multifaceted for an emerging writer in kindergarten or first grade to use. Emerging writers' editing needs also differ from the more advanced editing demands of students who are in second or third grade. Furthermore, the editing requirements of students at all grade levels change as students learn more about writing and editing over the course of an academic year. Therefore, I devised Personal Editing Checklists as a strategy that takes students' existing and changing individual editing needs into account. I shared my idea with Addie, who now supplies each of her students with a Personal Editing Checklist and, with her students' input, adds to their checklists when necessary.

I find that Personal Editing Checklists help students take charge of their self-regulated editing, especially when they proofread their compositions a number of times, each time with a single focus (for example, first spelling, then punctuation, followed by capitalization, and so on). I also share this single-focus editing process with my graduate students. It is impossible for them and even for me to notice and remedy all types of writing errors simultaneously (see Crimi & Tompkins, 2005; Cunningham & Cunningham, 2010; Davis & Hill, 2003).

The SCAMPER Model for Personal Editing Checklists

Survey and Assess

The first step in this strategy is to **survey and assess** students' editing needs. When I work in primary classrooms, I document in my Writing Strategies Notebook what individual students need to learn next about editing. Then I group students according to their editing stages and needs. For example, as Addie, the student in my graduate class, noted, not every student is ready to engage in the same editing processes as every other student in the class (refer to the concept of zone of proximal development, Vygotsky, 1978). For example, in one of my writing tutoring sessions, David, a second grader, wrote one sentence in which he neglected to leave spaces between words, did not capitalize the first word of the sentence or a proper noun ("Grandma"), and did not attempt to edit for spelling. He also wrote in the transitional stage of spelling. His writing looked like this: *spngbrakisnxtweekandIwill staebimgama.* ("Spring break is next week, and I will stay by my Grandma.") However,

Janitha, another second grader, wrote: *I didnt know I wasnt going to school Iforgt we had a spring vacashon.* Janitha wrote two connected sentences, used two contractions, and spelled many words in standard spelling. However, she neglected to place apostrophes in the contractions ("didn't" and "wasn't"), did not place a punctuation mark after the first sentence, and wrote two words in nonstandard spelling ("forgot" and "vacation").

Clearly, although both students were second-grade classmates, David's and Janitha's writing portrayed different stages of writing development; therefore, they had different editing needs. Other students in their classroom also had diverse editing requirements. For instance, I noted that five second-grade students did not capitalize the first word in sentences and wrote run-on sentences, whereas three other students neglected to check their spelling but capitalized the first word in sentences.

Confer

I **confer** with small groups of students who have similar editing requirements. I find that group work saves time, and students have opportunities to share ideas. I explain how editing one's writing helps readers understand what one has written. We also talk about some of the group's typical editing problems. After our group meeting, I confer with individual students. I carefully go through one or two pieces of their writing and point out some of their editing needs. Then I help students list their writing errors and set some personal editing goals. Initially, some students choose to concentrate on a single editing issue, whereas others share two or three editing concerns depending on their developmental writing stages.

Assemble Materials

I **assemble materials,** including blank copies of the Personal Editing Checklist (see Figure 18.1) and my own sample checklist (see Figure 18.2), black fine-line markers, and heavy cardboard or card stock with previously drawn horizontal lines.

Name: _____ Date: _____

When I complete a draft, I need to check that I . . .   I checked!

1._____

_____   _____

2._____

_____   _____

3._____

_____   _____

Figure 18.1 Personal Editing Checklist

Name: _____Dr. Janet Richards_____ Date: ____1/13/2010____

When I complete a draft, I need to check that I . . .   I checked!

1. Spell all of the words correctly, because sometimes I forget   _____
to use spell check on my computer.

2. Use appropriate punctuation, because sometimes I place   _____
two periods at the end of sentences instead of one.

3. Use a thesaurus to vary vocabulary, because sometimes I   _____
use the same word two or three times in the same paragraph.

Figure 18.2 Teacher's Sample Personal Editing Checklist

Model

I model how to create and use my own Personal Editing Checklist. I first talk about how I determine what I need to include on my checklist based on what I'd like to improve in my writing. Next I show students a piece of my writing and model how I use my checklist to improve it. I say, "Every time I complete something I have written, I use my Personal Editing Checklist to make sure I have fixed the editing problems in the writing."

Finally, I supply students with heavy cardboard or card stock and fine-line markers and help them make their own Personal Editing Checklists according to their individualized editing needs. I help students copy their designated editing goals on their copies of their Personal Editing Checklists. In this way, students take responsibility for determining and following through with their editing goals. For example, David (refer to the previous example of David's writing) decided to place on his checklist:

1. Leave spaces between words.
2. Check spelling.

Janitha (refer to the previous example of Janitha's writing) listed on her Personal Editing Checklist:

1. Place apostrophes in contractions.
2. Use punctuation at the ends of sentences.
3. Check spelling.

As you can tell by comparing David's and Janitha's writing samples and their statements on their Personal Editing Checklists, they had different editing goals. At this time, Janitha was more advanced than David in her understanding of and facility with written language conventions.

Practice

In our next session, I help students choose examples of their writing they wish to edit. Then I help small groups of students apply their Personal Editing Checklists to **practice** editing their work. At this stage of the strategy learning process, I find most students need considerable assistance to pinpoint their writing problems. Therefore, I often have to repeat these practice sessions. During these practice sessions I also make sure that students recognize their writing achievements. For example, I might point out that they already know how to capitalize proper nouns, or place appropriate punctuation marks at the ends of sentences.

Execute

When students are ready to **execute** the strategy on their own, I provide opportunities for them to ask me questions about their editing decisions in a risk-free environment (for example, "I think I need to place an apostrophe in this word. Am I right?"). I also rotate among the students, helping them identify their editing needs. In addition, I encourage students to confer with their peers for advice and to use other classroom resources, such as information found on our word and sentence walls.

Further, I make notes in my Writing Strategies Notebook about students who need to modify their Personal Editing Checklists, either because they have learned something new about editing or because it is time for them to develop additional editing skills. For example, after a few weeks, David is ready to add two more goals to his Personal Editing Checklist:

3. Use punctuation at the ends of sentences.
4. Vary sentence length.

Janitha is ready to add three more goals to her Personal Editing Checklist:

4. Use an exclamation point when appropriate.
5. Provide titles for stories, personal accounts, and other types of writing.
6. When writing a personal letter to someone, such as a book author or a friend, include the date at the top of the letter.

Reflect

I always enjoy talking with small groups of students as they develop and **reflect** about their writing abilities, and as their editing needs evolve. For example, when we talk at midyear, David reflects on how proud he is that his Personal Editing Checklist now contains six editing reminders. He says his writing is getting better because he knows how to edit his work with the checklist, which now reads

1. Leave spaces between words.
2. Check spelling.

3. Use punctuation at the ends of sentences.
4. Vary sentence length.
5. Capitalize words at the beginnings of sentences.
6. Vary vocabulary.

Janitha's checklist had also developed to

1. Place apostrophes in contractions.
2. Use punctuation at the ends of sentences.
3. Check spelling.
4. Use an exclamation point when appropriate.
5. Provide titles for stories, personal accounts, and other types of writing.
6. When writing a personal letter to someone, such as a book author or a friend, include the date at the top of the letter.
7. Check the use of appropriate verb tenses.
8. Check subject-verb agreement.

Adapting the Strategy

Adapting the Strategy for Emerging Writers

I use Personal Editing Checklists with emerging writers. However, the listings on their checklists begin as simple statements followed by visuals to assist their understanding. For example, an emerging writer's Personal Editing Checklist may contain two listings: (1) Circle the first letter of the first word in each sentence and make sure it is a capital letter followed by a simple sentence, and (2) Circle the final word in each of your sentences and make sure a punctuation mark follows it (either a period [.], a question mark [?], or an exclamation point [!]).

Adapting the Strategy for Writers Who Struggle

Writers who struggle need to develop and strengthen personal feelings of self-confidence and self-efficacy in regard to their writing abilities. Therefore, I work often with small groups of these students. I ask students to tell me an experience we have shared together. As they dictate, I write what they say on the board or on a large sheet of paper placed on an easel. I deliberately neglect to capitalize the first word in a sentence, or I misspell a few common words. Then we work together to discover some of the editing concerns in our composition. This lesson becomes the basis for a Personal Editing Checklist designed specifically for writers who struggle.

Adapting the Strategy for English Language Learners

As exemplary teachers know, all instruction, including strategy instruction, can be adapted to suit diverse learners' needs. Teachers who model the use of Personal Editing Checklists and offer them to English language learners should help these students initially set one editing goal, such as ''Use one (or two, or three) English words in a sentence that you originally write in [Spanish, Urdu, or whatever language applies]." Another initial editing goal might be to capitalize the first word in a sentence.

Adapting the Strategy for Advanced Writers

As students advance in their writing, the editing needs addressed in their checklists naturally develop. Therefore, I teach mini-lessons on homophones and pairs of words that are easily confused (for example, "than" and "then," "it's" and "its"). I also guide advanced writers to develop Personal Editing Checklists that highlight both the appropriate use of headings, titles, and features and the organization of various types of writing genres.

Extending the Strategy

I have noticed that Personal Editing Checklists help students learn more about writing than just editing skills. As I talk with students about editing, I find we use advanced writing vocabulary terms, such as *proofread, subject, verb,* and *agreement.* I help students add some of these vocabulary terms to their lists of weekly spelling words. They also enter these words into their personal dictionaries in complete sentences with the targeted words highlighted. We add these words to our large class dictionary for easy reference as well.

When I use new vocabulary, such as *proper noun,* I offer on-the-spot mini-lesson sessions about the new term. Extensions for Personal Editing Checklists thus include mini-lessons on other related topics that focus on writing and the English language. (See Chapter Six, Noun Charts.)

Once students have mastered the art of self-editing, I set up labeled editing stations in the classroom (Crimi & Tompkins, 2005), such as locations organized around punctuation, spelling, and commas. Students visit the various labeled editing stations that contain posted directions and such materials as colored markers and highlighting pens. They work with classmates, editing one another's writing. I update the stations as students learn more sophisticated editing skills, such as checking for cohesive paragraph structures. (Refer to Chapter Twenty-Five, Comprehensive, Step-by-Step Composing for Nonfiction Writing.)

EVIDENCE CONNECTIONS

Crimi, F., & Tompkins, G. (2005). Editing stations: Enhancing the readability of writing. In G. Tompkins and C. Blanchfield (Eds.), *50 ways to develop strategic writers* (pp. 37–40). Upper Saddle River, NJ: Pearson/Merrill/Prentice Hall.
These authors state, "Editing is the final housekeeping chore of the writing process" (p. 37). Writers need to check for standard spelling, punctuation, capitalization, overuse of common words, apostrophes, and syntax (order of the words in a sentence).

Parsons, L. (2001). *Revising and editing: Using models and checklists to promote successful writing experiences.* Markham, Ontario, Canada: Pembroke.
Parsons provides many examples of fiction and nonfiction that teachers can use to help students identify and fix editing problems.

REFERENCES

Cunningham, P., & Cunningham, J. (2010). *What really matters in writing: Research-based practices across the elementary curriculum.* New York: Allyn & Bacon.

Crimi, F., & Tompkins, G. (2005). Editing stations: Enhancing the readability of writing. In G. Tompkins and C. Blanchfield (Eds.), *50 ways to develop strategic writers* (pp. 37–40). Upper Saddle River, NJ: Pearson/Merrill/Prentice Hall.

Davis, J., & Hill, S. (2003). *The no-nonsense guide to teaching writing.* Portsmouth, NH: Heinemann.

Vygotsky, L. (1978). *Mind in society: The development of higher psychological processes* (M. Cole, Trans.). Cambridge, MA: Harvard University Press.

Chapter 19

Adding Dialogue to Fiction and Nonfiction

LORI CZOP ASSAF

Using this strategy, students will understand how dialogue can enhance a character's feelings and intentions and bring life to writing. Students will also learn how use mentor texts and Dialogue Charts to add dialogue to their independent fiction and nonfiction writing.

Why This Strategy Is Important

This strategy helps students become skilled at adding dialogue to their writing, thus increasing their ability to make a piece of writing interesting and evocative for readers. Students who learn to add dialogue to their writing become more able writers.

When I was a second-grade teacher, many of my students started the year by writing simple, formulaic sentences, such as "I like my mom" and "I like my dad." First-grade teachers often reinforce these predictable sentence structures because they help students both feel successful and gain control over a variety of sight words. These simple sentence structures also resemble those found in many of the little books first-grade students read in their guided reading groups.

In second grade, students are expected to move beyond writing simple sentences and discover, develop, and exhibit voice in their writing. At the same time, they need to become aware of audience and revise their writing for varied purposes. Transitioning from writing simple sentences to writing complex sentences with voice challenges my students. Even though I spent a considerable amount to time encouraging my students to use their oral language in their writing, it rarely worked. Instead, I realized that my students were in the habit of only writing sentences with words they could spell correctly. Even when I encouraged invented spelling and reminded students that they would edit their writing at the end of the writing process, they often refused to take such risks.

In an attempt to understand how to enhance my students' writing abilities, I turned to such workshop advocates as Graves (1983), Calkins (1986), and Ray (1999). Calkins believes that a young writer's voice is displayed by talk. Children's verbal expression or dialogue can help move their writing forward: "A lilt of oral language begins to appear in their stories," and it is as if "we can almost hear the author's voice come through" (p. 74). Graves adds that students must be given the freedom to share themselves, take risks, and avoid a need for correct writing in order to develop and convey personal meaningfulness in writing. After reading Graves, Calkins, and others, I knew I needed to find a systematic and consistent strategy to help my students take risks and use dialogue in their writing. I needed to move beyond simply encouraging students to add voice to their writing to explicitly teaching them a strategy that they could use independently to meet their individual writing needs.

Ray (1999) suggests that one way to help students develop individual writing styles and add dialogue is to examine and evaluate a writer's craft with them, using what she calls mentor texts. Ray recommends using multiple mentor texts to evaluate the art of using dialogue and then helping students envision new ways to use dialogue in their own writing. It was clear to me that my students needed to learn how other writers engage the reader and how adding dialogue could make a piece of writing more interesting and powerful. I devised Adding Dialogue to Fiction and Nonfiction as a strategy to help students use Dialogue Charts to not only identify and evaluate the varied uses of dialogue in mentor texts but also add dialogue in their writing.

The Dialogue Chart helps my students learn from other writers and experiment with adding dialogue to their writing. When they confer with one another during Writers' Workshop, they begin to make specific suggestions as to what kinds of dialogue to add to their writing—and where. Students take more risks, become more aware of audience, and begin to develop personal styles as writers. This writing strategy mini-lesson is the perfect approach to help students learn what voice is and how to use dialogue in their writing.

The SCAMPER Model for Adding Dialogue to Fiction and Nonfiction
Survey and Assess

The first step in this strategy is for the teacher to **survey and assess** students' writing needs. In my second-grade classroom I use a Writing Strategies Notebook in which I document students' writing strategies and needs on sticky notes. As I collect multiple notes on one student, I move these notes to a separate sheet on which I write evaluative comments, such as "José seems to be experimenting with new vocabulary. He uses the word 'thrilled.' Make sure to encourage the use of new words." Because not every student is at the same place in his or her writing development, I group students according to their needs and tailor the writing strategy mini-lesson to enhance individual writing growth. Prior to beginning teaching this dialogue strategy, I collect my students' writing notebooks and examine their writing for evidence of dialogue. For example, Carrie uses snippets of dialogue between her and her best friend Maya in a notebook entry titled "The Day We Made Up." Her writing looks like this: *You wre meen to me no I wasnot yes u wre.* ("You were mean to me. No I was not. Yes you were.") Carrie seems to understand the importance of adding dialogue to a story but is unclear on how to support dialogue with action. Eric uses dialogue in his story about Superman. He writes this: *pow, bang, boom superman was exauset.* ("Pow, bang, boom. Superman was exhausted.") In individual conferences, I ask Carrie and Eric what they are trying to convey in their writing. Eric explains he wants to write down the sounds of the Joker getting hit, and Carrie wants to illustrate her frustration when she and Maya fight. Although both students add small snippets of dialogue to their writing and have specific reasons for doing so, it is clear to me that they need to develop an explicit strategy for using language to elaborate the thoughts and feelings of characters and for identifying ways to make dialogue relevant to their stories.

Confer

I **confer** with small groups of students who use and approximate dialogue in their writing, because I want to build on their strengths. Small-group conferences save time and give students opportunities to help one another. I explain how dialogue enhances a story and brings life to characters. We carefully go through one or two pieces of their writing and discuss the use of dialogue. Then we brainstorm different ways dialogue can be used in their writing. I ask such questions as "What would the main character say about this event? Is that how people talk to each other? What words would the character say at this point? Is your dialogue in between action?" I help students write dialogue by using talking bubbles and cartoon captions.

Assemble Materials

I **assemble materials** needed, including a large copy of the Dialogue Chart (see Figure 19.1), students' Writing Strategies Journals, large chart paper, markers, and multiple picture books previously read in class with examples of dialogue in each text. A list of recommended books follows.

Picture Books with Dialogue

Anzaldúa, G. (1996). *Prietita and the Ghost Woman.* San Francisco: Children's Book Press.

Bloom, B. (1999). *Wolf!* New York: Orchard Books.

Cole, J., & Degen, B. (1990). *Magic School Bus Inside the Human Body.* New York: Scholastic Press.

Henkes, K. (1988). *Lilly's Purple Plastic Purse.* New York: Greenwillow Books.

Johnson, A. (2005). *A Sweet Smell of Roses.* New York: Simon & Schuster Books for Young Readers.

Ketteman, H. (1997). *Bubba the Cowboy Prince: A Fractured Texas Tale.* New York: Scholastic Press.

Lachtman, O. D. (1995). *Pepita Talks Twice/Pepita Habla Dos Veces.* Houston, TX: Arte Publico Press.

Levine, E., & Nelson, K. (2007). *Henry's Freedom Box.* New York: Scholastic Press.

Polacco, P. (1998). *Thank You, Mr. Falker.* New York: Philomel Books.

Short Chapter Books with Dialogue

Kline. S. (1989). *Horrible Harry Moves Up to Third Grade.* New York: Scholastic Press.

Osborne, M. P. (2010). *Good Morning, Gorillas* (Magic Tree House Series, no. 26). New York: Scholastic Press.

Sharmat, M. W. (1981). *Nate the Great and the Lost List.* New York: Yearling Books.

Directions: In the third column, use the numeral from the following list to identify the student's level.

1. Dialogue is used to elaborate the thoughts and feelings of a character.

2. Dialogue gives insight into the character's personality and intent.

3. Dialogue is relevant to the character and story.

4. Dialogue is broken up between action parts.

5. Word choices (language and vocabulary) are appropriate and bring life to the story.

6. Dialogue is effectively punctuated.

Student's Name	Date	Using Dialogue	Notes

Figure 19.1 Blank Dialogue Chart

Figure 19.2 shows a sample Dialogue Chart filled out for two students. I select numerals from the list at the top of the chart to identify how students are using dialogue and put them in the Using Dialogue column.

1. Dialogue is used to elaborate the thoughts and feelings of a character.

2. Dialogue gives insight into the character's personality and intent.

3. Dialogue is relevant to the character and story.

4. Dialogue is broken up between action parts.

5. Word choices (language and vocabulary) are appropriate and bring life to the story.

6. Dialogue is effectively punctuated.

Student's Name	Date	Using Dialogue	Notes
Natalie	11/30/09	3, 5, 6	Natalie uses dialogue that is relevant to the story. She uses interesting words to show fear, and effectively punctuates her sentences. I would like to encourage Nat to add more dialogue to elaborate the intent of a character or to get into the character's head.
Javier	1/15/10	2, 3	Javier loves to use dialogue in his writing! His dialogue brings life to the story. It is usually relevant but isn't always punctuated correctly. I need to help Javier use dialogue with more than one character.

Figure 19.2 Sample Filled Out Dialogue Chart

Model

I **model** how to examine mentor texts for dialogue, how dialogue can enhance a character's feelings and intention, and how to use the Dialogue Chart in my own writing. I begin by speaking to my students in various voices through a skit and a conversation. The students listen and identify different characters' voices.

After the students get a feel for the different voices in a conversation, I read the picture book *Henry's Freedom Box* (Levine & Nelson, 2007). I ask students to identify different voices represented in the text and notice how they differ based on each character's personality and purpose in the story. I record students' responses on a large piece of chart paper, modeling correct punctuation for dialogue. Next I read another picture book to the class. I model a think-aloud to identify different examples of dialogue. I write examples of mentor text dialogue on a large piece of chart paper and ask students to help me describe how each example enhances the story. Much like Ray (1999) suggests, I encourage students to name various uses of dialogue and to write these critical elements in their Writing Strategies Journals. Following my modeling of mentor texts, I pass out multiple picture books and ask students to read at least two books with partners and to explore ways the authors include dialogue in the stories. Students share their findings with the class, and we record all dialogue examples on a large piece of chart paper.

Finally, I model how to use dialogue in my own writing. I describe a character from my writing, and then we brainstorm words and phrases the character might say in a given story (Lane, 1993). I draw a large rectangle around this dialogue on the chart paper. Then I write an action sentence that describes what the character is doing in relation to the dialogue and the character's interaction with other characters. I draw a circle around this action sentence (see Figure 19.3). I explain to students the importance of breaking up dialogue with action sentences. Next I read a section of my writing from my Writing Strategies Notebook and ask students to help me add dialogue and action. I make sure that my word choice is appropriate and that the dialogue gives insight into each character's personality and intent.

"You don't do it right. Stop that and give me back the hammer." "No." "Give me back the hammer!"

The siblings each held on to one end of the hammer and pulled in opposite directions until Atiyeh, the little brother, fell down on the cement and bumped his head.

Figure 19.3 Identifying Dialogue and Action Sentences

Practice

In our next session, each student chooses an example of his or her writing to add dialogue. We meet in small groups to **practice** inserting dialogue and action sentences into students' writing. Applying the same process I used in the modeling phase, each student brainstorms words and phrases to add voice to a character in his or her writing, draws a large rectangle around this dialogue, and then writes two action sentences that describe what the character is doing in relation to the dialogue and interaction with other characters. I encourage students to help one another and to use the Dialogue Chart, which I have hung in the room for students to see easily, to evaluate their writing. At this stage, students need individual assistance to develop relevant dialogue and appropriate vocabulary that elaborate the thoughts and feelings of a character. Therefore, I repeat these practice sessions several times throughout the year.

Execute

When the students are ready to **execute** the strategy on their own, I provide opportunities for them to confer with their peers and practice adding dialogue and action sentences to their writing. I take notes in my Writing Strategies Notebook about students who need more support and those who are ready to develop more advanced dialogue skills and use standard editing. For example, after several weeks I note that Carrie is ready to add dialogue between four different friends in the continuation of her story "The Day We Made Up." I have made a note in my Writing Strategies Notebook that Carrie needs to identify tone and word choice in talk, so I ask Carrie to audio-record her friends and write down their conversation. Carrie is able to identify how each of her friends uses unique vocabulary, such as "cool" and "no way." She then adds these words and other phrases to individual comments in her story.

Reflect

After teaching this writing strategy mini-lesson, I encourage students to **reflect** on their writing. Students make connections between their own craft and that of mentor authors. For example, Eric shares, "When I just add dialogue like 'bang' and 'pow,' my story is confusing. Edgar didn't understand anything. But when I added action statements and dialogue, my story became alive and exciting!" He adds, "Now everyone knows this story is about Superman beating up Joker, and Joker is getting whipped!"

Adapting the Strategy

Adapting the Strategy for Emerging Writers

When I work with young writers, I begin by inviting them to draw pictures in their Writing Strategies Journals. As students finish their drawings, I ask them to tell me about their stories. As we talk about their journal entries, I ask them how they could add dialogue to their writing. For example, when Wendy draws a picture of a dog and a little girl, I ask her what the little girl is saying to her dog. Wendy replies, "That is my dog Pandy. Pandy is saying 'bark, bark.' That's me (pointing to the picture of the girl), and I am telling Pandy to go outside. I'm saying, 'Go outside Pandy. Go potty.'" As Wendy describes the conversation between her two characters, I write her words and reread them to her, explicitly stating that her characters are using dialogue.

At other times, students cut out images from magazines and newspapers and glue them into their Writing Strategies Journals. Together we add dialogue and action. As with all different levels of writers, I model the SCAMPER strategy with emerging writers and use interactive writing to scaffold their understanding of dialogue and action in writing.

Adapting the Strategy for Writers Who Struggle

For students who struggle with writing, I give them word banks and sentence frames. For example, in small writing groups, we reread our mentor texts and identify words and punctuation marks used in dialogue. We create a word bank chart, and I model how to use these words in writing dialogue and adding action. In addition to word banks, I use sentence frames based on the mentor texts. For example, I use the sentence *Then she said, "I did find something. I think it is a candy bar!"* Students are invited to notice the structure and punctuation of the sentence and to write similar sentences. We then create a chart with sample sentence frames for students to use in their writing. For instance, we have used the sentence frame "*Let's go* (action verb) *and* (action verb) *because* (reason)'' *said* (name of person doing talking). (Name of person doing talking) (action verb) *and* (action verb).

Adapting the Strategy for English Language Learners

This strategy can be adapted for English language learners of all levels. When students are learning English, they need to be encouraged to use their first languages as resources for writing (Cummins, 2001). I model code switching—that is, changing from formal to a more informal mode of speaking based on the context of a conversation—in dialogue in each student's native language, and I read a mentor text, such as *Pepita Talks Twice/Pepita Habla Dos Veces* (Lachtman, 1995), to highlight the effective use of different languages in dialogue. I encourage all students to employ their first languages as well as English in their writing so they will respect and consider legitimate languages other than English.

Adapting the Strategy for Advanced Writers

When using dialogue in their writing, many advanced writers use clever synonyms for "said" or "asked," but their sentence patterns can be predictable and unvaried. To help advanced students move from unvaried dialogue structures, the teacher can model how to chart out sentence structures with text clumps or "squiggle text" (Bernabei, 2007), and then copy or mimic and modify the mentor sentence structures. For example, in the *Percy Jackson and the Olympians Book Five: The Last Olympian* (Riordan, 2009, p. 32), Riordan uses varied sentence structure when adding dialogue and action:

> *"Mrs. Dodds," I said.*
>
> *She bared her fangs. "Welcome back, honey."*
>
> *Her two sisters—the other Furies—swooped down and settled next to her in the branches of the poplar.*
>
> *"You know Alecto?" Nico asked me.*
>
> *"If you mean the big hag in the middle, yeah," I said. "She was my math teacher."*

We can map these sentences out using squiggle text or text clumps, and I ask students to vary their sentence structures in similar fashion.

> *"xxx xxxxx," x xxxx.*
>
> *xxx xxxxx xxx xxxxx. "xxxxxxx xxxx xxxxx,"*
>
> *xxx xxx xxxxxxx—xxx xxxxx xxxxxx—xxxxxxx xxxx xxx xxxxxxx xxxx xx xxx xx xxx xxxxxxxx xx xxx xxxxxx.*
>
> *"xxx xxxx xxxxxx?" xxxx xxxxx xx.*
>
> *"xx xxx xxxx xxx xxx xxx xx xxx xxxxxx, xxxx," x xxxx. "xxx xxx xx xxxx xxxxxxx."*

These text clumps illustrate how speakers' voices change with the visual clues (how the text is laid out) provided by paragraph and punctuation changes. A student can see that words spoken by a character are marked within quotation marks. Tags, or punctuation marks, following or preceding speech are often included in the sentence with the speech. Some sentences contain neither speech nor tags. These sentences usually represent action or thought. Students can use these text clumps to apply different sentence structures in their writing.

Extending the Strategy

I find that my students become linguistic ethnographers by listening carefully to conversations and taking note of different word choices and tones in dialogue. It is important to note not only what people say but also how they say it. As my students become experts at adding dialogue to narrative essays, they begin adding dialogue to their expository writing. I also use books from the *Magic School Bus* series, such as *The Magic School Bus Inside the Human Body* (Cole & Degen, 1990), as mentor texts. We examine how the author adds character dialogue to elaborate facts and information about science-related topics. My students initially learn to mimic this craft.

I also extend this writing strategy by teaching students how to write storyboards and screenplays. Storyboards use comic book–like graphics to show what a story will look like onstage or on-screen. Storyboards are used in film, television, video art, and animation. Each storyboard includes dialogue that reveals the thoughts of and words between characters. Students create paper storyboards or electronic storyboards by using Comic Life or other similar software.

EVIDENCE CONNECTIONS

Lane, B. (1993). *After the end: Teaching and learning creative revision.* Portsmouth, NH: Heinemann.
In this book, Lane includes multiple strategies and activities to help students revise their writing by using dialogue. In fact, he argues that using dialogue as a revising tool should be a natural process and that students must be empowered to revise their writing in meaningful and authentic ways. The vignettes of students included in the book are entertaining and informative, and form the basis of many mini-lessons to guide students through the revision process painlessly and effectively.

Ray, K. W. (1999). *Wondrous words: Writers and writing in the elementary classroom.* Urbana, IL: National Council of Teachers of English.
Ray gives examples and specific explanations of how to help students study the writing craft and how to use mentor texts with young writers. She includes techniques for teaching language choice, grammar conventions, and sentence structure. More important, she illustrates how to teach students to read like writers. Her book includes a variety of excellent children's books, including picture books and some young adult novels to use as mentor texts. Ray invites teachers to bring inquiry and reading-writing connections into their classrooms.

REFERENCES

Bernabei, G. (2007). The chicken dance and advanced dialogue [online handout]. *Trail of breadcrumbs.* Retrieved August 11, 2010, from www.trailofbreadcrumbs.net/grammar.html.

Calkins, L. M. (1986). *The art of teaching writing.* Portsmouth, NH: Heinemann.

Cole, J. & Degen, B. (1990). *The magic school bus inside the human body.* New York: Scholastic Press.

Cummins, J. (2001). *Negotiating identities: Education for empowerment in a diverse society* (2nd ed.). Los Angeles: Association for Bilingual Education.

Graves, D. (1983). *Writing: Teachers and children at work.* Portsmouth, NH: Heinemann.

Lachtman, O. D. (1995) *Pepita talks twice/Pepita habla dos veces.* Houston, TX: Arte Publico Press.

Lane, B. (1993). *After the end: Teaching and learning creative revision.* Portsmouth, NH: Heinemann.

Levine, E. , & Nelson, K. (2007). *Henry's freedom box.* New York: Scholastic Press.

Ray, K. W. (1999). *Wondrous words: Writers and writing in the elementary classroom.* Urbana, IL: National Council of Teachers of English.

Riordan, R. (2009). *Percy Jackson and the Olympians book five: The last Olympian.* New York: Hyperion Books.

Chapter 20

Following Conventions for Writing Dialogue

DEBORAH GUIDRY AND NEVA ANN MEDCALF

Learning to write dialogue in stories and drama scripts is challenging for primary students. This strategy provides a format students can follow to help them write dialogue according to the conventions of written language.

Why This Strategy Is Important

Writers use dialogue to develop characters in stories. However, primary students are just beginning to develop an understanding about the written language conventions required for writing dialogue. The conventions for writing dialogue with which students have the most difficulty are indenting for each character's voice and using appropriate punctuation. The Following Conventions for Writing Dialogue strategy teaches primary students how to be successful with integrating dialogue into their writing using the proper conventions.

We have always been convinced that our first priority as teachers is to create independent writers. By the end of the school year, our students should be able to create real, vivid writing using the tools that writing strategy mini-lessons and subsequent activities offer them. We should become as-needed resources for students as they work, with their Writing Strategies Journals close at hand, toward independence in their use of writing strategies. If students aren't working toward independence, we aren't doing our job. This strategy will help students become confident in their use of conventions in written dialogue.

The SCAMPER Model for Following Conventions for Writing Dialogue

Survey and Assess

In general, we find that primary students infrequently use dialogue in their writing, so that is where we begin with our series of dialogue-writing sessions.

Before we present the actual mini-lesson on the conventions of writing dialogue, we ask students to focus on the way the characters in the student-choice books speak to one another. These books are selected from the classroom library for independent reading and have dialogue written in various ways. This leads to whole-class discussion in regard to these differences. They note that each character gets his or her own paragraph and how the dialogue tags are used. We check for understanding by having students respond in writing or in discussions to specific questions, such as "What did you notice when your main character spoke? Where was the dialogue tag, the beginning, the middle, or the end? Why do you think it was done this way?" At this point, we tell students we are teaching them to be writers. In other words, their writing is the same as professional writing; the only difference is experience. Expect your students to be surprised by this because they think professional writing and school writing are two different things. However, you can also expect them to rise to the challenge once they understand.

We **survey and assess** students' understanding and use of dialogue by reading and analyzing samples of their writing. This helps us document students' use of direct and indirect dialogue and correct punctuation for both. The documentation is done with a rubric, such as the one shown in Figure 20.1, and a student portfolio system. We model the use of the rubric for assessing their writing with a number of examples, and then students review their writing to self-assess the strategies they used and to reflect on their writing experiences. The rubric is holistic and based on curriculum standards. Specific revision strategies may be added to the rubric to address individual student needs and goals for improvement.

Confer

After we determine which students would benefit from learning a strategy that focuses on writing dialogue with appropriate punctuation and spacing, we form small groups made up of students with similar needs. We **confer** with students and share examples of strong dialogue from age-appropriate literature. We find it is vital to use literature students are interested in and find exciting. If the material is not engaging, students will be bored and will not learn what they need to learn about dialogue. Engaging material will vary from class to class, age to age, and year to year, which is why it is so important for teachers to continually seek out contemporary examples for both boys and girls.

During conferences with each small group, we ask students questions that lead them to recognize the importance of dialogue and its proper punctuation in good writing. We begin the sessions with such prompts as

How can you tell who is talking? How does this character's dialogue help you know more about her? How can you tell what the character is feeling from the words she says and the punctuation used? Can you tell where

the character is from or how old the character is by her speech? What helps you know these things? Can you tell what two characters think about each other based on what they say and how sentences are punctuated?

5
- Demonstrates an understanding of conventions for written dialogue
- Has a written piece that is complete and goes beyond what is expected
- Uses dialogue in several different ways
- Uses several examples of both direct and indirect dialogue
- Presents more than two speakers
- Uses correct punctuation for all dialogue

4
- Demonstrates an understanding of conventions for written dialogue the majority of the time
- Has a written piece that is complete
- Uses dialogue in more than one way
- Uses at least two examples of both direct and indirect dialogue
- Presents more than one speaker
- Uses correct punctuation for the majority of the dialogue

3
- Demonstrates some understanding of conventions for written dialogue
- Has a written piece that is fairly complete
- Uses dialogue in at least one way
- Uses at least one example of both direct and indirect dialogue
- Presents at least one speaker
- Uses correct punctuation for at least half of the dialogue

2
- Attempts to show understanding of conventions for written dialogue but is unclear
- Has a written piece that is incomplete
- Does not use dialogue correctly
- Does not use an example of either direct or indirect dialogue
- Does not present any speakers
- Does not use correct punctuation for dialogue

1
- Demonstrates no understanding of conventions for written dialogue
- Has a written piece that shows no attempt at being complete
- Does not use an example of either direct or indirect dialogue
- Does not present any speakers
- Does not use correct punctuation for dialogue

Figure 20.1 Rubric for Writing Dialogue

After several minutes of discussion about dialogue and writing conventions, we tell them about this strategy. We explain how applying the strategy will help improve their writing such that when their friends read what they've written, these friends will be able to understand who is talking. We also note that using this strategy to write dialogue will help with all of the issues we just discussed about showing characters' feelings and thoughts and providing information about the characters.

Assemble Materials

We **assemble materials,** which include markers, students' Writing Strategies Journals, student-choice books, and either transparencies and an overhead projector or a document camera, sentence strips, colored typing paper and markers, a wall chart, elbow macaroni, and glue. For this example, we have decided to use the story *Ira Sleeps Over* (Waber, 1972). The reason we chose *Ira Sleeps Over* as an example to use with this strategy is that most of the pages of the book each contain only one person's dialogue.

Model

We **model** the proper use of dialogue conventions, specifically by indenting and using quotation marks and dialogue tags. Depending on the students' needs in our small groups, we might teach all of the following techniques in one session or we might teach each one on a separate day.

We begin by reading *Ira Sleeps Over* aloud to students. The format of the book shows students that each character has his or her "space" for what is said. After we've read the book, we say, "Did you notice that Ira has his own page when he speaks and that his dad has his own page? Why do you think this is?" We lead the students to discuss and discover the organization of text for dialogue. We have them compare how in *Ira Sleeps Over* each character has his own page, whereas in their student-choice reading each character has his or her own paragraph. This is what we mean when we say that each character has his or her own space when speaking. Then we tell them, "Today you will learn how to do this in your own writing." Don't expect your students to get this the first time or to get it perfectly. That is why writing is a lifelong learning process. The important thing is that students are moving beyond their comfort zones and expanding themselves as writers.

We demonstrate how, in another piece of writing, this giving of each character's space is done by indenting. After we explain this to students, we model indenting dialogue for each character by projecting a block of text with multiple examples of unindented dialogue. As a class, we decide where to indent and discuss why and we do it, and we make the changes on the screen so students can see them. If students question why the class has made some correction to the text, we can go back and discuss further, and can edit or change it right there for everyone to see on the screen.

Once this demonstration is complete, students will need practice and support to apply indenting dialogue to their writing.

The next issue most students have with dialogue is putting quotation marks around the words being spoken. One of the reasons students are confused is they don't know the difference between direct and indirect dialogue. Direct dialogue is speech that quotes exactly what the character says; in other words, it will have quotation marks around it. Indirect dialogue is an approximation of what the character says and does not have quotation marks. To model this, we go back to several pages of *Ira Sleeps Over* and turn the direct dialogue from the book into indirect dialogue.

On a wall chart, we create a dialogue chart that has the indirect dialogue in a column on the left-hand side (see Figure 20.2). Then students identify the direct dialogue that matches each indirect passage from the book. We always emphasize, at this point, that you can recognize the direct dialogue because the author has put it in quotation marks. We have students glue elbow macaroni to the chart as quotation marks to punctuate direct dialogue. At this point, we emphasize that because indirect dialogue is not "exactly" what the character said, it has no quotation marks (elbow macaroni). We do several examples as a class, then students complete the exercise independently.

Directions: For each example of indirect dialogue, find the direct dialogue that matches and write it in the Direct Dialogue column. Be sure to punctuate your example using quotation marks. One example has been done for you.

Indirect Dialogue	Direct Dialogue
My sister asked me if I was going to take my teddy bear with me when I go to sleep over at my friend's house.	"Are you taking your teddy bear along?"
My sister wanted to know how I will feel sleeping without my teddy bear for the very first time.	
I told my father that Reggie would laugh and think I was a baby if I took my teddy bear.	
I asked Reggie what he thought about teddy bears.	
Reggie talked about telling ghost stories.	
My family said goodbye when I left to go to Reggie's house for the night.	
I tried to wake Reggie up so he could finish telling the ghost story.	

Figure 20.2 Dialogue Chart for *Ira Sleeps Over* (Waber, 1972)

Finally, we model how to use dialogue tags. We explain that dialogue tags are words that identify who is speaking and how the dialogue is expressed (in other words, "whispered," "snickered mischievously"). We do examples on the board or overhead with the whole class, asking for student input. Then we ask various students to come up and model the use of dialogue tags. In the following sentences, the dialogue tags appear in italics.

"I'm here!" *shouted Jill.*

Ann snorted, "Are you kidding?"

"My goodness," *exclaimed Kelly.* "It's beautiful!"

To reinforce the use and punctuation of dialogue tags, we group students into three sections; one each to practice dialogue tags at the beginning, at the end, and in the middle. The third group should consist of students who are strong readers and have a talent for language, because dialogue tags in the middle of dialogue are the most difficult for students to understand. Each group is given a sentence strip and a piece of dialogue with a clear dialogue tag. Then, as a group, they decide how to correctly punctuate the dialogue and put it on the strip, which will be posted on the wall. Then we discuss the choices each group made as a whole-class activity. All of the components of this strategy are to prepare students to approach their own writing.

Practice

The next step is to have students **practice** this strategy by inserting dialogue into their existing writing pieces. They can accomplish this task through a "pair and share" in which students read their pieces to each another and ask for places in which dialogue might make the writing more interesting.

The protocol for this type of revision (adapted from Carroll & Wilson, 2008) is as follows:

1. Writer reads piece aloud.
   Reader listens.
2. Writer reads piece aloud again.
   Reader listens, jotting down notes about where the writer can include useful dialogue.
3. Reader shares ideas with writer.
   Writer listens.
4. Writer jots down notes in his or her manuscript draft.

The physical revision itself is done with revision strips created by cutting different-size strips from colored typing paper. Once a student decides where to include dialogue and change his or her writing, the student highlights the section to be changed, then tapes a revision strip on the left side of the draft so it covers the highlighted section. The student physically writes the change on the revision strip. This revision approach allows students and the teacher to see what was originally written and what was changed.

Then students write their clean drafts with their revisions included. Ultimately, students should own their writing and make the decisions about whether the revisions "work" in their pieces or not. They can try certain revisions, but if these do not enhance their pieces of writing, students can and should remove them. The student is the ultimate editor of any piece of writing.

We expect that, when students first learn to insert dialogue with correct punctuation, they will overuse dialogue as they experiment and create. Early on this type of risk taking should be encouraged. Once students have practiced with several pieces of writing, it is the teacher's job to redirect students by asking, "What is the purpose of this dialogue? Do you need it?" We intervene only when students have had an opportunity to practice and master the strategy in various pieces of writing over time.

Execute

Students return to their writing to **execute** these new skills in their own independent work. We ask them to demonstrate what they have learned by requiring them to include one example of direct dialogue and one example of indirect dialogue in their pieces so we can assess their understanding and reteach if necessary. We look for the students to indent, use appropriate punctuation, and insert dialogue tags. The beauty of teaching dialogue this way is that it does not matter what genre the student is using, because dialogue can be effective in any piece a primary student creates.

At this point, dialogue has become a requirement for whatever writing assignment students are working on, and we expect dialogue to show up in their final products; however, it is always the authors' decision as to where this writing tool will be used in their writing. As we progress through each stage of the conventions of dialogue (indenting, punctuation, and using dialogue tags), students take notes in their Writing Strategies Journals so they can review the strategy later and implement it in future writing projects.

Reflect

Throughout the writing process, students are reminded to **reflect** on what they have learned and also that it is always *their* writing, and they have the final say on how it changes. Once this project is completed, we expect to see them adding dialogue that follows writing conventions throughout future writing projects. As a final reflection, our students enter their new understandings about writing dialogue in their Writing Strategies Journals by responding to such questions as "How did including dialogue in your writing paint a clearer picture for your reader? Does the dialogue you include help the reader understand what's happening in the story? How does including dialogue develop your characters?" Students also add "Use appropriate commas and quotation marks" to their Personal Editing Checklists (see Chapter Eighteen).

Adapting the Strategy
Adapting the Strategy for Emerging Writers

For emerging writers, we put examples of dialogue on sentence strips without the appropriate punctuation. Students then glue elbow macaroni on the strips to represent quotation marks and commas. Even very young writers enjoy this activity, and it reinforces the concept of "marking off" the words that are said by a character in a story. After students glue all the quotation marks and commas, they can put the strips together to make a story. Then they can copy the story into their Writing Strategies Journals and add additional pieces of dialogue.

Adapting the Strategy for Writers Who Struggle

The examples we use for this mini-lesson are a source of help for students who struggle with writing. We use them to design individual instruction for students who have dysgraphia or similar difficulties with handwriting. These students are still required to write during the mini-lesson (because writing something down helps them to remember), but we can provide them with typed versions of their previously written pieces before the next class. They can insert typed handouts into their Writing Strategies Journals next to their notes.

We record actual conversations in which struggling writers engage to demonstrate how dialogue is generated. These conversations can be compared with those in *Ira Sleeps Over* to bolster the students' understanding of what written dialogue represents.

We also model by placing a story on transparencies and highlighting the quotation marks and commas in the dialogue as we read it together. Then we have the students dictate some sentences that we write, or we ask students to write on the transparencies. We read and highlight the dialogue in those. Modeling is the most effective technique for helping those who struggle.

Adapting the Strategy for English Language Learners

English language learners tend to have little trouble with this strategy because of the modeling and repetition. If some do have more trouble than others, we use the adaptations for emerging writers and for writers who struggle, and also begin teaching dialogue punctuation using the students' first languages alongside English examples.

Adapting the Strategy for Advanced Writers

We encourage advanced writers to write pieces that include multiple characters who use considerable dialogue. We urge each advanced writer to employ the appropriate quotation marks and commas that designate direct dialogue and to begin new dialogue by moving to the next paragraph to write. We also encourage them to author skits with multiple characters. We help advanced writers become "directors" and work with members of the class as they practice dramatic enactments (for example, in Readers' Theater) based on their work. We also use these dialogue pieces for whole-class practice with reading dialogue.

In addition, advanced writers serve as mentors to their classmates who are just learning to write dialogue with appropriate written language conventions.

Extending the Strategy

This strategy can be used in students' future writing assignments. It has to be revisited, modeled, and practiced multiple times and in multiple ways (using differentiated instruction, in other words) for students to *own* the technique.

To check whether students understand what they have done over the course of learning to use dialogue with proper conventions, we introduce narrative poetry and have them examine and discuss the uses of dialogue in the piece. A good piece to use is "Casey at the Bat" (Thayer, 1888) because (1) many students are baseball fans; (2) it's an excellent narrative poem; (3) it's a sports poem, so it helps male students in particular connect to poetry as something other than "girlie" or "touchy-feely"; and (4) it shows dialogue to students in a less traditional format and provides additional examples for them. This "Casey at the Bat" project incorporates several mini-lessons in addition to this one, but the important thing for students to do is reflect on their own pieces.

Other extensions we use include centers through which students rotate. One center has them apply the conventions of writing dialogue to the creation of scripts for Readers' Theater based on various stories. Another center has them apply the conventions to additional examples of unindented and unpunctuated dialogue on a computer. Students edit and correct the examples, then save or print their corrections while leaving the example unchanged for the next student. Another center has additional sentence strips, elbow macaroni, and pieces of dialogue for students to practice adding dialogue tags and punctuating correctly.

EVIDENCE CONNECTIONS

George, J. (1998, November/December). Writing dialogue (with a little help from Norman Rockwell). *Teaching Pre K–8*. Retrieved March 20, 2009, from http://findarticles.com/p/articles/mi_qa3666/is_199811/ai_n8809476.

"At times, the ability to write dialogue seems to border on art in addition to language skills, because the result can be viewed in a beautifully created picture" (p. 1). This is the challenge that teachers of writing face—teaching the skill *and* the art of dialogue. The first step is to choose pieces that are engaging and are excellent illustrations of characters' using dialogue. Students need practice in identifying dialogue and recognizing how it is punctuated. After many sessions of meaningful practice, they really do begin to use dialogue in their writing much more effectively.

Carroll, J. A., & Wilson, E. E. (2008). *ACTS of teaching: How to teach writing* (2nd ed.). Portsmouth, NH: Heinemann.

Carroll and Wilson point out that dialogue "permits the reader to hear the authentic voice" (p. 1) of both the piece of writing and the characters. In short, any piece of writing that fits into the narrative genre—from a narrative poem to one from the vast majority of prose—cannot be perfected without dialogue.

REFERENCES

Carroll, J. A., & Wilson, E. E. (2008). *ACTS of teaching: How to teach writing* (2nd ed.). Portsmouth, NH: Heinemann.

Thayer, E. L. (1888, June 3). Casey at the bat. *San Francisco Examiner.*

Waber, B. (1972). *Ira sleeps over.* Boston: Houghton Mifflin/Walter Lorraine Books.

Chapter 21

Color-Coding Editing

JANET RICHARDS

This strategy motivates students to review their drafts to pinpoint and resolve their editing needs.

Why This Strategy Is Important

Conventions of written language are the surface features of writing that minimally include capitalization at the beginnings of sentences, punctuation at the ends of sentences, commas in a series, and spelling. Conventions of written language are not relevant to spoken language. Consequently, students know little about editing until they enter the primary grades and learn how to identify and fix editing trouble spots in their writing (Gardam, 2009).

Primary students often are reluctant to edit what they have written. They think this process will alter or destroy their writing rather than refine and fine-tune it (Clemens, Crimi, & Tompkins, 2005). In addition, they tend to be in the preoperational stage of development and are naturally egocentric—unable to see other's views and perspectives (Piaget, 1990). They believe that their audience will understand what they have composed, and thus that they do not have to make any improvements in their writing. Moreover, young students find the physical task of handwriting laborious, and as a result they understandably resist the chore of editing their work (Graham & Harris, 2005). Another obstacle is that editing is a cognitive task that often overwhelms primary students because they do not know how to either identify and locate errors in their writing or keep track of the edits they have attempted. In terms of development, they are just learning to organize, manage, and apply conventional mechanics, spelling, and linguistic skills. Nonetheless, primary writing curricula stress editing skills, and annual writing tests require primary students to edit their final drafts (Gardam, 2009). Therefore, primary students need to learn how to edit.

One of my graduate writing students teaches second grade. During our class sharing time, she told us she had concerns about her students' apparent lack of motivation and ability to edit their writing. She said,

> *No matter how I tell my students otherwise, they think when they compose something they do not have to revisit it to improve it. I tell them editing is a courtesy to their readers. I have talked to them about punctuation, capitalization, spelling, and sentence formation, but my students disregard these conventions of written language. They write sentence fragments and run-on sentences, use nonstandard spelling, and overlook punctuation. They write a draft, and then they think the composing process is completed. So I have to edit their writing for them. I simply do not know how to teach my students to edit independently.*

When I was a primary teacher, I did not know how to teach my students to edit independently either. And, just like this teacher in my writing class, I edited my students' writing for them and required them to look over my right shoulder as I edited their work, hoping they would somehow pick up some editing tips from me as I marked unconventional grammar, spelling, and so on in their papers. Since then I've learned much more about writing theory and pedagogy. I now suggest to teachers that, in addition to helping their students use Personal Editing Checklists (see Chapter Eighteen), they teach their primary students color-coding as an editing strategy, either as an independent editing plan or in conjunction with Personal Editing Checklists. Color-Coding Editing has been used in a variety of ways to assist secondary students' literary analysis (Olson, 2003). I have adapted the strategy to fit primary students' editing needs.

The SCAMPER Model for Color-Coding Editing

Survey and Assess

Early in the semester when I am out in schools, I know who might benefit from the Color-Coding Editing strategy because I **survey and assess** students' editing efforts and keep track of students who either neglect to edit their writing or decide editing is unnecessary. Yetta Goodman's notion of "kidwatching" (1978) is relevant here. "Put simply, kidwatching includes direct, intentional, and systematic observations by teachers" (O'Keefe, 1996, p. 4). During my daily kidwatching routine, I make anecdotal notes about each student in my Writing Strategies Notebook, such as "Noah: needs to learn to edit for capitalization, punctuation at the end of sentences, commas in a series, and spelling." Recording these notes helps me determine who will benefit from participating in Color-Coding Editing mini-lesson sessions. For instance, primary students who are in the precommunicative, semiphonetic, and phonetic stages of spelling would not benefit from learning how to edit because editing is beyond their current zones of proximal development with respect to writing (Vygotsky, 1978). Some students, however, are ready to learn how to independently capitalize the first words of sentences and use punctuation at the ends of sentences—but that is all they are able to manage until they develop additional writing competencies.

Confer

To initiate the strategy I call up a small group of students I have identified as ready and needing to learn how to independently check for capital letters at the beginnings of sentences and punctuation at the ends of sentences. We sit together as a group on carpet squares, or around a circular table. We **confer** and talk together about how authors often write stories, poems, and nonfiction for others to enjoy and to gain information. We also talk about how editing makes our writing easy for others to read.

Assemble Materials

I **assemble materials** that include anonymous examples of former students' unedited writing, a black marker, red and green crayons, and chart paper.

Model

To **model** the strategy, I first display the examples of former students' writing that are missing capitalization and end-of-sentence punctuation. We read these examples aloud as a group and conclude that the writing is hard to comprehend because the written messages look like one long sentence. We also consider how good writers begin each sentence with a capital letter and end each sentence either with a period, question mark, or exclamation point.

Then I model the Color-Coding Editing strategy. I write a short story on chart paper, reading it as I compose. I deliberately "neglect" to capitalize the beginnings of sentences and "forget" to place punctuation marks at the ends of sentences. When my story is complete, we review it and look for the capitalization and end-of-sentence punctuation problems. I point out the required beginning-of-sentence capitalization and end-of-sentence punctuation, highlighting these two written language conventions. I use two colored crayons so that these two editing concerns stand out. I always use the color green (go) for capitalization and red (stop) for punctuation at the ends of sentences.

Practice

The following day I review the strategy with my students, and then each writes a short narrative of his or her choice. When they have completed their writing, I help them **practice** locating the beginning word of each sentence and then highlighting the first alphabet letter of the word with a green crayon. I also help them locate and highlight with a red crayon where end punctuation is required. Then we go back through their writing and look for green and red color-coding to help them capitalize and punctuate at the ends of sentences.

Execute

In the next step, students **execute** color-coding on their own, shifting from assisted learning to writing with minimal assistance. I circulate among the students, helping them with the strategy when necessary.

Reflect

I have discovered that students are good teachers. Therefore, once they have become expert in color-coding capital letters at the beginnings of sentences and using end-of-sentence punctuation, I encourage them to model the strategy for other students who are ready to learn how to color-code as an editing strategy. Going through the strategy to assist their peers helps students review the strategy and **reflect** on its benefits. I have students make and continually update posters that highlight the writing strategies they know and use independently, so they add the Color-Coding Editing strategy to their posters.

Adapting the Strategy

Adapting the Strategy for Emerging Writers

We practice this strategy as a group. With me assisting as needed, students identify and color-code beginning- and end-of-sentence editing problems in fiction and nonfiction texts I have authored. I do not insist that emerging writers learn and use this strategy with their personally created texts until they can write compositions with ease.

Adapting the Strategy for Writers Who Struggle

I work one-on-one with writers who need extra help. I write a sentence that has no beginning capitalization or end punctuation, and I show students how to color-code these omissions and then edit with the appropriate capitalization and punctuation. I continue with this type of lesson until students are able to move on to comma usage and spelling, as suggested later in this chapter.

Adapting the Strategy for English Language Learners

The approach I use with struggling writers also works well with English language learners (ELLs). I have found it is more productive for a small group of English language learners to work together with me. Collaboration provides opportunities for ELLs to expand their English language vocabulary and helps them begin to understand the syntax (the order of the words in a sentence) used in English.

Adapting the Strategy for Advanced Writers

Advanced writers are usually able to move forward to color-coding and editing run-on sentences and limited or repetitious vocabulary, and to attend to the arrangement of transitions, topic sentences, and conclusions in their stories and nonfiction writing.

Extending the Strategy

When students have become proficient in using color-coding to edit their writing for capital letters at the beginnings of sentences and end-of-sentence punctuation, we move on to commas in a series and spelling. I teach students to highlight spaces between words in a series using yellow crayons and to place commas in these spaces. I also teach students to use orange crayons to highlight words they think are spelled in nonstandard English, and then to check these words in their primary-grade or personal dictionaries.

I often set up an editing station with supplies that include crayons, markers, synonym and antonym charts, a computer, a primary-grade dictionary, and a primary-grade thesaurus. I arrange for small groups or pairs of students to visit the editing station and engage in peer editing coupled with considerable peer discussion. I often pair an advanced writer with a struggling writer or an English language learner. As the school year progresses I introduce more sophisticated editing skills to the class for them to practice at the editing station (see Crimi & Tompkins, 2005).

EVIDENCE CONNECTIONS

Nitscheke, F. (2005). Color-coding: Using color as a revision tool. In G. Tompkins & C. Blanchfield, *50 ways to develop strategic writers* (pp. 18–21). Upper Saddle River, NJ: Pearson/Merrill/Prentice Hall.

Nitscheke offers tips about teaching editing to students in grades 4 through 12. She says teachers need to guide less-proficient writers through the editing process, whereas more proficient writers can use printed directions to help them analyze and edit their writing.

Piaget, J. (1990). *The child's conception of the world*. New York: Littlefield Adams.

Piaget identifies four stages of cognitive development. The preoperational stage (toddler and early childhood) is especially relevant to students' abilities to become self-directed writers and thinkers. This strategy helps guide students' development of self-directedness. In this period, which has two substages, the child demonstrates intelligence through the use of symbols (in this case, the use of colored codes), language use matures, and memory and imagination are developed, but the child thinks in a nonlogical, nonreversible manner. Egocentric thinking predominates (Huitt & Hummel, 2003).

REFERENCES

Clemens, Crimi, F., & Tompkins, G. (2005). Editing stations: Enhancing the readability of writing. In G. Tompkins & C. Blanchfield, *50 ways to develop strategic writers* (pp. 37–40). Upper Saddle River, NJ: Pearson/Merrill/Prentice Hall.

Gardam, B. (2009). The vision of Paul Gauguin. #2. Namaste. *Dragongate*. Retrieved October 6, 2010, from http://gardheim.blogspot.com/2009/11/vision-of-paul-gauguin-2-namaste.html.

Goodman, Y. (1978). Kidwatching: An alternative to testing. *Journal of National Elementary School Principals, 574*, 22–27.

Graham, S., & Harris, K. R. (2005). *Writing better: Effective strategies for teaching students with learning difficulties*. Baltimore: Brooks.

Huitt, W., & Hummel, J. (2003). Piaget's theory of cognitive development. *Educational Psychology Interactive*. Valdosta, GA: Valdosta State University. Retrieved September 7, 2010, from http://chiron.valdosta.edu/whuitt/col/cogsys/piaget.html.

O'Keefe, T. (1996). Teachers as kidwatchers. In K. G. Short, J. C. Harste, & C. L. Burke, *Creating classrooms for authors and inquirers* (2nd ed., pp. 63–80). Portsmouth, NH: Heinemann.

Olson, C. B. (2003). *The reading/writing connection: Strategies for teaching and learning in the secondary classroom*. Boston: Allyn & Bacon.

Piaget, J. (1990). *The child's conception of the world*. New York: Littlefield Adams.

Vygotsky, L. (1978). *Mind in society: The development of higher psychological processes* (M. Cole, Trans.). Cambridge, MA: Harvard University Press.

Chapter 22

Turning Up the Volume of Voice in Poetry

CINDY LASSONDE

This strategy helps students detect action words (verbs) and describers (adverbs and adjectives) within poems of their creation. The strategy also helps students look for vocabulary they might revise to express their feelings in stronger language. Then they "turn up the volume" to strengthen their voices in the poems by using a children's online thesaurus to select vivid, active vocabulary.

Why This Strategy Is Important

Poetry is the perfect genre for teaching students to write with passion and voice. However, their vocabulary often limits their ability to have a strong voice in their poems. *Voice* refers to the writer's unique style as projected through choices in vocabulary, tone, expression, and syntax (Pritchard & Honeycutt, 2007). I like to help students write in ways that project their personalities so their writing reflects their voices, but sometimes I have to show them how to find just the right words to express their points of view or emotions. This strategy walks them through that process. I show them how to use the strategy when they write poetry so they can turn up the volume of voice in their independent writing.

I find students are highly motivated to use the computer as a resource to help them with their writing. At the primary level, I don't expect or see much purpose in having students type final drafts of their poems as a way to integrate technology. To me, that's not a wise use of students' time in school; and it isn't meaningful to students. However, it is meaningful for them to type single words into the search box of an online thesaurus to find better word choices. Using the online thesaurus not only is motivating and helpful but also teaches them that revision doesn't have to be a chore. Often I've found my students are resistant to revising. They have the attitude of "I've written it. It's how I like it. I don't need or want to work on it anymore. I'm ready to leave this behind and go on to something else." Praising them for the poems they have written and then introducing the computer and Internet as a means to make the poems even better often causes them to side-step the resistance. Students become interested and eager to have their turns on the keyboard.

This opportunity to use the online thesaurus also begins to teach students how to focus in on the information they seek within the context of multifaceted electronic text. At first they need me right beside them to find the lists of synonyms they've searched for on the site; but they soon learn to key into the synonyms. In this chapter, I use the Wordsmyth Dictionary-Thesaurus Suite (www.wordsmyth.net). I like using it at the primary level because the synonyms are the only words in a definition that appear in a large rectangle. They are easy to find. Also, on this site I can click the desired level—beginner's, children's, or advanced—appropriate for my students.

We know vocabulary is best taught in context rather than in isolation. This strategy adds words to students' vocabulary in an authentic way that is motivating and exciting for them. What more could educators ask for?

The SCAMPER Model for Turning Up the Volume of Voice in Poetry

Survey and Assess

I **survey and assess** students to determine which students could benefit from learning this strategy. I do this as we read, write, and discuss poetry.

I spend time reading a variety of poems to my class. I purposely select poems that have a loud voice, ones that strongly express the authors' feelings about the topics. I ask,

"How do you think the poet feels about (the topic of the poem)?"

"How do we know the poet feels this way?"

"Does it sound like the poet is talking to you? Can you almost hear the poet's voice because the poet is trying to tell you how he or she feels?"

I survey and assess students' evidence of voice and the extent of their vocabulary in the poems they write. In particular, I look at the verbs, adverbs, and adjectives they select. In general, I listen to hear if there is any evidence that they make their word choices carefully rather than just writing down the first things to come into their heads. I keep anecdotal notes, and I list words I see in their writing and noteworthy words I hear students use in their everyday speech. I note evidence of selectivity in their word choices as well as the revision tactics they use. Over time, I look at the vocabulary they use in the poems they create to determine if Turning Up the Volume of Voice in Poetry would be a helpful strategy to teach. Once I have determined which students might benefit from learning this strategy, I form a small learning group and begin our writing strategy mini-lesson.

Confer

Now that I have a small group of students, I **confer** with them. I begin by asking, "What are some ways we can improve our poems by revising them?" I lead the discussion to the topics of word choice and voice. I say,

> *When I write, sometimes I like to take one word out and put another one in that I think is better. It's a better way to say what I mean so my reader will understand my feelings. For example, if I wrote, "The day was good," I might want to change the word* good *so my reader will know what I mean by that. What might we say instead of "The day was good"?*

Then I explain that we will learn a new strategy to help us choose better words so our readers will really know what we are feeling, just like we knew how the poets felt in the poems we read earlier. I tell them we'll do this by using the computer to help us find and learn new words, and that they will want to learn this strategy so they can use it when they write poems independently.

Assemble Materials

I **assemble materials,** including some of the students' favorite poems that are models of strong voice and vocabulary. I also have enough copies of the Turn Up the Voice Volume graphic organizer (see Figure 22.1) for every student to have two copies: one to add to their Writing Strategies Journals to use when they write poems independently and the other to use when they first execute this strategy as part of the mini-lesson. Students take their journals to the small group so they can add their new graphic organizers. I write a model poem (my poem about Cocoa in the next section) on easel paper ahead of time in black marker and gather several markers of various colors, enough for me and each student in the small group. I also prepare enough copies for everyone of a second model poem that students will use during the practice part of the mini-lesson. Of course, we'll need at least one computer that has access to the Internet. I have the Wordsmyth Web site up and ready to go. I refamiliarize myself beforehand with how the site works.

Model

I **model** by sharing a poem I've written about my cat Cocoa. The poem is written in black marker on easel paper so everyone can see it.

> *Cocoa lies in the sun spot on the floor.*
> *I get out of bed to get ready for school.*
> *Cocoa slowly licks his fur.*
> *I quickly get dressed and go out the door.*
> *While I'm gone, Cocoa sleeps*
> *And sleeps*
> *And sleeps*
> *While I work*
> *And work*
> *And work.*

Cocoa wakes and sits by the door
For me to come home.
I pick him up and give him a great, big hug.
My hug-a-bug Cocoa.
My big boy. My friend.

I want people who read my poem to know I _____.

To **TURN UP THE VOICE VOLUME,** I will change these words:

<u>Action Word I Want to Change</u>   <u>Vivid Verbs!</u>

<u>Describing Word I Want to Change</u>   Active Adverbs or Adjectives!

I will use these words to **TURN UP THE VOICE VOLUME** in my poem.

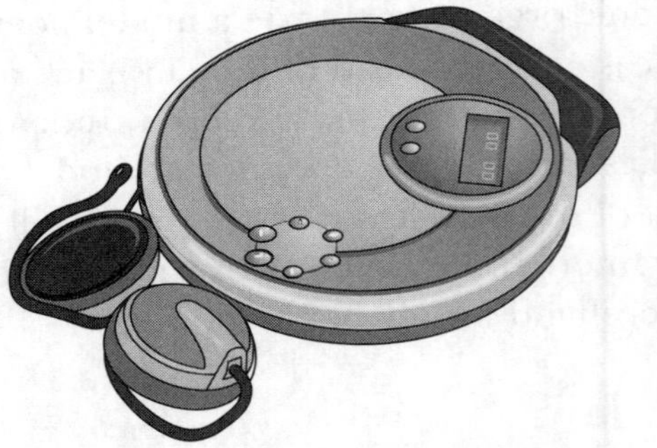

Figure 22.1 Turn Up the Voice Volume

Then, I say,

I like my poem about Cocoa, but I think I can make it better. First, I ask myself,
What do I want people who read my poem to know? I want people to know how
I feel about Cocoa. I love my Cocoa; and I want my readers to love him, too.
I want my readers to hear my voice saying, "My poem is about Cocoa having
the Good Life. He can sleep and hang out all day, but I can't. I have things I
have to do all day. But that doesn't matter. I still love Cocoa." That's what I
want my readers to get out of my poem. (I fill in the first blank on the worksheet.)

The next thing I'm going to do is put a solid rectangle around the action
words, or verbs, in my poem. Will you help me find the words that are doing,

or action words? (We go through the poem finding them.) When I look at the words we just found, I think, Which one could I change that would better show that Cocoa is kind of lazy and I have to work hard BUT I still love him? How can I make my voice louder? I think I could probably change the word lies *to find a word that tells that he isn't just lying there—he's really sprawled out and lazy. So I'm going to put the word* lies *in the solid rectangle on my Turn Up the Voice Volume sheet. Later I'll use the computer to help me find a better word for* lies. *(I write the word* lies *in the solid rectangle on the sheet.)*

And now, I'm going to find some describing words in my poem and put dashed rectangles around them. Will you help me? (We go through the poem finding them.) Again I ask myself, Which one could I change that would better show that Cocoa is kind of lazy and I have to work hard BUT I still love him? How can I make my voice louder? I think I could probably change the word slowly. *It's an adverb because it describes how he licks his fur. I want a better word that says he does it slowly because he has all day to lick his fur if he wants to. He has nothing else to do! So I'm going to put the word* slowly *in the dashed rectangle on my Turn Up the Voice Volume sheet. Later I'll use the computer to find a better word for* slowly. *(I write* slowly *in the dashed rectangle on the sheet.)*

Next we go to the computer and look at the Wordsmyth Web site together. I say, "I want to change the words *lies* and *slowly*, but I don't know any better words. This online Web site called Wordsmyth will help me." Then I show them how to type in one word at a time into the search box, click on the beginner's dictionary, then GO. I tell them to look at the big rectangle that says "Similar Words" to find better words. I tell them to pick two synonyms for each word to go into the circles on the worksheet.

Finally, we decide which choices we will use and write them in the two circles at the bottom of the worksheet. We have made our decision. We go to our poem and replace the words with the better words we have found (for example, *relaxes* for *lies*, and *leisurely* for *slowly*). We reread the poem to see if it has a louder or stronger voice. I emphasize the new words as I read those lines. I ask if readers will get a better idea that Cocoa is kind of lazy and doesn't have much to do.

Practice

I review the strategy with the students and ask them to **practice** using the strategy and Web site with a short poem reproduced on cards I have given them. Each working with a partner, they take a red and green marker and begin the process of circling action and describing words and filling in the Turn Up the Voice Volume worksheet.

I stand by to scaffold and support their progress, prompting them with suggestions of questions to ask themselves to self-monitor their skill in using the strategy. I help them use the graphic organizer and the Web site. I help them identify the verbs, adverbs, and adjectives. When two students have identified the words to replace, I let them input the words into the computer and complete the graphic organizer. Partners then collaborate to choose the best words to help the poem come alive and express the author's intended feelings.

Execute

In the next step, students **execute** the strategy and work toward independent, self-regulated writing. Students at this point may use poems they have written. I support their efforts and remind them to use the Web site and their graphic organizers, and to select the most appropriate words.

Reflect

In the final step, I encourage students to **reflect** on their use of the strategy. We talk about how they could use the worksheet and the Web site to turn up the voice volume in their poems. I ask them to talk about how this strategy made their word choices better. Then we talk about poetry and the use of technology as a writing tool. For example, I ask,

"How did the computer help you today?"
"What did you like best about what we did today?"
"What do we mean when we say we want to hear our voices in our poems?"
"What do we have to remember when we want to make our voices louder in our poems?"

I want them to reflect on the importance of integrating their voices into their poems and on how technology can be used as a tool to help us improve our writing.

Adapting the Strategy

Adapting the Strategy for Emerging Writers

Emerging writers who may not yet be confident readers might need extended scaffolding in using and navigating the Wordsmyth Web site. I find they need assistance in word selection when I give them a list of synonyms on the Web site. I read the list of words to them and explain what some of them mean. Often I select two appropriate words from the list of synonyms and encourage students to choose from those two. Eventually they are able to self-regulate their use of this strategy in their independent writing as their literacy skills develop.

As a registered user of the Wordsmyth Web site, I have access to the "spelled-like" search mode. This feature is great for students who use invented spelling because they only have to approximate the way the word is spelled for the word to pop up.

Adapting the Strategy for Writers Who Struggle

This strategy is effective with struggling writers because they think the computer does the work for them. It's like magic! I have found, though, that sometimes struggling writers have difficulty identifying what words they want to replace. They tend to circle words haphazardly, which is why initially I started using red and green markers to detect action words and describing words. With struggling writers, I scaffold this part by first circling the words in the poem for them, then teaching the rest of the strategy. Little by little, I bring them into the selection process.

Adapting the Strategy for English Language Learners

I bring in poems in each student's first language so he or she has models of voice. The worksheet may be written in the student's first language in his or her journal to reinforce the English version. Also, if the computer text is too difficult for the English language learner to navigate, a hard copy of a primary thesaurus can be substituted or used additionally to support the concept.

Adapting the Strategy for Advanced Writers

I encourage advanced writers to change more than a couple of words in their poems to strengthen their voices. Wordsmyth allows students to select from beginner's, children's, and advanced dictionaries. I have advanced writers search for more difficult vocabulary to use by choosing a higher-level dictionary. When they come across words they do not know at the higher levels, I direct them to use a dictionary—either online or hard copy—to distinguish what synonyms are the best choices for their poems.

Extending the Strategy

Voice is not identified and displayed solely by the word choices we make when we write. I extend this strategy by creating other mini-lessons on strengthening voice in our poems by considering the tones, expressions, and syntax we use. Strategies for revising for each of these characteristics are taught and practiced following the SCAMPER model and in the contextualized, interactive manner demonstrated in this strategy.

EVIDENCE CONNECTIONS

Pritchard, R. J., & Honeycutt, R. L. (2007). Best practices in implementing a process approach to teaching writing. In S. Graham, C. A. Macarthur, & J. Fitzgerald (Eds.), *Best practices in writing instruction* (pp. 28–49). New York: Guilford Press.
Pritchard and Honeycutt help educators think about the writing process. For example, in their guidelines for best practices using the process approach, they tell us to ''address the emotional issues surrounding writing'' (p. 31) by providing time for students to practice writing and be part of a writing community in which they can experience a positive, nonthreatening social climate for composing and creating. The poetry-writing process can become a bit hazy for students unless we discuss the uniqueness of the process involved in writing poetry. Here's why: on the one hand, we as educators want students to be creative in their writing. On the other hand, we don't want them to make any errors in their writing. Sometimes these two wishes can be contradictory in the poetry genre because we don't always follow the rules of mechanics and grammar in poetry. Poetic freedom allows us to use sentence fragments, run-on sentences, and even capital letters in the middle of a sentence! Sometimes we use chunks of words rather than clear narrative to express thoughts. Pritchard and Honeycutt tell us to help students develop an understanding of the complexity of the writing process as it pertains to the intentions of the writer. I would add to this that we also need to help students understand how the writing process should be adapted to the genre of poetry.

Milard, E. (2003). Towards a literacy of fusion: New times, new teaching and learning? *Reading: Literacy and Language, 37*(1), 3–8.
There is no doubt that students are engaged with technology. Even very young children play educational and not-so-educational games online in school and, if they have access to computers, at home as well. Milard's study looked at new ways fifth graders made meaning based on their interactions with technology. She found evidence that students developed a sense of empowered agency. They shaped and transformed meanings through their participation in educational games online.

Turning Up the Volume of Voice in Poetry allows students to interact with technology in a way that is functional but that can also be transformative as they become aware of the possibilities technology offers them as a tool for improving their writing.

REFERENCE

Pritchard, R. J., & Honeycutt, R. L. (2007). Best practices in implementing a process approach to teaching writing. In S. Graham, C. A. Macarthur, & J. Fitzgerald (Eds.), *Best practices in writing instruction* (pp. 28–49). New York: Guilford Press.

Chapter 23

STEP into the Shoes of a Reader

NOREEN S. MOORE

STEP into the Shoes of a Reader is a strategy to help students revise their descriptive writing. STEP stands for **S**witch roles, **T**hink, **E**valuate, and **P**lan. After writing brief descriptions of objects, students become readers of peers' similar descriptions. As readers, students have the opportunity to think about what makes their peers' writing effective and provide suggestions for what their peers could change or add to make their writing even better.

Why This Strategy Is Important

Young writers' lives are filled with authentic reading and writing experiences: writing birthday cards to friends, reading notes that parents or guardians pack in their lunch boxes, writing and reading e-mails, and delivering notes from teachers to parents. Implicit in many of these early literacy experiences is the relationship between a writer and his or her audience, or readers. Young writers understand they must write in such a way that their readers can comprehend their messages. Yet when young writers are crafting written texts, they spend so much cognitive effort transcribing their messages that they often forget to consider their readers (McCutchen, 2006). Because reading-writing connections are inherent in writing, writing instruction for young writers that emphasizes the role of reading and readers, while deemphasizing the energy required for transcription, is necessary (Nystrand, 2006; Prior, 2006).

This strategy gives students the opportunity to think about the needs of readers (develop audience awareness) by stepping into their readers' shoes. It combines several effective writing instruction practices: making reading-writing connections, collaborating with peers, and studying written texts (Graham & Perin, 2007). In addition to the recent research that informed the development of STEP into the Shoes of a Reader, my observations over time in an elementary school classroom also informed STEP. As a teacher and researcher, I noticed my students were better able to identify characteristics of effective writing than to include them in their writing. More specifically, my students could easily distinguish a great description from a mediocre description, but they struggled to write great descriptions. I suspected they were not able to write great descriptions as easily as they were able to identify them because they had to exert a lot of cognitive energy transcribing their messages—and they did not have many cognitive resources to spend on other aspects of writing, such as audience awareness. I wanted to create a strategy that would enable my students to practice higher-level writing skills after they transcribed their original messages. Revision is an activity that not only helps writers improve the quality of their writing but also allows writers to practice different aspects of the composing process. I also found that my students were motivated to work with their peers as well as motivated by their peers. Therefore, I sought to design a strategy to give students opportunities for peer collaboration in writing.

The SCAMPER Model for STEP into the Shoes of a Reader
Survey and Assess

Before teaching the strategy, I collect writing samples from my students to **survey and assess** the informational adequacy, or detail level, of students' descriptive writing. In addition, to make sure the task is appropriate for my students (in other words, within their zones of proximal development, Vygotsky, 1978), I informally interview my students in regard to their knowledge about the characteristics of descriptive writing.

All students write about the same topic for the writing sample I collect. First, I display four pictures of different (but similar) seashells, with varied shapes, sizes, and colors, in front of the classroom (see Figure 23.1). I label the seashells *A, B, C,* and *D* on individual index cards. I tell students they can choose one seashell to describe. I ask students not to tell anyone what seashells they chose to depict. Next I give students three sheets of paper. On the first sheet, each student writes his or her name and indicates the letter of the seashell he or she chose to describe (when I collect students' writing, their name sheets are stapled to the back of the other two sheets). On the second sheet, lined paper for writing, the student describes the shell he or she chose. On the third sheet, blank paper for drawing, each student makes a picture of the chosen seashell (see Figure 23.2).

It is important to note that before I ask students to write independently, I have already introduced descriptive writing by reading aloud descriptive writing and modeling how to write descriptions. In addition, morning meetings consist of shared writing and interactive writing activities focused on descriptive writing. During these activities I ask students to tell me about the characteristics that define effective descriptive writing. I record the characteristics students identify on chart paper and display it by the writing and library center. Informally assessing students' knowledge of characteristics of descriptive writing helps me determine if students are ready to write descriptively on their own.

Once students are able to identify the characteristics of effective descriptive writing and have participated in several modeled and collaborative writing experiences, I ask them to do the seashell writing task. I use two formal writing assessments to evaluate students' writing. First, I read students' descriptions myself (as a reader, not a teacher-evaluator). I try to match each student's description to the correct seashell without knowing what seashell each child describes. This helps me gauge overall how successful students were at accomplishing the goals of descriptive writing. Next I use a primary trait rubric I designed for descriptive writing (see Figure 23.3). This rubric is a modification of the Six-Traits primary trait rubric for young writers (Spandel, 2008). This type of rubric helps educators assess writing more analytically by focusing on six different areas related to writing quality: ideas, organization, voice, word choice, sentence fluency, and conventions. The primary trait rubric allows me to see what specific aspects of students' descriptive writing interfere with their effective communication of ideas. The two formal writing assessments coupled with the earlier informal assessment of students' understanding of descriptive writing give me information I can use to decide whether my students know more about descriptive writing than they are able to show in their actual writing.

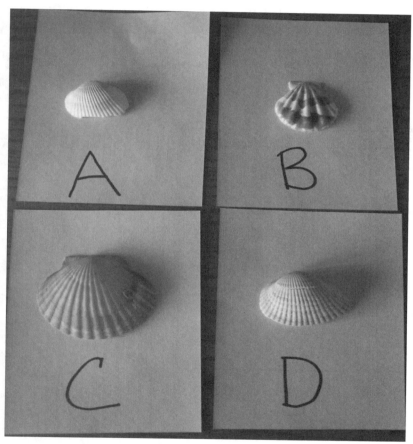

Figure 23.1 Seashells Displayed on a Desk

Confer

When I **confer** with students, I say, "We have been talking about descriptive writing, and you just wrote a description. What makes a good description?" After I ascertain students' ideas, I tell them,

> *I am going to describe our classroom and you tell me if I can improve it by adding more or better details. We know that a good description has lots of great details. Sometimes after we write a description we think of more details or better details that we could add. Then we can go back to our writing and add them. This makes our description even better!* (Discussion with students follows.)

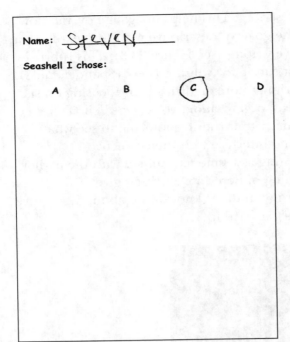

Name: STEVEN

Seashell I chose:

A   B   (C)   D

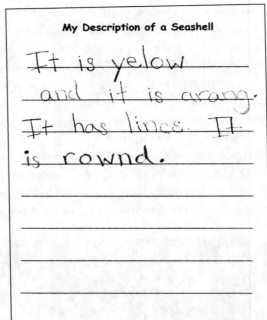

My Description of a Seashell

It is yelow
and it is arang.
It has lines. IT
is rownd.

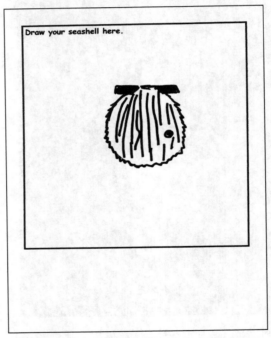

Draw your seashell here.

Figure 23.2 Student Description and Drawing of Seashell C

Assemble Materials

Next I **assemble materials.** In addition to the materials used for the seashell activity (four different shells purchased at a craft store or found at a beach, a packet for each student of three papers on which they write their descriptions and draw their pictures, and copies of the descriptive writing scoring guide), I gather the following supplies: (1) two pictures of trees, photographed in my backyard; (2) chart paper and colored pens for modeling the strategy; (3) sample descriptions; (4) paper and pencils for students to use to revise their seashell descriptions; (5) the Steps of the STEP into the Shoes of a Reader classroom poster and handouts for students (see Figure 23.4). I type up each student's seashell description so that handwriting does not interfere with students' comprehension during peer review. I also assign each student a number code at the top of his or her description. Even though these steps ensure that peers do not know whose papers they are reading, we refer to everyone in the class as a friend so peers respect that they are reading a friend's writing. Finally, I match students with partners for peer review. I record in a Word document students' names, their number codes, the seashells they described, and their partners to facilitate the STEP into the Shoes of a Reader strategy.

Descriptive Writing Scoring Guide

Ideas: Ideas are the "meat" of the description. When scoring for ideas, you look to make sure the writing includes a mention of the main components that make up the object, person, or event described.

2: All main points related to the topic are discussed. I have a complete sense of the object, person, or event described.

1: Most but not all main points related to the topic are discussed. I have a fuzzy sense of the object, person, or event described.

0: Significant information pertaining to the main ideas of the topic is missing. I have a weak (or no) sense of the object, person, or event described.

Organization: Organization refers to the coherence and understandability of the writing. When scoring for organization, you look to make sure ideas are in a logical order and that the writer gives the reader clues about the order using transition words.

2: The description is easy to follow. The writer includes transitions. I rarely had to reread to figure out what the writer was trying to say.

1: The description can be followed, but some effort is required on the part of the reader to piece information together in a cohesive way. I often had to reread parts of the writing to understand it.

0: The ideas are difficult to follow and understand. I had to reread several times. And even after several reads, it was difficult to understand the main ideas.

Word choice: Word choice refers to the precision of the words used to describe the object, person, or event. When scoring for word choice, you pay attention to the extent to which the language helps you experience (see, feel, smell, taste, hear, and so on) the object, person, or event being described.

2: The words are vivid and precise. The word choice helped me paint a picture in my mind.

1: The words convey most of the ideas, but some words, phrases, and sentences lack specificity. I was not able to visualize all parts of the object, person, or event.

0: The words are general and vague. I could not picture any part of the event, object, or person in my mind.

Figure 23.3 Descriptive Writing Scoring Guide

Sentence fluency: Sentence fluency refers to the sentence structures and variation in the writing. When scoring for sentence fluency, you pay attention to how easy or difficult it is for you to read the writing fluently. (Choppiness, run-on sentences, and repetitive structure can all interfere with a reader's ability to read and understand writing.)

2: The sentences are well formed, varied, and interesting. I did not stumble over the sentence structure as I was reading.

1: The sentences are well-formed, but may lack variation in structure and length. I felt like the description was repetitive at points.

0: The sentences are sometimes incomplete and lack variation. Errors in sentence structure impeded my understanding of the writer's message.

Conventions: Conventions refer to the grammar, syntax, spelling, and punctuation used. When scoring for conventions, you pay attention to these elements in terms of how much they interfere with your understanding of the writer's message.

2: The writing is free from errors that impede my understanding of what I am reading.

1: There are a few errors, but I can still understand what I am reading without much effort.

0: There are major errors that impede my full understanding of the writing.

Scoring Sheet

Element	Score			Name/Draft
Ideas	2	1	0	
Organization	2	1	0	
Word choice	2	1	0	
Sentence fluency	2	1	0	
Conventions	2	1	0	
Notes:				

Figure 23.3 Continued

Model

During two whole-group sessions, **I model** the strategy. First I tell students they will learn a strategy that will help them improve their descriptive writing. Then I tell them that the strategy they will learn is called the STEP into the Shoes of a Reader strategy, or STEP for short. I invite students to speculate about what the title of the strategy might mean. Next I tell students that the strategy is one a writer can use with a friend or fellow writer. I then post the mnemonic "STEP" and the corresponding strategy steps on a colorful chart at the front of the classroom (see Figure 23.4). I explain the steps of the strategy as I refer to the chart. I also provide a handout of the poster for each student. Students save their handouts in their Writing Strategies Journals.

1. **Switch roles**—After you write a description, you switch papers with a friend. Now you have *switched roles* and become the reader.

2. **Think**—As a reader you *think* about the characteristics that make a description effective.

3. **Evaluate**—As you read your friend's writing, you *evaluate*. Ask yourself, Does this description contain all of the characteristics of effective descriptions? What details and information were missing?

4. **Plan**—Next you check the writing again and decide whether more or different details and information should be included. Give the writer a *plan* to add more specific details and information. Think about if you can use any of the advice you gave your friend to improve your writing.

Figure 23.4 Steps of the STEP into the Shoes of a Reader Strategy

Finally, I tell students they can use this strategy any time they write descriptions and want to make sure they have included all of the important details and information.

After explaining the strategy, I model its use. I tell students I am going to show them how to use STEP with a friend. I present two pictures of similar (but different) trees, as shown in Figure 23.5. I tell my students I wrote a description of a tree and my friend wrote a description of a tree. On the back of our written descriptions we specify the tree we were trying to describe. I explain that my friend and I are going to use STEP into the Shoes of a Reader to help us improve our descriptions. I explain that good writers use strategies, and that they talk to other writers to help them improve their writing.

Friend's description: "The tree is tall. There are a hundred leaves or more! The leaves are green. There are a lot of branches, too."

My description: "The tree is very green. There are so many leaves I can hardly see the branches. The leaves look soft. I would like to sit under this tree."

Figure 23.5 Two Pictures of Trees with Sample Descriptions

Next I perform a think-aloud in which I go through the STEP procedure.

1. **Switch roles**—I read my friend's tree description aloud, noting good and poor characteristics of the description. I make a guess about which tree my friend is describing. I ask students to contribute their own evaluations of the writing and to guess which picture matches the description.

2. **Think**—I list the characteristics of good descriptive writing, and I talk about what characteristics the description we read contains. I invite students to help.

3. **Evaluate**—I talk about what I think is missing from the description. I talk about the reasons I would have difficulty matching the description to the correct picture. I ask students to help.

4. **Plan**—Finally, I make a list of two pieces of additional information that could be added to the description to improve the overall quality. In addition, I think aloud about how I might be able to use these two suggestions in my own writing as well.

When I flip over the paper that contains the description, we learn as a class which tree my friend was describing. I summarize by stating the difficulties the reader would have in picturing the tree described in the writing. As a class, we brainstorm more suggestions to help my friend improve the description.

I remind students of the steps in the STEP into the Shoes of a Reader strategy, and I refer to the chart displaying the mnemonic. I tell students that we are going to use the strategy today to help me revise my description of a tree. I scaffold students through the STEP process with my writing (see Figure 23.4). I monitor comments and make sure students understand what makes an appropriate comment. Finally, I make one revision to my writing from my students' suggestions.

I wrap up the session by talking about how good writers can STEP into the shoes of their readers and read their descriptive writing the way their audience might read it. I explain that as readers, writers can learn important information about what makes writing effective.

Practice

Now we **practice** the strategy. I remind students that they learned how to STEP into the shoes of a reader. I say,

> When you step into the shoes of a reader, you switch roles *and become a reader. You* think *about the characteristics of descriptive writing. You* evaluate *what works and doesn't work with a piece of writing, and you* plan *ways the writing you read can be improved and ways your own writing can be improved.*
>
> We read two different descriptions and you talked about what the writers did well and what they needed to improve. Today you are going to have the opportunity to STEP into the shoes of a reader again. This time you will read a description of a seashell authored by one of your friends in class. You are not going to know who this friend is or what seashell he or she was trying to describe. You are going to read this friend's writing and guess what seashell he or she described. Think about the characteristics of good descriptive writing, evaluate this friend's writing, and create a plan for him or her that includes one thing that could improve the description.

I give students approximately thirty minutes to work on this task.

Next I say, "Now I am going to put you in pairs: your partner wrote the description you just read." I must facilitate this part because the writing is coded; as stated previously, I use predetermined pairs to help make this part of the procedure go smoothly. I say, "Now turn to your partner and tell him or her which seashell you think matches his or her description. See if you were correct." I give students a few minutes to talk. "Now tell your partner why you matched the description to the seashell you did." I give students a few minutes to talk. "Now tell your partner one or two things he or she could do to improve the description—What would make it easier for you as a reader to match his or her description to the correct seashell?" I give students a few minutes to talk. I tell students to record the suggestions their partners give in the area underneath their written descriptions.

Execute

How might these writers **execute** this strategy independently? During writing time, I suggest they work with partners to revise their writing. Also, I provide opportunities for students to execute this strategy on their own. I ask them to write and then pretend they are the readers, not the writers. I tell them all exemplary writers do this.

After students have time to use the strategy with a partner or independently, they share what they learned about their writing with a friend, a partner, a small group, or the whole class. Finally, students revise their original descriptions to incorporate the suggestions of their partners as well as anything they learned by being readers. I give students thirty to forty minutes to complete their revisions.

Reflect

I collect student revisions, reread, score the descriptions, and determine whether the information students provided was more detailed and complete in the second drafts. I also ask students to self-evaluate their writing. I do this by randomly handing out the revised drafts to new readers (in the same class) and asking the new readers to try to match the descriptions to the objects again. If there are more correct matches, the students know they revised to make their writing more effective. Finally, I ask students to **reflect** on what they learned by stepping into the shoes of readers and on when they could use this strategy again. This informal discussion allows me to assess their strategy knowledge.

Adapting the Strategy

Adapting the Strategy for Emerging Writers

So that emerging writers can learn the STEP into the Shoes of a Reader strategy, I help them complete an interactive writing activity in which I share a description (already written) of a seashell, and students help me determine which seashell is described. After students vote on which seashell they think the writing describes, we talk about the reasons for their guesses. I record each child's vote in a graph on chart paper. Next we flip the description over and learn which seashell it matches. We talk about how it was not easy for everyone to guess the correct match because the writer needed better details to help us out. As a group we brainstorm a list of details that could be used to describe the shell. Next we do an interactive or shared writing activity to revise the description to make it better. We conclude the lesson by talking about how we improved the description.

Adapting the Strategy for Writers Who Struggle

This strategy is especially helpful for writers who struggle with issues of self-regulation as they write. However, when my students have difficulty with transcription skills, I do a collaborative writing activity in which students work in pairs (stronger writers paired with writers who struggle) and do the activity collaboratively. Alternately, students can record their descriptions on cassette tapes or audio files on the computer.

Adapting the Strategy for English Language Learners

Prior to having students write their descriptions of seashells of their choice, I lead students as a group to brainstorm descriptive words to describe the seashells. Then I record these words on chart paper to help facilitate English language learners' use of new vocabulary and spelling.

Adapting the Strategy for Advanced Writers

My advanced students provide more formal advice to their partners about why a description works or doesn't work. Their advice is either in a verbal or written format. Advanced writers can also work together to perform think-alouds for each other. As one student reads his or her partner's description, he or she thinks aloud about what makes the description effective or not. The partner records places in the description that the reader finds confusing or thinks could benefit from more detail or information.

Extending the Strategy

The strategy can be used with different genres: procedural text, summaries, narratives, and persuasive writing. For example, after students write the steps for procedures or recipes, they can use STEP with their peers who wrote similar texts. As readers, students can attempt to follow the steps of the procedures and note where they were confused or needed more information. Next they can use what they learned to improve their own procedures. Similarly, after students write persuasive letters, they can use STEP. As readers, students can think about whether or not their peers' writing persuaded them or not. This works well when the writing topics are controversial so that peers have different opinions (for example, which book, city, team, movie, pet, or food is better). When students have different opinions, they learn about including counterarguments and rebuttals. Peers can provide suggestions about what would make the writing more persuasive.

EVIDENCE CONNECTIONS

Englert, C. S., Mariage, T. V., Dunsmore, K. (2006). Tenets of sociocultural theory in writing instruction research. In C. A. MacArthur, S. Graham, & J. Fitzgerald (Eds.), *Handbook of writing research* (pp. 208–221). New York: Guilford Press.
Englert, Mariage, and Dunsmore outline three tenets of sociocultural theory that underlie instruction designed to facilitate writers' development: sociocognitive apprenticeships, procedural facilitators and tools, and participation in communities of practice. The STEP into the Shoes of a Reader strategy allows teachers and students to create a classroom environment that embodies these tenets. Sociocognitive apprenticeships involve social interaction (students' observing expert writers modeling their thinking, or students' engaging in problem-centered conversations around text with teachers or peers) as a way to acquire cognitive processes. Englert and colleagues assert that collaboration, whether among teacher and students or students and other students, is the ''heart'' (p. 211) of writing development. Procedural facilitators and tools, including teacher-designed prompts, graphic organizers, mnemonics, and writing strategies, scaffold students' use of higher-level mental functions. Over time these external tools become internalized and alter students' thinking as they develop into more expert writers. Communities of practice are groups of students engaging in authentic, text-centered discussions. These groups give students practice negotiating, conversing about text, reflecting, and providing feedback. When writing pieces become tools for thinking and reflection, students are more likely to develop higher-order thinking and critical literacy.

Holliway, R. D., & McCutchen, D. (2004). Audience perspective in young writers' composing and revising. In L. Allal, L. Chanquoy, P. Largy (Eds.), *Revision: Cognitive and instructional processes* (pp. 157–170). Kluwer Academic.
Several studies provide evidence that when students have opportunities to become readers under structured conditions, they learn more about audience needs and are subsequently able to revise their writing to improve its overall quality. Holliway and McCutchen found that elementary-age students revised their descriptive writing to improve its overall quality and level of detail after they participated in a special reading activity. Specifically, students read descriptions of tangram figures and tried to match the written descriptions to the correct figures from a set of four. After students

formed a match, they learned if the match was correct. Through this activity, students learned the characteristics that made descriptions effective, and they were able to apply this information to improve their own descriptive writing.

REFERENCES

Graham, S., & Perin, D. (2007). *Writing next: Effective strategies to improve writing of adolescents in middle and high schools* (Carnegie Corporation Report). Washington, DC: Alliance for Excellent Education.

McCutchen, D. (2006). Cognitive factors in the development of children's writing. In C. A. MacArthur, S. Graham, & J. Fitzgerald (Eds.), *Handbook of writing research* (pp. 115–130). New York: Guilford Press.

Nystrand, M. (2006). The social and historical context for writing research. In C. A. MacArthur, S. Graham, & J. Fitzgerald (Eds.), *Handbook of writing research* (pp. 11–27). New York: Guilford Press.

Prior, P. (2006). A sociocultural theory of writing. In C. A. MacArthur, S. Graham, & J. Fitzgerald (Eds.), *Handbook of writing research* (pp. 54–66). New York: Guilford Press.

Spandel, V. (2008). *Creating young writers: Using the six traits to enrich writing process in primary classrooms.* New York: Pearson.

Vygotsky, L. (1978). *Mind in society: The development of higher psychological processes* (M. Cole, Trans.). Cambridge, MA: Harvard University Press.

Section V

Comprehensive Strategies

The chapters in Section Five offer strategies that guide students through several writing processes. Please refer to the introductions to Sections Two, Three, and Four for descriptions of inventing, drafting, and polishing.

The four chapters in Section Five provide K–3 students with comprehensive plans to help them move through phases of the writing process from beginning to end. Chapter Twenty-Four, Making Pictures, encourages students to use images to plan, write, and edit stories. Chapter Twenty-Five, Comprehensive, Step-by-Step Composing for Nonfiction Writing, provides a format students can follow independently to improve their abilities to plan, organize, write, revise, and edit their nonfiction compositions. Chapter Twenty-Six, Mentoring Authors' Voices Through Readers' Theater, helps students learn to recognize voice in others' writing and develop a sense of voice in their own writing through the scaffolded development of Readers' Theater scripts. Finally, Chapter Twenty-Seven, Think Back, Look Forward, encourages students to self-analyze their strengths as writers and to set goals for improvement. The strategy is a recursive process to which students return as they begin and end writing projects.

Chapter 24

Making Pictures

GAIL VERDI AND SUSAN POLIRSTOK

This strategy encourages students to use imagery and drawings to help them plan, write, and edit their stories.

Why This Strategy Is Important

Primary students love to draw and to tell stories about pictures. Therefore, the strategy we call Making Pictures mirrors primary students' natural tendency to use visual imagery when they write. As they practice this strategy over time, young authors internalize both the concepts presented in the stories (friendship, families) and how stories are structured (beginning, middle, and end). Similarly, using imagery helps primary students write rich, descriptive narratives. By reflecting on the process, they develop metacognitive awareness of how the strategy can facilitate successful completion of writing tasks (Zakin, 2007).

As teachers of students with linguistic, cognitive, and other special needs, we view the use of scaffolding and strategy instruction as an approach that promotes active learning in classrooms (Chamot, Barnhardt, Beard El-Dinary, & Robbins, 1999; Lerner & Johns, 2009). And as teacher educators, we integrate activities into our courses that help future and in-service teachers engage in strategy instruction that will enhance primary students' writing and empower them to develop strong writing voices. In the summer of 2009, we had the opportunity to demonstrate this strategy for teachers participating in the Kean University Writing Project, which is part of the National Writing Project. The lists, dialogue, and pictures included in this chapter represent the outcomes of that workshop.

The SCAMPER Model for Making Pictures
Survey and Assess

To begin, we **survey and assess** students' use of writing strategies. The first form of assessment we use with students at the primary level is a checklist (see Figure 24.1). This list includes specific behaviors students exhibit as they move toward becoming competent writers. By having this list available, teachers are able to note the "writerly behaviors" their students possess. These behaviors help define the writing phases, or developmental stages, students have achieved as young authors. For example, a student might begin the school year at the pre-emerging phase of writing, using scribbling or drawing to communicate. As the year progresses, this student may move closer to becoming a more fluent primary writer, using a distinct voice with language structures and word choices appropriate for his or her grade level (Spandel, 2008). This checklist also includes space for teachers to make anecdotal comments about their observations.

By using the checklist to assess student writing behaviors, we can identify which students would benefit from practicing the use of imagery to recall stories. The survey also helps us decide what types of scaffolding or adaptations we will use to support students with special needs. We begin this process by asking each student to tell us a story and then write it. While the young authors are at work, we observe them and review the traits and phases in the left-hand column of Figure 24.1. We stop and spend some time with N'Jinga, one of our brightest and most verbal students, and note the writerly behaviors she exhibits. She loves to talk and is able to describe events, but has trouble sequencing. In addition, when she tries to write down her story, she has control over letter formation and writes from left to right, but cannot write simple sentences. We make comments in the Anecdotal Notes column as we observe her at work. We determine that she is at the emerging writer phase, and we decide that N'Jinga would benefit from practicing the strategy for using imagery to recall stories. From our observations, this strategy works best with emerging writers like N'Jinga, because students at this phase can talk about the meaning of a text but might still have trouble with sequencing. However, it is also important to note that pre-emerging writers who are taught this strategy can listen to stories and begin to internalize story structure, whereas self-reliant and fluent writers can continue to practice this strategy as they read and write more complex texts (Fountas & Pinnell, 2006; McCarrier, Pinnell, & Fountas, 2000). What is most important is that the mini-lesson is challenging, but not beyond students' zones of proximal development (Bandura, 1986, 1997; Vygotsky, 1976, 1978). The second assessment, a post-writing reflection (see Figure 24.2), helps students evaluate their own writing by asking a series of questions. By engaging in conversations about these questions, students begin to understand how to talk about and think about their writing while teachers note their responses. Teachers can create a section of a student's portfolio to keep track of these notations in order to map the child's metacognitive thinking over time.

In primary classrooms, this is a challenge because we have to incorporate some pretty complex concepts about writing into a discourse style appropriate for young authors. Teachers who believe in a strategy approach to teaching writing need to instruct students in metacognitive skills that facilitate meaning making. We have therefore developed assessments for determining whether students in our classrooms are emerging writers who are just beginning to make marks on paper or experienced (primary) writers who are able to create clear messages through text and art (Spandel, 2008).

Writing Phases and Behaviors	Yes/No/Developing	Anecdotal Notes
Pre-Emerging Writer • Scribbles or draws • Shows interest in letters or words **Emerging Writer** • May recognize letters or words • Uses letter forms to label • Writes from left to right • Connects sounds and symbols • May be able to talk about the meaning of text **Post-Emerging Writer** • Experiments with invented spelling • Utilizes environmental print • Includes new vocabulary • Attempts to leave spaces between words • Can retell a story using sequence • Can create text a reader will understand **Novice Writer** • Includes vowels in some words • Writes simple sentences • Attempts to tells stories using details • Reads his or her own writing • Reads writing to revise • Uses connecting words like *first* **Self-Reliant Writer** • Connects oral language and writing • Uses writing for a variety of purposes • Attempts to plan and organize writing		

Figure 24.1 Phases of Writing Development and Behaviors for Picture Making

Writing Phases and Behaviors	Yes/No/Developing	Anecdotal Notes
• Creates writing to which readers can connect; shows a sense of audience • Writes multiple sentences • Begins using such story elements as sequenced events and character and setting descriptions when telling or retelling stories Fluent Writer • Tells or retells a story using story elements and includes a clear beginning, middle, and end • Has clear organization • Uses strategies like showing rather than telling by including dialogue and details • Writes independently • Revises writing • Edits writing by checking grammar and spelling • Writes in a variety of genres and styles		

Figure 24.1 Continued

Confer

After the assessment phase, we **confer** with students to help us develop a qualitative view of what students know about writing. Peregoy and Boyle (2008) encourage teachers to get to know their students before making decisions about instruction, especially when working with students with special needs and English language learners. We are often surprised at what students teach us about themselves as writers when we sit with them and talk about their experiences.

Name: _____ Date: _____

What pictures helped me tell my story?
What details are in my pictures?
What details are in my writing?
What words helped me tell my story?
Who are the most important people in the story?
What ideas do I have for writing/drawing my own story?

Figure 24.2 Post-Writing Reflection: Using Retelling as a Strategy for Rewriting and Recognizing Story Structure

According to Hancock (2007), it is important, when developing portraits of these learners, to ask students a variety of student-centered questions that will help with decision making in regard to their instruction. We revised the questions Hancock recommends to reflect the type of discourse level we believe is most appropriate for primary students in terms of their understanding of what writing means to them, the kinds of writing they observe people doing, and how they use writing. The revised questions include

- What is writing?
- Who do you see writing?
- What is writing for? Why do people write?
- What kinds of things do you write?
- How do you feel about writing?
- What kind of writer are you?
- What would you like to be able to write?

We understand that students may not be able to answer all of these questions. Student responses can be quite variable based on each student's level of sophistication and language development.

Assemble Materials

We **assemble materials.** Our materials include a story titled *And Tango Makes Three* (Richardson & Parnell, 2005), newsprint paper, crayons, markers, paints, and music. *And Tango Makes Three* has won both the ASPCA Henry Bergh Award (2005) and Bank Street Students' Book of the Year (2006). We chose this text because we believed it would fit into a thematic unit on families and because it provides an excellent model of story structure and vivid imagery. It has a clear beginning, middle, and end (plot). It is easy to determine where the story takes place (setting). Young authors can describe who and what the story is about (characters). The story has a message (theme). There is a problem that needs to be solved (conflict), and the characters find a way of solving the problem (solution). It is also important to note that this story models language functions and forms, including a highly descriptive text incorporating lots of adjectives and the use of present- and past-tense verbs to describe the action in the story.

Model

When we teach the Making Pictures strategy, we engage students in an interactive session. We play gentle, calming music and speak softly to help students focus on the strategy we **model.** We introduce the objectives and rationale for the lesson. We present these content, language, and strategy objectives (Chamot, 2009):

Content Objectives
- Recognizing and accepting that families are different
- Developing tolerance and empathy toward people who are different

Language Objectives
- Listening and recalling a story in preparation for retelling it
- Visualizing and rewriting the story in one's own words

Strategy Objectives

- Using mental imagery, or visualization, and drawing to recall a story
- Retelling a story orally and in writing through paraphrasing

We prepare for our initial reading of the story by gathering students in a circle. We model making mental images by telling a short story or nursery rhyme and then closing our eyes and sharing all the images we have about the story or rhyme. For example, we might tell the rhyme "Jack and Jill." Then, with our eyes closed, one of us says,

> *I saw green grass, a hill that was not too tall, two kids holding hands as they went up the hill, a well with a triangular top over it, a bucket or pail used to scoop up water from the well, and a large spoon to enable people to ladle water from the pail.*

Then we show students the front cover of *And Tango Makes Three,* and ask the following questions to help them activate their schemata, make predictions, and think about what they do to remember stories:

Gail: The title of the story is *And Tango Makes Three.* What do you think the story is about?
Lisa: Friends.
Cathy: A family.
Cara: Someone joining a family.
Gail: Oh, these are all good answers. When I read the story to you, we will find out if you were right. When I wanted to remember the rhyme "Jack and Jill," I made pictures of the rhyme in my mind. Now I was wondering, what might you do to remember this story? (We list students' comments on an overhead projector, chart paper, or an interactive whiteboard. Students' comments might include that they think about the people in the story, try to pay attention, make movies in their minds, write about it, or make pictures.)
These are all good strategies for remembering. Now I want you to close your eyes while I read the story the first time. (I read the whole book without showing pictures.) "In the middle of New York City there is a great big park called Central Park. Students love to play there. Best of all, it has its very own zoo. . . ." (After reading the complete book, I prompt them with a question.) What do you imagine the character or characters look like?

Mary: Silo and Roy wore baseball caps and bow ties.
Cara: The caretaker has a mustache.
John: Silo and Roy looked like all the other penguins.
Gail: What do you imagine the characters are doing? What do the scenes look like? (After students respond to the questions, we reveal the strategy.) To remember these parts of the story, you were using a learning strategy called Making Pictures. When you use imagery to recall a story, you are making pictures in your mind's eye. (Then we help students articulate why they use the strategy.) Why do you make pictures or use imagery?
Various Students: The picture in my head helps me remember the story; It's sort of

like watching TV; I live near a big park and I was thinking about the park when I was listening to the story.

Gail: (After the group answers, we summarize the strategy.) Your answers are all right! Yes, making pictures helps us remember what we hear, see, taste, read, or study. The clearer we make the image, the better we remember it.

Practice

To help students **practice** this strategy, we retell the story again. As we refocus on the strategy, one of us says, "As I tell you the story of *And Tango Makes Three,* practice using imagery or making pictures to remember what you hear. You can close your eyes while you listen." After reading the story, we ask, "What images or pictures do you have in your mind? Has anything changed now that you are making pictures in your mind?"

We note what students say on chart paper, and draw some of the images to demonstrate drawing as part of the strategy (see Figure 24.3).

Next we create groups of about three students. We direct them to fold large pieces of newsprint into the number of sections that reflect the various scenes and to draw (as teams) what they remember about the story. We usually try to group together students with different strengths. Sometimes a student with less communicative competence,

Figure 24.3 Gail Draws Families in the Central Park Zoo with Silo, Roy, and Tango

Figure 24.4 Making Pictures and Retelling *And Tango Makes Three*

for example, might be great at drawing. To evaluate whether students can successfully use this strategy, we ask the groups to write their versions of the story and to share them with the rest of the class. Cara and Richard made the picture in Figure 24.4 and retold the following story:

> *Central Park is in New York. It has a zoo and a merry-go-round. There are lots of different animal families. There is a penguin family with two boy penguins. Their names are Silo and Roy. They were sad and wanted a baby penguin like the other penguin families. The man gave them an egg. They lived happily ever after when Tango came. They are a happy family.*

Execute

In this phase of the SCAMPER model we work closely with students as they **execute** the strategy to plan, write, and edit stories. We work with individual students or small groups and remind them to make pictures in their heads or on paper as a comprehensive writing strategy. We make sure to work individually with students who need extra support.

Reflect

We have group members **reflect** about how the strategy helped them invent (plan), write, and edit their stories. To help guide their reflection, we ask,

''When you made pictures in your mind or drew pictures, did it help you imagine ideas for your story? In what way? What helped you the most, making images in your head or drawing pictures?''

"How did making pictures in your head or on paper help you think of ideas for your story? Share your ideas with your group or partner."

"How did making pictures in your head or on paper help you write your story?"

"How did making pictures in your head or on paper help you edit or fix your story?"

Students' reflections can range from drawing pictures to making detailed verbal comments. We often encourage students to reflect on this phase of the SCAMPER strategy as a think-pair-share activity, in which each student writes a reflection in his or her journal and shares the journal entry with a small group.

Adapting the Strategy

Adapting the Strategy for Emerging Writers

For emerging writers to understand what writing is, they need to be able to make the connection that a story someone tells can be written down to become a story in a book—in other words, that narrative text is really made up of words that someone spoke. Making this connection to text helps students see themselves as "makers of text." This concept is best facilitated by a language experience approach, in which students tell stories and we scribe for them. In our visualization strategy, students can draw pictures to recall the story *And Tango Makes Three*, and then dictate sentences to us to create a summary of their pictures. This process of dictating sentences about text is called creating a language experience story. The children are asked several times to take turns reading the dictated story the teacher has written down, with the teacher helping them pronounce some words they may not know. Once they have practiced reading this language experience story, we can then omit words from the story, asking students to supply the original word or words omitted or to substitute different words as long as the text continues to make sense and convey meaning. This vocabulary activity is referred to as a "cloze procedure"; it helps students recognize how words contribute to ideas, how ideas tell a story, and how they can use the context of a story to derive the meaning of words.

Adapting the Strategy for Writers Who Struggle

Students who struggle with writing often have difficulty with language processing and attentiveness. In fact, about 40 percent of the time, students with learning disabilities also have attention deficit disorder (Polirstok, 1999). Therefore, students who present with both learning disabilities and attention deficit disorder need to be engaged in the task, because their attention may quickly wane. One way we increase students' active involvement is to use echo reading and choral reading. For example, with the story *And Tango Makes Three*, we first ask some questions to activate students' schemata. Then we read the story completely. Following the first reading, we ask questions about the story. After the questions, we implement echo reading: we read two sentences, and students echo-read those sentences back until the whole story has been read again, with appropriate voice inflection to convey meaning. If students can hear the teacher and then hear themselves, the images we want them to visualize will be strengthened in their minds. We then transition to the visualization activity.

Adapting the Strategy for English Language Learners

For primary-grade students who are English language learners (ELLs), moving directly to drawing as a tool for prewriting and recall of a story may be too broad a leap from their first language systems. Given that it can take up to seven years for a child to become fully fluent in a new language and that language competency begins with acquisition of language as it relates to daily life contexts, being able to process an entire story and derive meaning from it may require lots of scaffolding and support depending upon where the student is in the acquisition process. Therefore, we adapt the Making Pictures strategy by using gestures or visual cues to model and prompt students to devise their own pictures. Similarly, using concrete objects to evoke the story can be an effective initial step in moving to a visualization process. Labeling the physical prompts in students' first languages and then in English will help them create pictures about a story. Once the physical prompts are in place, drawing the actual pictures then becomes the repetition, practice, and reinforcement that scaffold this strategy. As Brice, Miller, and Brice (2006) suggest, "Allow for code switching and code mixing behaviors to occur. Code switching, code mixing, and native language use have been shown to promote and accelerate English language learning" (p. 246).

Adapting the Strategy for Advanced Writers

This strategy is designed to allow all students, including ELLs, struggling writers, emerging writers, as well as advanced writers, to participate in making pictures and in retelling and writing stories. For advanced writers, the use of the Making Pictures provides numerous opportunities for enrichment and creative thinking. From an enrichment perspective, advanced students may be asked to provide more details in their drawings and to label the details to extend their vocabulary development. They could also be encouraged to develop alternate endings to the story, to draw them, and to pick one ending from these alternates that would be even more interesting than the actual ending of the story. Here the teacher can probe students to reveal what contributed to their thinking about particular alternate endings. In this way, advanced students can extend both their vocabulary and their ability to make inferences about the text.

Advanced writers can also have a more extensive role in class when the teacher uses cooperative learning groups. When students are asked to take on roles during group work (for example, leader, recorder, time keeper, presenter, artist), advanced students can become leaders and help guide the group through the practice activities. (For examples of group roles, see "Cooperative Group Roll Cards," n.d.). In addition, advanced students can work as partners with a less-able writer to help point out ideas about the characters or the plot that the student may have missed. This can be done with an oral explanation, a series of pictures, or a paragraph the students write together.

Extending the Strategy

We encourage students to use this strategy when they read literature throughout the year. Students can also employ imagery with other types of text. For example, young writers can view a television show and use visual imagery to recall and retell what happened, and indicate what they liked and didn't like about the outcome of the show. They can also use the Making Pictures strategy to contextualize new and unusual vocabulary words in a story. Once the teacher has read these words to them and they have discussed the meaning in the context of the story, the students' ability to include these words in the Making Pictures strategy and in their speaking vocabulary will be an indication that the words have been incorporated into their schemata.

EVIDENCE CONNECTIONS

Krashen, S. (2003). *Explorations in language acquisition and use.* Portsmouth, NH: Heinemann.

Krashen proposes that when learners feel anxious, their affect level or the affective filter is raised, resulting in missed opportunities for learning. Anxiety interferes or competes with a student's ability to focus attention, especially if the student perceives that he or she is not academically competent. The increased affect level functions as a defense against feelings of not being up to a given task. By providing students with strategies to help them engage and to be successful in class, their levels of anxiety decrease, the filter is subsequently lowered, and students have a better chance to participate fully. For visual learners, English language learners, and students with learning disabilities, the Making Pictures strategy is quite helpful in moving students beyond the defensive posture they often adopt to insulate themselves from a task.

Spandel, V. (2008). *Creating young writers: Using the six traits to enrich writing process in primary classrooms* (2nd ed.). Boston: Allyn & Bacon.

Spandel notes that organization for young writers may be as simple as linking picture writing (imagery) with text. She argues that drawing helps primary writers organize their thoughts, particularly at the early stages when they are learning how to group ideas together, tell plot elements in an order that makes sense, and coordinate picture writing with text.

REFERENCES

Bandura, A. (1986). *Social foundations of thought and action: A social cognitive theory.* Englewood Cliffs, NJ: Prentice Hall.

Bandura, A. (1997). *Self-efficacy: The exercise of control.* New York: Freeman.

Brice, A., Miller, K., & Brice, R. (2006). Language in the English as a second language and general education classrooms. *Communication Disorders Quarterly, 27,* 240–247.

Chamot, A. (2009). *The CALLA handbook.* New York: Pearson Longman.

Chamot, A., Barnhardt, S., Beard El-Dinary, P., & Robbins, J. (1999). *The learning strategies handbook.* New York: Pearson Longman.

Cooperative group role cards. (n.d.). *Read, write, think.* Retrieved December 2009, from www.readwritethink.org/lesson_images/lesson277/cooperative.pdf.

Fountas, I., & Pinnell, G. S. (2006). *Teaching for comprehension and fluency: Thinking, talking, and writing about reading: K–8.* Portsmouth, NH: Heinemann.

Hancock, M. (2007). *Language arts: Extending the possibilities.* Upper Saddle River, NJ: Pearson/Merrill/Prentice Hall.

Lerner, J., & Johns, B. (2009). *Learning disabilities and related mild disabilities: Characteristics, teaching strategies, and new directions* (11th ed.). Florence, KY: Wadsworth/Cengage Learning.

McCarrier, A., Pinnell, G. S., & Fountas, I. C. (2000). *Interactive writing: How language and literacy come together, K–2.* Portsmouth, NH: Heinemann.

Peregoy, S., & Boyle, O. (2008). *Reading, writing, and learning in ESL: A resource book for teaching K–12 English learners.* Boston: Allyn & Bacon.

Polirstok, S. (1999). The co-morbidity of attention deficit hyperactivity disorder: Co-occurrence with disorders of conduct, oppositional defiance, anxiety, somatization and learning disabilities. *Ciclo Evolutivo e Disabilità (International Journal of Life Span and Disability)*, *2*(1), 1–9.

Richardson, J., & Parnell, P. (2005). *And Tango makes three*. New York: Simon & Schuster.

Spandel, V. (2008). *Creating young writers: Using the six traits to enrich writing process in primary classrooms* (2nd ed). Boston: Allyn & Bacon.

Vygotsky, L. (1976). *Thought and language* (A. Kosulin, Ed. and Trans.). Cambridge, MA: Harvard University Press.

Vygotsky, L. (1978). *Mind in society: The development of higher psychological processes* (M. Cole, Trans.). Cambridge, MA: Harvard University Press.

Zakin, A. (2007). Metacognition and the use of inner speech in student thinking: A tool teachers can use. *Journal of Education and Human Development*, *1*(2), 1–14.

Chapter 25

Comprehensive, Step-by-Step Composing for Nonfiction Writing

JANET RICHARDS

This strategy provides a format students can follow independently to improve their abilities to plan, organize, write, revise, and edit their nonfiction compositions.

Why This Strategy Is Important

Many primary students can plan and write stories independently because they learn to read with fiction and are familiar with the basic elements in stories: characters, settings, problems, solutions, and encompassing themes. However, primary students have difficulty writing nonfiction compositions because they have limited exposure to this genre, which for the most part provides factual information.

A number of years ago as a beginning teacher, I recognized that most of my primary students had difficulties planning and writing nonfiction compositions independently. Developmentally they had not yet acquired a personal awareness of what steps to take to write a good expository composition (see Vygotsky, 1978, for a discussion of zones of proximal development). They had little experience with nonfiction writing because they learned to read mainly with fictional material rather than from content text. In addition, I did not know how to teach them to write nonfiction compositions. Therefore, my students did not plan their work, and began writing before they figured out what they knew and needed to know about a topic. They also did not understand how to group and categorize information to help them organize cohesive paragraphs. They were confused about the appropriate style and voice to use when they wrote to explain, describe, or convince. In addition, as they wrote they inserted "just thought of'' ideas out of place into inappropriate paragraphs. Equally serious, they did not recognize organizational inconsistencies in their final drafts. As a result, they made limited and inadequate revisions of their writing, assuming that the text was clear and readers would understand their intended meaning. In an effort to help my students I taught whole-class lessons devoted to writing nonfiction, and I also modeled my thinking for my students as I planned and created my own "explain," "describe," or "convince" manuscripts on chart paper or on the board. However, my lessons were all too often ineffective.

Because of my failure in teaching whole-class lessons on how to write nonfiction, I decided to help each student individually. You can imagine how quickly I learned the complexities of working one-on-one with twenty-five or more students who were in different stages of the nonfiction composing process. To solve my dilemma I devised a step-by-step, comprehensive inventing, drafting, and polishing strategy that I could model for my students, and that they could use as a guide as they wrote nonfiction texts independently. Now I am a literacy teacher educator who works each summer with graduate education majors as they tutor at-risk students in a literacy camp. We model the Comprehensive, Step-by-Step Composing for Nonfiction Writing strategy because it helps our primary students take charge of their writing when they want to explain, describe, or convince.

The SCAMPER Model for Comprehensive, Step-by-Step Composing for Nonfiction Writing

Survey and Assess

To **survey and assess** students' writing, I analyze their expository writing initiatives and observe students as they engage in nonfiction writing, which informs me about each student's need to learn and use the strategy. For example, does a student do any of the following?

- Brainstorm to discover what he or she knows about a topic (for example, by making a concept map)
- Determine what else he or she needs to know about a topic and determine where to find that information
- Write in the style and voice appropriate for nonfiction
- Organize paragraphs using the information in his or her concept map
- Revise and edit

Confer

Once I ascertain who needs to learn the strategy and their developmental readiness for learning the strategy, I gather a small group of students in order to **confer** with them. I tell them I notice they have difficulties with writing compositions that explain. We talk about the differences between fiction (characters, settings, problems, solutions, and encompassing themes) and nonfiction (mostly facts and information). Then I explain I will teach them a strategy to help them write nonfiction compositions independently.

Assemble Materials

I **assemble materials** that include a large chart, large sheets of paper, tape, and a black marker. I occasionally write on the board rather than on a chart. I also provide copies of the steps to the strategy for students to add to their Writing Strategies Journals.

Model

I **model** the strategy through these steps:

1. With the students' help, I develop a prewriting concept map on the chart, such as the concept map about horses shown in Figure 25.1. We jot down everything we know about horses. I also explain that we can find more information about horses by using the Internet, and by reading fiction and reference books about horses. (Go to www.thehorse.com/viewArticle.aspx?ID=5270 for an example of an online resource.)

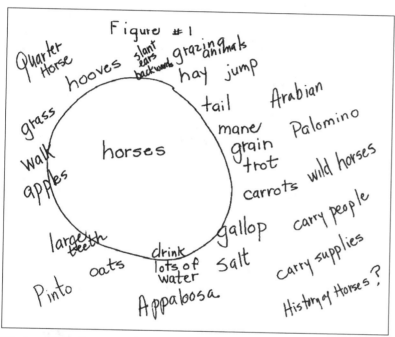

Figure 25.1 Concept Map About Horses

2. With the students' help, I categorize and label the concepts in the concept map (for example, breeds of horses, history of horses, horses' activities, what horses eat, and horses' physical attributes; see Figure 25.2). Students usually require considerable help with this step in the strategy because the content vocabulary might be unfamiliar to them, and students often have difficulty with categorizing information.

3. Then we talk about how we can organize the composition into an opening paragraph, subsequent informational paragraphs, and a closing paragraph, with the final order depending on what we think is a good way to order the informational paragraphs.

Students may decide the opening paragraph should tell why we decided to write about horses, or they may want the opening paragraph to describe what information the composition will provide. There are many ways to begin a nonfiction piece. Subsequent paragraphs equal the number of categories included in the concept map (for example, a paragraph each about the history of horses, breeds of horses, horses' physical attributes, horses' activities, and what horses eat), unless students decide to eliminate one of the categories (and therefore eliminate a paragraph). A closing paragraph might present a summary of the ideas in the composition.

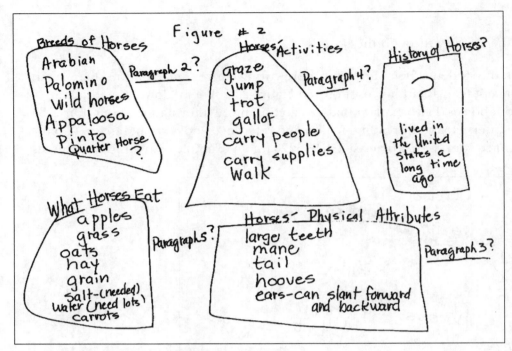

Figure 25.2 Categorized and Labeled Concepts

4. We then evaluate what we have so far. I ask students,

Do we know enough about horses to write a good composition? Is there sufficient information included in all of our clusters? Do we need to learn more about the history of horses? How can you tell? Where might we obtain more information?

At this point we may decide not to write about the history of horses because we have limited information about this topic, and because the history of horses is a broad and extensive topic that students might later develop as other pieces of nonfiction.

5. Because writers usually discover new or "just thought of" ideas as they write, I show students how to incorporate these new ideas into the appropriate categories of the concept map. I particularly emphasize that writers cannot add "just thought of" ideas into their drafts until they enter these ideas into the appropriate places in the categorized and labeled concept map (see Figure 25.2). Also, ideas that do not fit into any category should be saved for another piece of writing. In this way, students can consciously incorporate these new ideas into the appropriate categories on their maps before they include the ideas in the corresponding paragraphs in their compositions.

6. In this step I use large sheets of paper to model how to organize our nonfiction composition into an opening paragraph (an overview of the topic), subsequent paragraphs, and a closing paragraph (perhaps a summary of the ideas we presented—see Figure 25.3). We can move the sheets of paper around to determine in what order we wish to have our informational paragraphs.

Opening Paragraph

Overview of horses

Second Paragraph

Breeds of horses

Third Paragraph

Horses' physical attributes

Fourth Paragraph

Horses' activities (what horses do)

Fifth Paragraph

What horses eat

Closing Paragraph

Summary of the ideas presented

Figure 25.3 Organizing Our Nonfiction Composition

Because we deleted the history of horses, we now have four labeled clusters (breeds of horses, horses' physical attributes, horses' activities, and what horses eat). Thus we have four informational paragraphs plus an opening and closing paragraph.

Next we talk about our intended audience—such as peers, parents, extended family, teachers, and publications—and the importance of directing our writing to that audience.

Practice

In the **practice** step of the strategy, I scaffold students as they plan and write their own first drafts of nonfiction pieces. I help them make concept maps and categorize information. I also help them write and read through their first drafts and revise paragraph order or sentence structures. I assist them as they edit as well, showing them how they can delete redundancies; combine short, choppy sentences; and devise interesting clauses. Finally, we check spelling and punctuation. We also use a thesaurus and dictionary to vary vocabulary. I find that even students who are moving along at a nice pace in their writing development (I call them "writers in progress") need considerable practice with this comprehensive strategy before they can follow it independently. We therefore practice different parts of the strategy, such as categorizing and labeling concepts, writing opening paragraphs, and adding "just thought of" ideas to the appropriate categories in concept maps before students can execute the entire strategy on their own.

Execute

When students are able to **execute** this strategy independently, I rotate among groups or work with single students to assist them as they write. I also work one-on-one with struggling writers.

Reflect

Students like to join small-group discussions in which they **reflect** and talk about how a strategy works for them or what they find difficult about a strategy. The

Comprehensive, Step-by-Step Composing for Nonfiction Writing strategy is a comprehensive (inventing, drafting, and polishing) strategy, and therefore we talk considerably about students' concerns or accomplishments using different parts of the strategy. I also type and run off the steps to the strategy so that students can enter them into their Writing Strategies Journals for easy access whenever they need to use the strategy and for referral when we discuss and reflect on this strategy.

Adapting the Strategy

Adapting the Strategy for Emerging Writers

I have found that emerging writers can definitely benefit from engaging in the first two parts of this strategy. Although they may be budding writers, their cognitive abilities and background knowledge are usually commensurate with their ages and grade levels. They therefore enjoy brainstorming with me as I take their dictation and jot down their ideas and understandings about a content topic. We also work as a team to categorize the concepts in our first map into a paragraph-by-paragraph organizational scheme. As emerging writers hone their abilities to brainstorm and categorize content pertinent to a topic, I encourage them to work in pairs and use their Writing Strategies Journals to draw pictures of what they know about a topic. Drawing pictures also works for categorizing the information into a paragraph-by-paragraph format. Over the course of the school year, emerging writers gradually add the entire strategy to their repertoires.

Adapting the Strategy for Writers Who Struggle

Struggling writers need considerable scaffolding and support to be able to plan, organize, write, revise, and edit their independent nonfiction compositions. One idea I have found helpful for struggling writers is to have them each write with a buddy (an advanced writer) to compose one composition. I also meet often with struggling writers to review the components of the Comprehensive, Step-by-Step Composing for Nonfiction Writing strategy. In addition, I offer reading-writing connections by reading informational books aloud and sharing nonfiction picture books. In our read-aloud book conversations we talk about how authors of these books use and explain vocabulary, write cohesive paragraphs, and sequence sentences and paragraphs. I provide examples of some of these books in the following list:

Cannon, J. (1997). *Verdi*. New York: Harcourt.

Carle, E. (2000). *Does a Kangaroo Have a Mother Too?* New York: HarperCollins.

Ryan, P. (1988). *A Pinky Is a Baby Mouse and Other Baby Animal Names*. New York: Hyperion.

Waddell, M. (2002). *Owl Babies*. New York: Candlewick Press.

Adapting the Strategy for English Language Learners

I spend a considerable amount of time on this strategy with English language learners (ELLs). The prewriting or invention stage of the writing process is especially crucial for ELLs to experience success with nonfiction writing. First I help ELLs write their brainstorming ideas in their concept maps in complete sentences rather than as one or two words or phrases. Then I help students organize the sentences in their concept maps and use these visual organizers to provide the structure they need to write nonfiction. I also offer considerable assistance during the revision and editing stages of nonfiction writing because it is difficult for ELLs to find their writing mistakes in the English language. An editing and revision checklist is helpful for ELLs. For example, the checklist might include "Check noun-verb agreement (the cat runs; the cats run)." (Refer to Chapter Eighteen, Personal Editing Checklists, and Chapter Six, Noun Charts.)

Adapting the Strategy for Advanced Writers

Usually my students learn this strategy quickly when I model a nonfiction piece that explains something. Once advanced writing students have mastered this strategy, I encourage them to extend their nonfiction writing repertoires and move on to nonfiction writing in which they offer opinions, instruct, describe, or convince.

Extending the Strategy

Vocabulary that students use in their nonfiction writing is vocabulary they might not use in their everyday oral communication. Therefore, content vocabulary is often unusual for them. In order to reinforce vocabulary pertinent to nonfiction text, I help primary students enter new and unusual words (in complete sentences) in their personal dictionaries under the appropriate alphabet letters, with the target words highlighted or underlined. For example, a student might write on the "A" page of his or her dictionary, *An appaloosa horse is brown with white markings.* In addition to having students compile personal dictionaries, each week I ask students to supply a word for our weekly spelling tests that they have used in their nonfiction writing. We keep a listing of all of these content words in our large class dictionary for easy reference.

EVIDENCE CONNECTIONS

Cunningham, P., & Cunningham, J. (2010). *What really matters in writing: Research-based practices across the elementary curriculum.* Boston: Allyn & Bacon.
Cunningham and Cunningham state that one of the goals of writing instruction is to teach students how to produce nonfiction writing. They say that *nonfiction writing* (in other words, expository writing) is actually a broad term for different types of composing other than narrative (in other words, fiction). The authors point out the benefits of graphic organizers for young authors of nonfiction, and they provide writing scales for students to self-evaluate their nonfiction writing initiatives.

Moore-Hart, M. (2010). *Teaching writing in diverse classrooms K–8: Enhancing writing through literature, real-life experiences, and technology.* New York: Pearson.
Moore-Hart notes that students' voices appear in their nonfiction writing when teachers give them choices about writing topics. She also states that students need to learn how to write nonfiction texts through mini-lessons that focus on strategies they can apply as they write.

REFERENCE

Vygotsky, L. (1978). *Mind in society: The development of higher psychological processes* (M. Cole, Trans.). Cambridge, MA: Harvard University Press.

Chapter 26

Mentoring Authors' Voices Through Readers' Theater

TIMOTHY V. RASINSKI AND CHASE J. YOUNG

This strategy helps students learn to recognize voice in others' writing and develop a sense of voice in their own writing through the scaffolded development of Readers' Theater scripts based on high-quality literature. In this comprehensive strategy we employ modeling (using authentic literature to demonstrate the process of writing for students); making associations (story mapping); planning, checking, and monitoring (revising); and verbalizing (reading orally to check for voice).

Why This Strategy Is Important

The goal of enhancing voice in writing affects readers directly. Student writing should evoke emotions, such as sadness, surprise, anger, and joy, and should invite the reader to get to know the writer through written discourse. However, developing voice in writing is a critical writing trait that is often difficult for students to master (Culham, 2003).

Readers' Theater itself is an enjoyable, engaging, and effective reading strategy. The comprehensive writing strategy in this chapter is integrated into a Readers' Theater instruction routine, so students have the opportunity to practice and perform the scripts they develop with proper elocution, or prosody. By having students develop their scripts, we engage them in authentic writing and reading that is inherently motivating and requires an awareness of voice. Well-written children's literature provides an excellent and authentic model for writing that we want students to emulate. It has been our experience that students love developing their scripts based on good literature and then performing them with appropriate verbalization (in other words, stress, pause, and intonation) for an audience.

We have implemented this strategy with students as a vehicle for developing a corpus of Readers' Theater scripts for the classroom. Here is how Chase, a classroom teacher, describes how he came to use Readers' Theater:

First I told my students what to do. Then I yelled. Finally, I tried the yell-and-stomp-while-clapping method. It was then I noticed students were not listening. My hope for a strategic lesson on integrating voice into students' writing was not strategic, nor was the lesson "mini"—it was actually quite lengthy. I thought yelling louder and for longer periods might be the answer, but luckily, as I matured in my teaching, the concepts of modeling and the gradual release of responsibility to students alleviated my preaching to students about using good voice in their writing. I had spent far too much time telling them what to do, instead of showing them. When I began supplying mentor texts, pointing out instances of good use of voice, and then employing Readers' Theater scripts to bring the voice embedded in the texts to life, students were able to reproduce voice in their writing.

The SCAMPER Model for Mentoring Authors' Voices Through Readers' Theater

Survey and Assess

We find it particularly helpful to **survey and assess** students' writing, and we usually find that it reveals the absence of voice. Voice is absent when a reader cannot "hear" the personal voice of the writer; when students' writing lacks heart or personality. In particular, we look for examples in which the writing reflects the author's own style or "flavor"; in which the author connects with the reader; in which the writing "pulls" the reader into the story; in which the writer's thoughts and point of view are reflected; and even in which the language reflects the writer's age, culture, or background experiences. We consider these characteristics as evidence of the writer's voice showing through in the writing. The goal of this strategy is to produce writers who communicate their ideas with strong voice.

Confer

We **confer** with students to discuss the features and strategies of voice used by authors of selected children's literature, and the presence or absence of voice in the students' written work. We ask students to verbalize the texts—that is, read them out loud—to become aware of and "hear" the ways authors create and use voice in their writing. For example, exemplary authors of fiction write the way they talk. Authors use their voices to bring stories to life. If Dr. Seuss had tried to write like Shakespeare, the cat never would have even found the hat. Dr. Seuss, however, loved rhyme and rhythm. Readers are entertained when they can "hear" the voice of a passionate writer.

Throughout the day we find opportunities to point out student voice in everyday classroom discussions. This helps students become aware of their unique voices so they can begin to incorporate them into their writing.

Assemble Materials

We **assemble materials** that include examples of children's literature—in particular, relatively short stories—that contain evidence of voice and can be easily transformed into scripts. Some books we recommend include the following:

Brett, J. (1997). *The Hat*. New York: Putnam.

Brett, J. (2000). *Hedgie's Surprise*. New York: Penguin Group.

Carpenter, S. (1998). *The Three Billy Goats Gruff*. New York: HarperFestival.

Cronin, D. (2000). *Click, Clack, Moo: Cows That Type*. New York: Simon & Schuster.

Kellogg, S. (1987). *Chicken Little*. New York: HarperCollins.

Lester, H. (1990). *Tacky the Penguin*. New York: Sandpiper.

Lobel, A. (1970). *Frog and Toad Are Friends*. New York: HarperTrophy.

Martin, B. (1983). *Brown Bear, Brown Bear*. New York: Holt.

Schachner, J. (2003). *Skippyjon Jones*. New York: Scholastic Press.

Scieszka, J. (1992). *The Stinky Cheese Man and Other Fairly Stupid Tales*. New York: Penguin Putnam Books for Young Readers.

Seuss, D. (1960). *Green Eggs and Ham*. New York: Random House.

Tolstoy, A. (1969). *The Great Big Enormous Turnip*. New York: Watts.

Trivizas, E. (1993). *The Three Little Wolves and the Big Bad Pig*. New York: Scholastic Press.

Literature that includes dialogue among characters often adapts easily to script writing. Sources for scripts vary according to the mini-lesson's objective, but can include trade books, poems, Web sites, or magazines. We also gather chart paper, markers, paper, highlighters, and colored and regular pencils. Finally, we assemble photocopies of several texts to be used during the modeling and practice parts of this lesson.

Model

To **model** the Mentoring Authors' Voices Through Readers' Theater strategy, we guide students through the process of transforming literature into a script. We write interactively with students as we think aloud through the process of developing a Readers' Theater script with voice. Students tend to take the task very seriously, knowing they will later perform the script.

To walk you through the steps, we will use the book *Skippyjon Jones* by Judy Schachner (2003). We chose this story to model script writing with students because of its strong voice. As you will see, if you are not already familiar with the book, there are many playful rhymes that capture the main character's loveable traits. The book is full of clever expressions and innovative uses of language, making the story ideal for the development of voice in writing and prosody in reading.

As we read the book aloud and analyze it multiple times, students become familiar with the characters, settings, problems, and solutions in *Skippyjon Jones*. Students also read it independently or with partners.

Then we give each student a photocopy of the text, and we analyze the story for text structure and other features used by the author to evoke voice. For example, Schachner infuses songs, rhymes, and humorous interjections throughout Skippyjon's fictitious adventure. Using chart paper and markers, we work with students to develop a visual story map of the original text that can then be used in planning their scripted adaptation of the passage (see Figure 26.1).

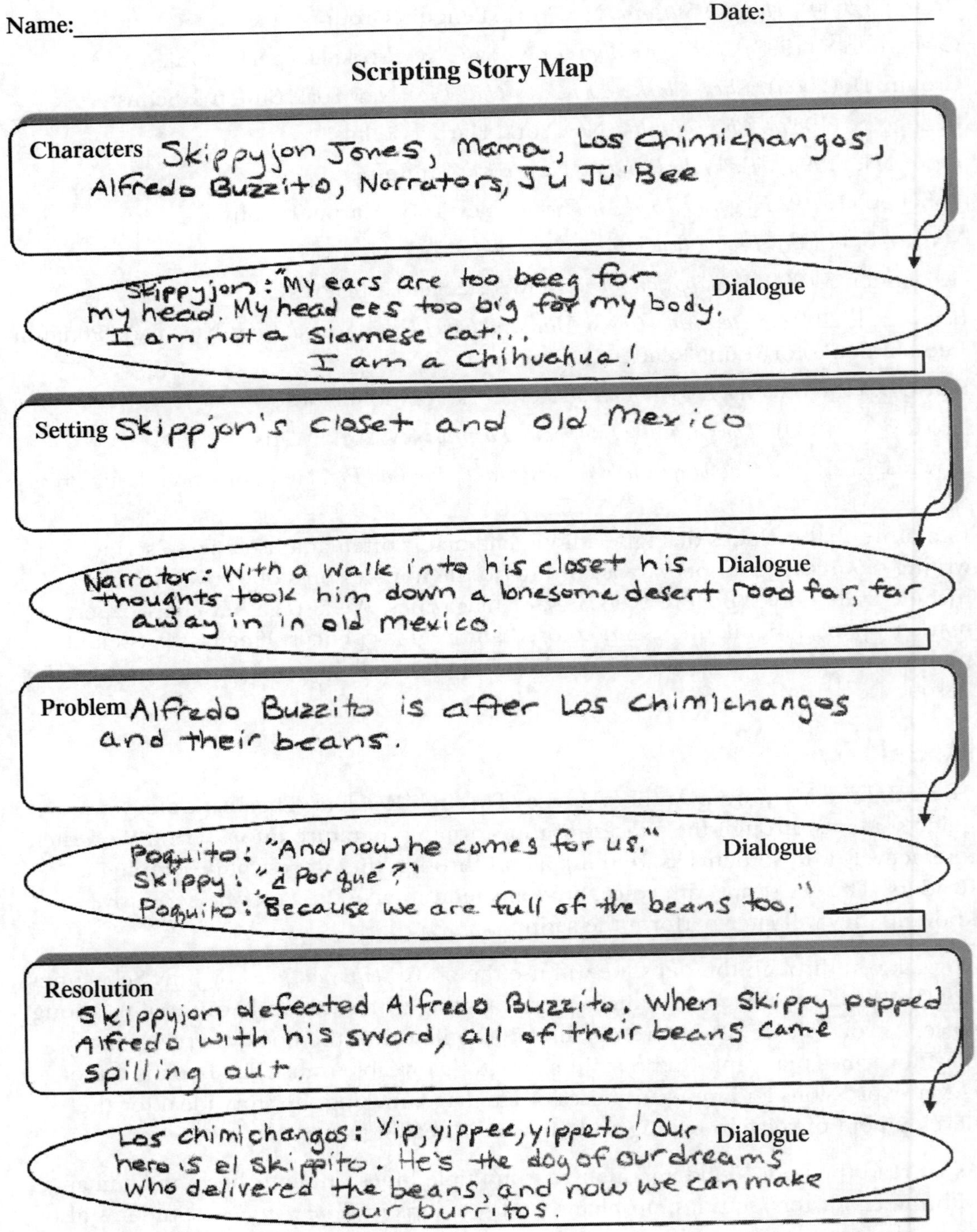

Name:_____ Date:_____

Scripting Story Map

Characters Skippyjon Jones, Mama, Los Chimichangos, Alfredo Buzzito, Narrators, Ju Ju Bee

Skippyjon: "My ears are too beeg for my head. My head ees too big for my body. I am not a Siamese cat... I am a Chihuahua! Dialogue

Setting Skippjon's closet and old Mexico

Narrator: With a walk into his closet his thoughts took him down a lonesome desert road far, far away in in old mexico. Dialogue

Problem Alfredo Buzzito is after Los Chimichangos and their beans.

Poquito: "And now he comes for us." Skippy: "¿Por qué?" Poquito: "Because we are full of the beans too." Dialogue

Resolution Skippyjon defeated Alfredo Buzzito. When Skippy popped Alfredo with his sword, all of their beans came spilling out.

Los chimichangos: Yip, yippee, yippeto! Our hero is el skippito. He's the dog of our dreams who delivered the beans, and now we can make our burritos. Dialogue

Figure 26.1 Scripting Story Map for *Skippyjon Jones*

Elements of our story map include setting, characters, problem, resolution, and dialogue elements that bring voice to the plot. A reproducible blank version of our story map appears in Figure 26.2. We have our students insert copies of this blank voice-highlighting story map into to their Writing Strategies Journals for use in their independent writing.

Name: _____ Date: _____

Scripting Story Map

Characters

Dialogue

Setting

Dialogue

Problem

Dialogue

Resolution

Dialogue

Figure 26.2 Reproducible Scripting Story Map

Through class discussion, we determine which characters to include in the script and the number of narrators needed. We model making notes and highlighting passages on our photocopies. For example, we might circle all of the characters we want to include. We also might highlight things a narrator might say or explain. For *Skippyjon Jones,* we determine a need for two narrators based on extensive narration by the author. Next we decide which episode or portion of the text to script. In this case, students choose to use the entire text. Then we think out loud to demonstrate the process of locating and highlighting quotations with strong voice that we want to use. We slowly include students in the process as we scaffold them toward independent, self-regulated writing.

Creating the script, dialogue, and narration is fairly easy. Depending on our students' writing abilities and needs, we may review story writing at this point. Other strategies in this book, such as those in Chapter Eight, Let's Tell a Story, or Chapter Seventeen, Act It Out to Discover the Details, might be helpful to include here as the story line is developed. Here is a portion of the script we created for *Skippyjon Jones.*

(Characters: Narrator 1 [N1], Narrator 2 [N2], Skippyjon Jones [Skippy], Ju Ju Bee, Don Diego, Poquito, Tito, Pintolito, Tia Mia, Rosalita, Junebug Jones [Mama])

N1: Every day Skippyjon woke up with the birds.

N2: This did not please his mother at all.

Mama: Get yourself down here right now, Mr. Kitten Britches. No self-respecting cat ever slept with a flock of birds, or ate worms, or flew, or did his laundry in Mrs. Doohiggy's birdbath.

N1: The lecture went on and on.

Mama: You've got to do some serious thinking, Mr. Fuzzypants, about just what it means to be a cat . . .

N2: . . . not a bird . . .

N1: . . . not a mouse . . .

N2: . . . or a grouse . . .

N1: . . . not a moose . . .

N2: . . . or a goose . . .

N2: . . . not a rat . . .

N1: . . . or a bat . . . .

Mama: You need to think about just what it means to be a Siamese cat. And stay out of your closet!

N1: . . . she added, closing the bedroom door.

N2: But once he was alone, Skippyjon Jones began to . . .

N1 & N2: . . . bounce, and bounce, and bounce . . .

N1: . . . on his big boy bed.

Skippy: Oh, I am Skippyjon Jones and I bounce on my bed. And, once or SIX times, I land on my head.

Finally, we ask several students to perform the script with us, modeling expressive, fluent reading to check for the author's voice. Through discussion of the script and voice, students begin to express and internalize how to write with voice.

Practice

At this point, we review the components of the strategy we used to write the script for *Skippyjon Jones*. Now that students are familiar with the process of script development, we give them the responsibility to **practice** the strategy to create their scripts independently.

To scaffold their writing as they work toward independence, we encourage students to work with partners or in groups. We select several children's books that we know lend themselves to script writing and allow students to choose from these titles. We provide the story maps and photocopied pages from the books to get them started. We stand by to guide them as needed as they are highlighting key dialogue exchanges that depict the authors' voices and parts they want their narrators to explain.

We listen as they verbalize the scripts throughout the process of drafting, helping them to revise and improve the presence of voice. As we collaborate with the students, we constantly ask where and how voice is represented or "heard" in their writing. We help them monitor how their readers or audience will interpret what they have written.

Execute

As students begin to **execute** this strategy independently, we rotate among partners or groups, providing feedback, modeling, and coaching as needed. Students who experience difficulty in writing are given more intensive and one-on-one support.

As students become more independent in their use of the strategy for script writing, we give them the choice of scripting literature; scripting responses to literature; creating expository scripts based on research; or scripting parodies of other scripts, literature, or poetry. The students, a teacher, or classroom volunteers then type the scripts, and students practice (verbalize). Once students draft and verbalize the scripts to check for voice and impact, they edit and revise their scripts. Students verbalize independently and perform for varying audiences.

Through ongoing practice with writing scripts, students ultimately and independently make every decision regarding script development. We facilitate student debates by encouraging them to take turns, respect ideas, and vote for their choices. The existing structure and content of the stories on which each script is based limit disagreements when students are working in groups and makes the tasks associated with this strategy relatively easy to perform independently as student proficiency in the process grows.

Reflect

Students intuitively **reflect** on their writing as they anticipate the impact of the performances on their audience. We make modifications to increase the entertainment value. After each performance we reflect with the students on their personal performances, especially their ability to create the voices of the characters; the impact of the script and the performance on the audience; the fidelity of the script in regard to the original story; and the creativity of the script writer or writers in editing and extending the original story. Script writers give suggestions to and ask for suggestions from other members of the class about how to improve their scripts.

Adapting the Strategy

Adapting the Strategy for Emerging Writers

We provide emerging writers with greater support in two ways. First, the stories on which the scripts are based should reflect the developmental levels of the students. Younger students can work with stories that are more familiar (for example, fairy- and folk tales) or stories that are simpler in nature, structure, and length (such as chapters from Lobel's *Frog and Toad Are Friends,* 1970).

Second, we provide greater support for emerging writers by extending the modeling portion of the learning process, and also by acting as scribe for students, taking their dictation and writing the script on chart paper or another form of display for the entire group of students to view and examine. The charted script can later be published in a more conventional format so each student can have her or his own copy of the script to practice.

Adapting the Strategy for Writers Who Struggle

We accommodate struggling writers with high-interest and developmentally appropriate material. We avoid difficult and overly complex material, because this may frustrate the already struggling learner. It is also important that the stories being adapted are high quality and match the students' interests. Allowing students to choose texts to transform into scripts from a limited list of books the teacher has preselected will enhance engagement. Still, the teacher needs to monitor student engagement and provide assistance and additional scaffolding where needed. In addition to directing struggling students toward appropriate books, the teacher can also help choose portions of books to adapt.

Adapting the Strategy for English Language Learners

Developing proficiency in writing and reading fluency are critical issues for English language learners (ELLs). Script development provides wonderful support for ELLs, because students have published stories as the basis or scaffolds for their writing. The rehearsal in anticipation of the ultimate performance provides ELLs with an authentic and motivational format, repeated readings, the goal of which is the making of meaning.

In addition, the development of vocabulary (word meanings) is a major concern for ELL students. Published stories that are the basis for the scripts, by their very nature, are filled with literary words that will expand students' vocabulary. As students are exposed to the stories, develop scripts based on the stories, and eventually practice and perform those scripts, they are given repeated exposure to words that authors use to make their stories more interesting. To provide additional focus on these words, we have students "harvest" words from the original stories and scripts and place the words on word walls; enter them into their word journals, defined and described; and use them in their oral and written language beyond the scripts they develop. In doing so, we are helping students use the reading and writing experience to grow their literary vocabulary.

Adapting the Strategy for Advanced Writers

We can easily adapt our writing strategy for advanced readers and writers. We do this by simply using more sophisticated stories as the basis for students' scripts. Moving from picture books to episodes and segments in chapter books provides students with more complex settings, characters, and plots, which they need to develop through the scripts. We also encourage our more advanced writers to take more risks in their script development—for example, adding characters, dialogue, and action that are not found in the original stories. We might also ask more advanced students to develop scripts that reflect prequels and sequels to the original stories.

Extending the Strategy

We reinforce the strategy over time through a Creative Response Workstation used throughout the year. In addition, we give students the option of creating Readers' Theater scripts to demonstrate and reinforce their knowledge in content areas or as the final products of a research assignment. For example, our students love developing (and practicing and performing) fictional dialogues between scientists who debate scientific theories and ideas, monologues that reflect critical decisions made by important figures from history, and fictional journal entries or letters written by famous and ordinary characters at significant junctures in history. When doing such tasks, students have less scaffolding available to them, but much more freedom to use their "creative juices" to make the voices of history and ideas heard.

Further, students love to turn silly poems into scripts and perform them. Visit www.gigglepoetry.com for humorous poems for kids. For examples of complete scripts, visit www.aaronshep.com/rt/RTE.html.

Other great Web resources for extending our strategy include

www.fictionteachers.com/classroomtheater/theater.html

www.readerstheatre.ecsd.net/collection.htm

www.readinglady.com

www.readingonline.org/electronic/elec_index.asp?HREF=carrick/index.html

www.teachingheart.net/readerstheater.htm

www.thebestclass.org/rtscripts.html

www.timelessteacherstuff.com

www.timrasinski.com

www.vtaide.com/png/theatre.htm

EVIDENCE CONNECTIONS

Worthy, J., & Prater, K. (2002). "I thought about it all night": Readers' Theater for reading fluency and motivation. *Reading Teacher*, *56*, 294–297.
Worthy and Prater make a convincing case for the use of Readers' Theater as an approach for improving students' reading fluency, a critical but often neglected goal of the reading curriculum, and at the same time for increasing students' motivation for reading. Students love to perform scripts for an audience, and the expectation of performing scripts gives students a natural reason for practicing the scripts to bring authentic voice to the characters therein.

Young, C., & Rasinski, T. (2009). Implementing Readers' Theater as an approach to classroom fluency instruction. *Reading Teacher*, *63*, 4–14.
Young and Rasinski demonstrate how Readers' Theater can be implemented in a primary-grade classroom. Moreover, the authors present evidence of the effectiveness

of Readers' Theater in improving students' reading proficiency. To develop the large corpus of scripts necessary for use in his classroom, Young had students transform familiar stories into scripts that could be practiced with voice and performed for classmates.

REFERENCES

Culham, R. (2003). *6+1 traits of writing: The complete guide.* New York: Scholastic Professional Books.

Lobel, A. (1970). *Frog and toad are friends.* New York: HarperTrophy.

Schachner, J. (2003). *Skippyjon Jones.* New York: Scholastic Press.

Chapter 27

Think Back, Look Forward

TRACY L. COSKIE AND M. MICHELLE HORNOF

This strategy encourages students to consider their strengths as writers and to set goals for improvement. It is a recursive process to which students return as they begin and end writing projects or units of study.

Why This Strategy Is Important

Teaching writers from primary through adult levels, we've seen the learning power that comes when writers develop a personal sense of what strategies they use and what they do well. Even more powerful is when writers know in what areas they need to improve. When writers reflect on their work on a regular basis, they gain more control over the writing process and often feel motivated to try new things (Schunk, 2003). We've also observed that when writers engage in this kind of metacognitive process, they are more able to take an active role in conferring with and learning from peers and teachers.

We have noticed how young writers often rush through the process, finishing one piece and then starting a new one moments later. They rarely think about why or how they are moving through and repeating the writing process. When we ask primary-level students to explain what they were writing about and whom they are writing for, they struggle to answer our questions. By asking these writers to slow down and think about the work they are doing as writers, we believe they become more purposeful as learners and more capable of talking about that learning with each other and their teachers. Although reflecting on and describing their work as writers can be a big challenge for primary students, who may still be developing the oral language skills or "mentalistic vocabulary" to communicate their thinking, they are still capable of practicing and developing such metacognitive strategies (Bereiter & Scardamalia, 1983; Desautel, 2009).

When we began using the Think Back, Look Forward strategy with young writers, an additional benefit became apparent. The writing process became more individualized for writers. Those who wanted to become better at planning spent more time in that part of the process, whereas those who wanted to remember to reread and "fix" their writing engaged in more revision and editing work. Because students could articulate their goals as writers, we were more able to meet students' needs in mini-lesson sessions and to differentiate our instruction in small groups and one-on-one conferences. For example, when many students in one class set goals related to stamina—"I want to write more" or "I want to write a longer story"—we incorporated sessions on stamina in the next unit of study to help these students reach their goals. This type of responsive instruction helps us in "maximizing the potential of each learner" (Tomlinson, 2003, p. 3). What's more, over the course of the year, students developed a sense of agency regarding what they were doing as learners (Johnston, 2004). Having this sense of agency provided a much-needed point of motivation for some of the writers who struggled more.

The SCAMPER Model for Think Back, Look Forward

Survey and Assess

Before we start the first unit of study at the beginning of the school year, we give students one to three days (depending on the grade level) in Writers' Workshop to each work on a piece (or pieces) of writing that will show us what they can do as writers. In addition to assessment of their process and their products, we use two tools that help us **survey and assess** students' self-assessment and goal setting. The first tool is a survey that we adapted from one that was designed for intermediate writers (Fountas & Pinnell, 2001). In addition to making it more primary focused, we added a question to begin getting information about students' ability to set goals (see Figure 27.1).

The second tool is a two-question reflection we have students complete after they finish their beginning-of-the-year pieces. The questions are

1. When you think about the work you did on this piece of writing, what are you most proud of? Why?
2. What would you like to learn how to do as a writer?

Students' responses to these questions provide us with an indication of how they refer to their work as writers. For example, do they focus on their final products? Do they talk about their processes? Are they aware of the effect their writing has on audiences? Their responses also help us see if students use goal-oriented language and whether that language is focused on their abilities or on what others think.

Confer

As we end the first unit of study, we **confer** with the small group of students we have selected that would benefit from learning this strategy. We follow up our assessment by engaging our small group of writers in talk about their strengths and goals as writers. As Anderson (2000) suggests, we keep our questions open-ended to foster students' ability to discuss their writing. We ask them, "How's your writing going today?" and "What are you trying to do?" The purpose of the questions is twofold. First, students' responses provide us with additional assessment information about what they know about themselves as writers and how they talk about that. Second, the conversations serve to "prime" students to begin thinking in this way before we even teach the mini-lesson. When asked these kinds of questions regularly and in an authentic way, "students can't help but see themselves as the kinds of people who ought to have the answers" (Ray, 2006, p. 59).

Name: _____ Date: _____

1. Are you a writer?

2. How do you feel about writing?

😊   ☹️

3. What do you like to write about?

4. Whom do you like to write for?

5. What is the best part of writing?

6. What is the hardest part of writing?

7. What do you want to learn about writing this year?

Figure 27.1 Beginning-of-the-Year Writer's Survey

After several minutes of conferring with students, we explain they are going to learn a new writing strategy that will help them advance their writing by thinking about their strengths and setting goals for improvement.

Assemble Materials

We **assemble materials** to ensure that the Think Back, Look Forward writing strategy mini-lesson goes smoothly. We ask students to bring pens and copies of their final pieces from the unit. At the carpet we have copies of the unit rubric on clipboards, and we make sure to have our own piece of writing. The rubric changes as we move through different units of study. For example, in this rubric the "seed story" row reflects our work to help students keep their writing focused or "zoomed in" rather than trying to write "watermelon" stories. Figure 27.2 provides an example of a personal narrative rubric we have used.

Students bring their clipboards and final pieces from the first unit of study. To create the Think Back, Look Forward poster during the reflection section of the mini-lesson, we use poster board or chart paper and 3-by-5 or 4-by-6 pink and green index cards.

Name: _____   Date: _____

		4	3	2	1
Independence	Getting Started and Generating Ideas	I used the strategies we learned in class to generate ideas. I got started right away and independently.	I used the strategies we learned in class to generate ideas. **Once in a while** the teacher had to remind me.	The teacher **often** needed to remind me to get started or to use the strategies to generate ideas.	I needed the teacher's support every day to get started or to generate ideas.
	Monitoring My Writing Process	I wrote at least twenty lines per day.	I wrote at least fifteen lines per day.	I wrote at least ten lines per day.	I wrote fewer than ten lines per day.
Content	Seed Story	I zoomed in on one small moment, starting with the first sentence.	I eventually zoomed in on one small moment.	I wrote a series of events.	I wrote a "watermelon" story.
Organization	Lead	I used action, dialogue, **and** setting in my lead to instantly hook the reader.	I used action, dialogue, **or** setting in my lead.	I have a "BLAH" lead, such as "One day I walked in the forest. . . ."	I did not try drafting a lead.
Conventions	Editing	I used **all of these** correctly: ❑ Capital letters at beginnings of sentences ❑ Ending punctuation ❑ Quotation marks I spelled **all** high-frequency words correctly.	I used **two** of these correctly: ❑ Capital letters at beginnings of sentences ❑ Ending punctuation ❑ Quotation marks I spelled **most** high-frequency words correctly.	I used **one** of these correctly: ❑ Capital letters at beginnings of sentences ❑ Ending punctuation ❑ Quotation marks I spelled **some** high-frequency words correctly.	❑ My piece is difficult to read because it lacks conventions. ❑ I forgot to put spaces between my words. ❑ I used a mix of capital letters and lowercase letters.

Figure 27.2 Personal Narrative Rubric

What do you like most about your piece? Why? _____

_____

_____

_____

_____

_____

What was the hardest part about writing this piece? _____

_____

_____

_____

_____

What is your <u>writing goal</u> to make your writing better next time? _____

_____

_____

_____

_____

Figure 27.2 Continued

Model

To **model** the strategy, we gather the small group of students together at the carpet. Following is a sample conversation we would use to begin modeling:

Michelle: You have all been working very hard in Writers' Workshop these past few weeks, and tomorrow we will be having our publishing celebration for the stories you wrote. I know you are looking forward to that! But before we do that, I want to teach you one more thing that writers do: they think back and they look forward. When writers finish a piece of writing, they think back about what they just did. They ask themselves some questions, like What did I do well? What did I work hard at? They also look forward and ask themselves, What do I want to do better as a writer? What do I want to learn next? . . . Why do you think writers do this?

Maria: They want to tell what they wrote.

Alex: Maybe so they can be better writers.

Michelle: That's right, they want to think back about what they did as writers and look forward so they can plan to be better writers. Let me show you what writers do when they think back and look forward.

Here is my story. You know I have been writing about the time when I accidentally hurt another player in soccer and how bad I felt.

Here is the rubric that I will use to help me look back at my writing. You have copies of the rubric on your clipboards. I am going to put the rubric here on the document camera so you can see what I am doing. I am going to start by covering up everything except the first row. I am going to read across the first row, and then I am going to circle the box I think best describes what I did as a writer in my story. This first row is about getting started and finding ideas. The first box says, "I used the strategies we learned in class to generate ideas. I got started right away and independently." Hmmm. Well, I used the strategies to come up with ideas, but I don't know if I got started right away. I'm going to read the next box. "I used the strategies we learned in class to generate ideas. Once in a while the teacher had to remind me." The next box says the same thing, except it says, "the teacher *often* needed to remind me." Hmmm. And the last one says that I needed "support every day to get started or to generate ideas." I think the box that best describes what I did is the one that says I used the strategies every day and once in a while needed to be reminded to get started. I'm going to circle that box right there. Think about the work you did on your stories and circle the box in the row that you think best describes what you did. Does anyone want to share?

Emma: It was really, really hard for me to start writing every day. I circled the box under number two.

Sean: I circled the box that says, "I used the strategies we learned in class. I got started right away," because I did.

We continue modeling and working through this self-assessment process with students until we complete the rubric and arrive at the reflection and goal-setting questions at the end.

Michelle: Now we have been thinking back as writers about the work that we have done. And sometimes writers ask themselves this question: What do I like most about what I did on this piece and why? This question asks me what I think I did well. One thing I can do is look at the rubric and see if there is something that I circled in the 4 or 3 column to indicate what I did well. I notice on my rubric that I did a good job on my lead, or beginning of the story. I am going to write: "I like my lead because I used action so that people would want to read my story." Remember, I said that writers also look forward and think about how they can do better. This question asks, "What is your writing goal to make your writing better next time?" I'm going to look on the rubric and see if there is something I did in the 3, 2, or 1 column that I could use to help me make a goal. Well, I said that once in a while I had to be reminded to work on my story, so I am going to make that my goal: "I am going to get started right away on my writing."

Think back and look forward about your writing. What will you say you like most about what you did on this piece and why? What will you say is your goal for making your writing better next time? Turn and tell a partner.

Practice

Now students get the opportunity to **practice** the strategy with our help. Michelle says,

> *Okay, writers, today we want you to reread what you circled on the rubric to see if you still think it is the best description of the work you did. If not, you can fix it. Then we want you to answer the Think Back and Look Forward questions at the bottom of the page. We are going to come around with a purple pen and circle the boxes we think best describe what you did. We can talk about that and about your Think Back and Look Forward sentences. If you know what you need to do, you can get started.*

If some students hesitate, we reteach enough for them to get started. Sometimes advanced primary writers will have trouble thinking about the Look Forward piece. They often are reluctant to recognize that they need to improve anything about their writing. We've found that asking them to think about things they are good at but want to get even better at helps them set goals.

Execute

Students **execute** the strategy while we confer with them about their self-assessments, their reflection, and their goal setting. We encourage students to use the strategy during their writing. They refer to their rubrics to help them remember what they need to do as they write. We take note of who needs the most support in being specific about what they have done well as writers and in setting goals for their next pieces.

Once students complete their statements, we hand them pink Think Back cards and green Look Forward cards on which they rewrite their statements in their best handwriting. Figure 27.3 shares two examples of students' responses to the Look Forward component.

Reflect

At the end of students' writing time we gather everyone back together. They bring their Think Back and Look Forward cards with them to the small group. Michelle says,

> *Today we have been using a strategy that many writers use. They think back and they look forward. I made this poster (she points to the poster) to help us **reflect** about our work and share and remember what we have learned as writers and what our goals are. At the top it says, "How Do Writers Improve?" and then this side says, "They think back at what they did well." The other side of the poster says, "…and look forward to new goals." Let's start by looking back. Each of you will bring your card to the front and read it. Then I am going to put it on the poster.*

Once we have all our strengths posted, we do the same with our goals. We reflect about the poster and give ourselves a big round of applause for thinking back and looking forward.

Think forward...what is your next writing goal?

Rite more evry Day.

Think forward...what is your next writing goal?

SLow down and Dont rush.

Figure 27.3 Two Examples of Student Goal Setting

As we begin the next unit, we incorporate the strengths and goals into our plans for lessons and into our conferences with students. Although we always include their names, we have found that it helps to put small pictures of each student next to their Think Back and Look Forward cards so that they can easily refer to the poster for reminders. Because this is a recursive strategy, we encourage students to use the Think Back, Look Forward strategy each time we begin and end a unit of study or whenever students finish a piece.

Adapting the Strategy

Adapting the Strategy for Emerging Writers

We believe that even emerging writers can benefit from the Think Back, Look Forward strategy. To support them, we often use a checklist (see Figure 27.4) rather than a rubric. Students circle or place an ecstatic face, smiley face, plain face, or frowning face next to each checklist statement.

During writing time we come around to talk about their checklists and to scribe a Think Back sentence for each student on his or her card. We might add an icon to help them "read" their own self-assessment. At the end of later units we begin adding the Look Forward element of goal setting.

Adapting the Strategy for Writers Who Struggle

Because it is so important that struggling writers maintain a positive attitude toward writing and see they are making progress, we work hard at helping these writers find appropriate and attainable goals. We review the identified goals frequently with struggling writers and make sure to teach strategies and skills that support them in meeting their goals. During conferences we try to use language that helps them see that their efforts and their use of the strategies we teach are helping them achieve as writers. When readers and writers attribute their successes and challenges to their efforts, they are more engaged and motivated as learners (Pressley, 2002).

Adapting the Strategy for English Language Learners

We often encourage English language learners to start with their first languages. If they have language buddies in class, they tell what they plan to write for their self-assessment and goals in their first languages. Then they try expressing their plans in English before writing. Sometimes students write their Think Back, Look Forward statements in their first languages, and we work with them to translate the statements into English.

Adapting the Strategy for Advanced Writers

Some students quickly learn to self-assess and set goals for their writing. To extend their thinking, we ask them to give examples or evidence of how they know they are good at particular elements of writing. We have them explain why the goals they chose are appropriate for them and how they plan to achieve those goals.

Name: _____ **Date:** _____

Rate your poem!

exceptional   good   so-so   needs improvement

My poem says something in a new and surprising way...
Explain.

blar creature spartly

My poem uses poetic words...........................
Explain.

I don't Now

My poem uses line breaks for a purpose..................
Explain.

to make the Ritham good

My poem has an important title..........................
Explain.

The title is about the pome

My poem uses repetition for a good reason...............
Explain.

I didn't want to Jous Repetiton for my pome

Figure 27.4 Sample Completed Checklist for Emerging Writers

Extending the Strategy

Because metacognitive activities like self-assessment and goal setting can be subject specific, we begin to have the same conversations and processes in reading once students have gone through a cycle or two in writing (Donovan, Bransford, & Pellegrino, 1999). We've found that students become interested in and naturally begin setting goals in other areas. Although they still need to develop the language to talk about their processes as readers and to learn to develop specific and relevant goals for reading, they can draw on their self-reflective experiences as writers to support their metacognitive work as readers.

EVIDENCE CONNECTIONS

Donovan, M. S., Bransford, J. D., & Pellegrino, J. W. (1999). Key findings. In M. S. Donovan, J. D. Bransford, & J. W. Pellegrino (Eds.), *How people learn: Bridging research and practice* (pp. 5–24). Washington, DC: National Academy Press.

In their synthesis of the research on human learning, the authors claim that one key finding relates to the role of metacognition in education. They say that taking a metacognitive approach "can help students learn to take control of their own learning by defining learning goals and monitoring their progress in achieving them" (p. 13). The research they reviewed showed that experts in a variety of areas were constantly monitoring their own understanding and recognized when they needed more information. The authors also highlight research that indicates that children can be taught to engage in this kind of monitoring, especially when teachers model and practice the strategies with children—providing scaffolds as they move toward independent use of the strategies. In order for transfer to occur, these strategies must be taught within the context of the subject the children are learning. Students must be taught to engage in self-assessment and goal setting in writing as well as in reading and other subject areas.

Marzano, R. J., Pickering, J., & Pollock, E. (2001). Setting objectives and providing feedback. In *Classroom instruction that works* (pp. 92–102). Alexandria, VA: Association for Supervision and Curriculum Development.

For this chapter, the authors reviewed the research on goal setting and feedback. One of the generalizations they drew from the research on goal setting is that "students should be encouraged to personalize the teacher's goals" (p. 94). Studies have shown that as long as teachers' goals are not too narrow, students can personalize them to meet their own needs and interests, and that when they do there is a positive effect on learning. A generalization the authors drew from the research on providing feedback is that "students can effectively provide some of their own feedback" (p. 99). It has been shown not only that students are capable of providing their own feedback but also that it is a feasible activity for the classroom. The authors note that although setting objectives and providing feedback are common practices in classrooms, they are "frequently underused in terms of their flexibility and power" (p. 102). By engaging the children themselves in self-assessment and goal setting, teachers can draw on a whole new dimension of these practices.

REFERENCES

Anderson, C. (2000). *How's it going? A practical guide to conferring with student writers*. Portsmouth, NH: Heinemann.

Bereiter, C., & Scardamalia, M. (1983). Child as co-investigator: Helping children gain insight into their own mental processes. In S. Paris, G. Olson, & H. Stevenson (Eds.), *Learning and motivation in the classroom* (pp. 61–82). Hillsdale, NJ: Erlbaum.

Desautel, D. (2009). Becoming a thinking thinker: Metacognition, self-reflection, and classroom practice. *Teachers College Record, 111*, 1997–2020.

Donovan, M. S., Bransford, J. D., & Pellegrino, J. W. (1999). Key findings. In M. S. Donovan, J. D. Bransford, & J. W. Pellegrino (Eds.), *How people learn: Bridging research and practice* (pp. 5–24). Washington, DC: National Academy Press.

Fountas, I. C., & Pinnell, G. S. (2001). *Guiding readers and writers (Grades 3–6): Teaching comprehension, genre, and content literacy.* Portsmouth, NH: Heinemann.

Johnston, P. H. (2004). *Choice words: How our language affects children's learning.* Portland, ME: Stenhouse.

Pressley, M. (2002). *Motivation and literacy.* In M. Pressley (Ed.), *Reading instruction that works: The case for balanced teaching* (2nd ed.). New York: Guilford Press.

Ray, K. W. (2006). What are you thinking? *Educational Leadership, 64*(2), 58–62.

Schunk, D. H. (2003). Self-efficacy for reading and writing: Influence of modeling, goal-setting, and self-evaluation. *Reading and Writing Quarterly, 19*(2), 159–172.

Tomlinson, C. A. (2003). *Fulfilling the promise of the differentiated classroom: Strategies and tools for responsive teaching.* Alexandria, VA: Association for Supervision and Curriculum Development.

About the Authors

Janet Richards, a former elementary teacher, is a professor of literacy in the Department of Childhood Education and Literacy Studies, College of Education at the University of South Florida, where she teaches graduate courses in reading and writing and qualitative methods. Her research interests include devising reading comprehension and writing strategies, and investigating changes in education majors' beliefs and cognitions. Richards is senior editor of the *Journal of Reading Education* and has published over 130 articles in scholarly journals. This is her eighth book.

Cindy Lassonde moved to teaching at the college level after over twenty years as a preschool and elementary teacher. For the majority of her career, she taught elementary language arts, and she especially enjoyed teaching children how to improve their writing. Currently she is an associate professor at the State University of New York College at Oneonta, teaching under-graduate and graduate literacy, early childhood, and special education courses. She was awarded the 2010 SUNY Chancellor's Award for Excellence in Teaching. As Editor of *Excelsior: Leadership in Teaching and Learning,* Lassonde enjoys working with researchers to polish their writing for publication. She has been published widely in professional journals, and this is her ninth book.

About the Contributors

Lori Czop Assaf is an associate professor in Literacy Education at Texas State University–San Marcos. She conducts research in writing instruction, teacher education, and literacy assessment. She is the director for the Central Texas Writing Project, a federally funded, professional development organization. Prior to getting her doctoral degree, Assaf was a reading specialist and classroom teacher for thirteen years in both elementary and middle school classrooms.

Ilene Christian is an associate professor and coordinator of the Graduate Reading Certificate Program in the Department of Teacher Development at St. Cloud State University. She currently serves as president of the Minnesota Reading Association. During her twenty-six years as a primary classroom teacher, Ilene promoted writing with her students and colleagues through classroom publishing, author events, children's literature, and professional development book clubs.

Tracy L. Coskie is an associate professor of literacy education in the Woodring College of Education at Western Washington University. She is a former classroom teacher and currently teaches reading and writing methods courses for the undergraduate and graduate programs. Her research interests include writing instruction and writing development, teacher learning, and content area literacy.

Joanne Durham has been a teacher, reading specialist, literacy staff developer, and Reading Recovery Site coordinator, and is a reading and language arts supervisor in Prince George's County Public Schools, Maryland, where she currently coordinates reading comprehension and writing workshop projects with a focus on Title I schools. She also teaches writing courses at Trinity University in Washington, DC. She has published her poetry in *Language Arts* and the *Journal of Reading Recovery*, and articles about teaching in the *Reading Teacher* and other publications.

Joyce C. Fine, associate professor of reading and language arts at Florida International University, is the program leader for reading education and teaches undergraduate and graduate courses. She has worked in school settings with teachers and students to develop reading and writing for diverse populations of students. She has published chapters in *Alternatives to Grading Student Writing,* edited by Stephen Tchudi (National Council of Teachers of English, 1997); *Scaffolding Literacy Instruction: Strategies for K–4 Classrooms,* edited by Adrian Rodgers and Emily M. Rodgers (Heinemann, 2004); and *Literacy Tutoring That Works: A Look at Successful In-School, After-School, and Summer Programs* (with Lynne Miller) edited by Janet C. Richards and Cynthia A. Lassonde (International Reading Association, 2009), as well as numerous articles in various professional journals.

Eva Garin is currently an associate professor of education at Bowie State University in Maryland, where she teaches graduate and undergraduate courses in reading and coordinates the Professional Development Schools. Her current research interests are in literacy; professional development; and teacher inquiry, including action research and inquiry groups that focus on literacy. She holds an M.Ed. from the Pennsylvania State University and an Ed.D. from the University of Maryland.

Steve Graham is the Currey Ingram Professor of Special Education and Literacy at Vanderbilt University in Nashville, Tennessee. His research interests include learning disabilities, writing instruction and writing development, and the growth of self-regulation. Graham is the editor of *Exceptional Children* and coeditor of *Handbook of Writing Research* (Guilford Press, 2006) and *Handbook of Learning Disabilities* (Guilford Press, 2003). He is coauthor of *Writing Better* (Brooks, 2005) and *Making the Writing Process Work* (Brookline Books, 1999).

Deborah Guidry, a writer for most of her life, graduated from the University of Texas at Austin in 2001, where she majored in English and received a minor in secondary education. She taught sixth grade at Northside Independent School District for five years, then worked toward her master's degree in English language and literature at St. Mary's University in San Antonio. Her coursework will be completed by December of 2009, and she is currently the English department coordinator at Sul Ross Middle School, where she is delighted to continue teaching her passion: literature and writing.

Jane Hansen, a professor at the University of Virginia who started to study children as writer-readers in 1981, morphed her research into the study of writer-readers as self-evaluators, and now researches students as writers across the curriculum. In her articles and books she writes in detail about what writers do in the natural settings of classrooms designed to promote their engagement.

M. Michelle Hornof has fifteen years of teaching experience that include positions as classroom teacher, reading specialist, English language learner teacher in the Peace Corps, adjunct lecturer at Western Washington University, and literacy consultant. She currently teaches in the Bellingham Public Schools in Washington. She received her M.A. in curriculum and instruction from Teachers College at Columbia University, and taught in New York City schools for five years, where she was fortunate to be mentored by Columbia University Reading and Writing Project staff. She recently celebrated earning National Board Certification in literacy.

Anne Marie Juola-Rushton, a primary educator and adjunct professor at University of South Florida–Sarasota, brings fifteen-plus years of teaching and literacy leadership experience to her knowledge of writing. As a literacy advocate, she presents her research nationally and internationally. She is enthusiastic about sharing her knowledge of the writing process and its application to designing and delivering comprehensive learning engagements in optimal learning environments. In addition to holding an M.S. in reading and a Ph.D. in curriculum and instruction with a focus on childhood education and brain research, Anne has recently completed her National Board Certification and continues to study with the Reading and Writing Project through Columbia University.

Susan Davis Lenski is a professor at Portland State University (PSU). Before becoming a professor, she taught for twenty years, working with children from kindergarten through high school. During her years as a teacher, Dr. Lenski was awarded the Nila Banton Smith Award from the International Reading Association (IRA) for integrating reading in content area classes, and she was on the IRA Board of Directors from 2004 to 2007. She currently teaches graduate reading and language arts courses at PSU. Her research interests focus on strategic reading, writing, and adolescent literacy.

She also conducts research on preparing teacher candidates. Dr. Lenski has published more than sixty articles and sixteen books, including *Improving Reading: Interventions, Strategies, and Resources* (Kendall Hunt, 2009) and *Reading Success for Struggling Adolescent Learners* (Guilford Press, 2008).

Cynthia B. Leung is an associate professor of literacy and childhood education at the University of South Florida St. Petersburg. Dr. Leung has extensive experience teaching writing at the college level through the University of Delaware Writing Center and English Language Institute. Changing her career focus to children's literacy development and teacher education, she has carried out classroom ethnographic research on young children's writing development and multimodal literacy. She currently teaches courses in early literacy, comprehension, literacy and technology, and literacy assessment, and works with graduate students in K–12 literacy practicum experiences. She has published articles in *Reading Psychology, Journal of Pragmatics, Canadian Modern Language Review, Asian Journal of English Language Teaching, Asia Pacific Journal of Language in Education*, and others.

Deborah G. Litt is an associate professor of education at Trinity Washington University in Washington, DC. Prior to teaching at the college level, she worked as an independent consultant, introducing Writers' Workshop to schools in the DC metropolitan area, and as a Reading Recovery teacher and reading specialist in Title I schools. Her current research interests are in the relationship between rapid automatic naming and reading difficulties, and in literacy teacher education.

Rochelle Matthews-Somerville is an assistant professor and coordinator of the Early Childhood and Special Education program, Bowie State University, where she joined the faculty in 2005. Dr. Matthews-Somerville's primary research interests are in the areas of the identification of motivational components of achievement in underperforming students, self-regulation in college students, effective strategy use in struggling students, and differential learning in online learning environments. Although most of her work has been based on the college level, Dr. Matthews-Somerville is still actively involved in clinically supporting teachers and students in the identification of strategies that maximize students' performance.

Neva Ann Medcalf is a professor of education and director of the Master of Arts in Reading program at St. Mary's University in San Antonio, Texas. She is the author of *Kidwatching in Josie's World: A Study of Children in Homelessness* (University Press of America, 2008) as well as numerous articles regarding the language development of children, the testing of young children, and the uses of technology in training future teachers.

Noreen S. Moore is an assistant professor of special education, language, and literacy at the College of New Jersey. Her current research interests are in K–12 writing strategies and instruction, writing and technology, and the vocabulary development of young children. She has presented her research at national and international literacy conferences. Her most recent publications include research on vocabulary instruction for preschool children.

Susan B. Neuman is a professor of educational studies at the University of Michigan specializing in early literacy development. Previously she served as the U.S. assistant secretary for elementary and secondary education. In her role as assistant secretary, she established the Reading First program and the Early Reading First program, and was responsible for all activities in Title I of the Elementary and Secondary Act. She has directed the Center for the Improvement of Early Reading Achievement (CIERA). Her research and teaching interests include early childhood policy, curriculum, and early reading instruction for pre-K through grade 3 children who live in poverty. She has written over one hundred articles, and authored and edited eleven books, including *Changing the Odds for Children at Risk* (Praeger, 2008); *Educating the Other America* (Brooks, 2008); as well as two volumes of *Handbook of Early Literacy Research* (Guilford Press, 2001, 2006).

Susan Polirstok is a dean of the College of Education and a professor of special education at Kean University in New Jersey. She taught language arts for special needs learners in the Bronx for eight years, and has also taught in-service and pre-service teachers in programs focusing on learning disabilities and attention deficit disorder at Lehman College of the City University of New York. While at Lehman College, she worked as acting dean of the Division of Education and professor of special education. Dr. Polirstok is the author of articles and book chapters on topics including peer tutoring, parent advocacy and training, social skill development, strategies for teaching students with learning disabilities, autism spectrum disorders, attention deficit hyperactivity disorder, self-monitoring, gentle teaching, and emotional intelligence. Dr. Polirstok is coeditor of *Language Disorders Versus Language Differences,* which will be published by Sage in late 2010.

Timothy V. Rasinski is a professor of curriculum and instruction in the Reading and Writing Center at Kent State University in Ohio. Tim is a member of the International Reading Hall of Fame. His major interests are in the development of reading fluency in students and in the writing materials that lend themselves to fluent reading and fluency instruction.

Todd Sundeen is an assistant professor at the University of Northern Colorado in the School of Special Education. The primary themes for his research are focused on written expression strategy instruction for students with diverse learning needs. He is specifically interested in the impact of explicit strategy instruction for students with mild and moderate disabilities who have difficulty planning and prewriting.

Frances Ramos Verbruggen is a literacy specialist with an interest in second language acquisition. She has taught reading at both the elementary and college levels, working with many English language learners. She has studied Spanish, French, and Dutch, and spent several years living in both France and Belgium. She is currently a doctoral student in curriculum and instruction at Portland State University, where her research focus is the development of language and literacy skills in English language learners.

Gail Verdi is an assistant professor of elementary and bilingual education at Kean University in New Jersey. Her research interests include literacy development, process writing, urban education, second language education, and the influence second languages and dialects have on student success. Dr. Verdi is a consultant for Kean University's Writing Project and is an executive board member of New Jersey Teachers of English to Speakers of Other Languages/Bilingual Education. She has published in *Language Learning* and the *Journal of Multicultural Discourses,* and has presented at the National

Council of Teachers of English Annual Convention and the Ethnography in Education Research Forum at the University of Pennsylvania.

Chase J. Young is an elementary reading specialist for McKinney Independent School District, and doctoral student at the University of North Texas. As a reading specialist, and previously a second-grade teacher, he has experience teaching writing and sharing his knowledge through professional development.

Acknowledgments

There are many people who have contributed to this book. We thank those who worked with us to refine their chapters. We also thank the many classroom teachers who invited authors into their classrooms to work with children and refine their writing strategies, such as Miranda Nelson, first-grade teacher at Ridgecrest Elementary School, Hyattsville, Maryland, and her first-grade students. Certainly, we appreciate the scholars who wrote chapters for the beginning section of the book. Their ideas helped to position the strategies within a scholarly foundation. We also are indebted to the people at Jossey-Bass who worked on this book with us. We especially appreciate the guidance and knowledge of Kate Bradford, our editor; Nana Twumasi, our editorial assistant; Francie Jones, our copyeditor; Pamela Berkman, our editorial production manager; Sophia Ho, our proofreader; and Michael Cook, our cover artist. Of course, we acknowledge our families for their love and support through everything.

Subject Index

nonrhyming poetry, 154–155; sample mini-lesson in, 37; to teach nouns, 77; to teach story features, 94, 132–133; to teach voice, 217

Assessing learners' needs, 24–25

Assessing Writers (Anderson), 35

Assessment, of struggling writers, 57–59, 64

Assigned topics, 40

Attention deficit disorder, 245

Attitude, positive, 275

Audience awareness, 223–234, 253

"Audience Perspective in Young Writers' Composing and Revising" (Holliway & McCutchen), 233–234

Authentic writing: considering audience in, 223; importance of, 15; in mini-lessons, 144

Author's Chair strategy: to add information to drafts, 146, 147; class guidelines for, 63f; description of, 62–63; for struggling writers, 62–63

B

Bank Street Students' Book of the Year Award, 241

Becoming Literate: The Construction of Inner Control (Clay), 128–129

Bed-to-bed stories, 174

"Best Practices in Implementing a Process Approach to Teaching Writing" (Pritchard & Honeycutt), 221

Beyond Reading and Writing: Inquiry, Curriculum, and Multiple Ways of Knowing (Berghoff et al.), 169

Board books, 125

Brainstorming, 103, 191, 194

Broadsides from the Other Orders (Hubbell), 10

Brown Bear, Brown Bear (Carle), 124

Brown Bear, Brown Bear (Martin), 259

Bubba the Cowboy Prince: A Fractured Texas Tale (Ketteman), 191

Buddy writing: description of, 60; for nonfiction writing, 254; for poetry, 83–90; for struggling writers, 60

C

Calvin and Hobbes cartoon (Watterson), 11, 12

Capitalization: in Color-Coding Editing strategy, 210–211; in Noun Charts strategy, 80; for struggling writers, 62

Caps for Sale (Slobodkina), 50

"Casey at Bat (Thayer), 206

Categorizing ideas, 251–252, 254

Centers, 206, 212

Chapter books, 191, 265

Characters: dialogue for, 136, 189–197, 199–206; for Readers' Theater, 262; strategies for teaching about, 135, 136, 137f, 139

Charts: to generate writing ideas, 107–114; to promote writing fluency, 124; to teach nouns, 76–81; for teaching grammar, 76

Checking and monitoring strategy, 22

Checklists, 35, 36; for editing, 181–187, 255; to plan compositions, 102; for rhymed versus unrhymed poetry, 155, 156; versus rubrics, 275, 276f; for struggling writers, 57, 61, 64; of writing behaviors, 238–240

Chicken Little (Kellogg), 259

The Child's Conception of the World (Piaget), 213

Choice Words (Johnston), 129

The Civil War (Burns), 10

Class books, 97–98

Classrooms That Work (Cunningham & Cunningham), 69–70

Click, Clack, Moo: Cows That Type (Cronin), 259

Closing paragraphs, 251, 252, 253f

Cloze activities, 245

Code mixing, 246

Code switching, 196, 246

Color words, 124–127, 128

Color-Coding Editing strategy, 209–213

"Color-Coding: Using Color as a Revision Tool" (Nitscheke), 213

Colored markers, 139

Comic books, 197

Comic Life software, 197

Common nouns, 80

Communities of practice, 233

Community of writers, 37

Comprehensive, Step-by-Step Composing for Nonfiction Writing strategy, 249–255

Computers, 215–216, 219

Concept maps, 251–252

Confer (C) component: for acting out stories, 174; to add dialogue, 191, 200–201; to add information to drafts, 143; for audience awareness, 225; to compose sentences, 118; for composition planning, 102; description of, 25; to edit writing, 210–211; to generate writing ideas, 109; for goal setting, 268–269; for nonfiction writing, 250; for poetry writing, 85; to promote writing fluency, 124; for rhyming versus nonrhyming poetry, 154; sample mini-lesson in, 35–37; to teach nouns, 76; to teach story features, 94, 132; to teach voice, 217, 258

Conferences, writing: adults' actions in, 48; to compose sentences, 120–121; evaluations and, 48; examples of, 17, 48–49; record keeping of, 35; with struggling writers, 59, 65; transcripts of, 178

Conferring with Primary Writers (Calkins et al.), 178

Conflict, of stories, 136, 137*f*

Cooperative learning groups, 246

Copying ideas, 41

Copying words, 165, 166, 168

Corduroy (Freeman), 133

Cover-copy-compare strategy, 61

Creating Young Writers: Using the Six Traits to Enrich the Writing Process in Primary Classrooms (Spandel), 247

Creative Response Workstation, 265

Cultures, of students, 113

D

Dandelion (Freeman), 37, 38

Deep processing, 140

Demonstration lessons, 144

Descriptive writing, 224–232

Detailed writing, 173–178

Diagramming sentences, 76

Dialogue, of characters, 136; charts for, 190, 192*f*, 193–194, 193*f*, 202–203; learning conventions for, 199–206; overuse of, 204; purpose of, 199; Readers' Theater and, 259; strategies for adding, 189–197

Dictation: to add dialogue, 205; to compose sentences, 120; for nonfiction writing, 254; for story retelling, 245; to teach story features, 97

Dictionaries, 80, 158, 221, 255

Direct dialogue, 199–206

Direct instruction, 68, 121, 131

Disabilities, students with, 245, 247

"The Discourse of Collaborative Creative Writing: Peer Collaboration as a Context for Mutual Inspiration" (Vass et al.), 89

Discussions, 254

Does a Kangaroo Have a Mother Too? (Carle), 254

Drafting strategies: in class guidelines, 63; to connect story features, 131–140; diversity in, 115, 116; examples of, 16–18; for struggling writers, 60–61, 65*t*; usefulness of, 115–116

Drama: to add dialogue, 193, 206; to develop details in writing, 173–178; developing scripts for, 257–266; effectiveness of, 173–174; to teach story features, 92, 97, 136

Dramatic props, 29

Drawing pictures: to add dialogue, 195; adding information and, 149; benefits of, 161, 247; to compose sentences, 118, 120; for detailed writing, 177; during free choice time, 162; to generate writing ideas, 112; importance of, 161; of nouns, 79; to plan compositions, 104, 105; role of, in emergent writers, 161; strategies to promote, 161–169; students' love for, 237; to teach story features, 97, 135*f*, 136; to write poems, 87; for writing process, 237–247

Dysgraphia, 205

E

Echo-reading, 245

Editing stations, 187, 212

"Editing Stations: Enhancing the Readability of Writing" (Crimi & Tompkins), 187

Editing writing: Color-Coding Editing strategy, 209–213; organization of, 61–62; personal checklists for, 181–187, 255; for struggling writers, 61–63; students' lack of knowledge of, 209; students' lack of motivation for, 209–210; zones of proximal development for, 182

"The Effect of Direct Instruction in Story Grammar Using Deep Processing on the Reading and Writing Achievement of Second Graders" (Fine), 140

Egocentric thinking, 213

Elaboration, 141–150, 173–178

"The Emergence of Visible Language: Interrelationships Between Drawing and Early Writing" (Dyson), 169

Emerging writers: Act It Out to Discover the Details strategy with, 177; Add Information strategy with, 149; Adding Dialogue to Fiction and Nonfiction strategy for, 195; Color-Coding Editing strategy for, 212; Comprehensive, Step-by-Step Composing for Nonfiction Writing strategy for, 254; description of, 2–3; editing needs of, 182; Following Conventions for Writing Dialogue strategy for, 205; Growing a Poem with Interview Buddies strategy for, 88; Interest Charts strategy for, 112; lack of rereading by, 117; Let's Tell a Story strategy for, 96–97; Making Pictures strategy for, 245; need for confidence in, 96–97; Noun Chart strategy for, 79; Personal Editing Checklists for, 186; Readers' Theater for, 264; Reread So You Know What to Write Next strategy, 120; To Rhyme or Not to Rhyme strategy for, 157; role of drawings in, 161; for STEP Into the Shoes of a Reader strategy, 232; Storyteller Blocks strategy for, 139; Think Back, Look Forward strategy for, 275; Think, Draw, Write, and Share strategy for, 167; Turning Up the Volume of Voice in Poetry strategy for, 220; Where Have I Seen That Word Before? strategy, 127; Writing Rockets and Other Graphic Organizers strategy for, 105

English language learners: Act It Out to Discover the Details strategy with, 177; Adding Dialogue to Fiction and Nonfiction strategy for, 196; Color-Coding Editing strategy for, 212; Comprehensive, Step-by-Step Composing for Nonfiction Writing strategy for, 254–255; evaluations of, 48; family support for, 99; Following Conventions for Writing Dialogue strategy for, 206; Growing a Poem with Interview Buddies strategy for, 88–89; Interest Charts strategy for, 112–113; Let's Tell a Story strategy for, 97; Making Pictures strategy for, 245–246; needs of, 3; Noun Chart strategy for, 77, 79–80; peer learning for, 113; Personal Editing Checklists for, 186–187; Readers' Theater for, 264; Reread So You Know What to Write Next strategy, 121; To Rhyme or Not to Rhyme strategy for, 157–158; small-group instruction for, 212; for STEP Into the Shoes of a Reader strategy, 232; Storyteller Blocks strategy for, 139; Think Back, Look Forward strategy for, 275; Think, Draw, Write, and Share strategy, 168; Turning Up the Volume of Voice in

Poetry strategy for, 220; Where Have I Seen That Word Before? strategy, 128; Writing Rockets and Other Graphic Organizers strategy for, 105

Evaluations: case studies of, 45–53; English language learners and, 48; examples of, 18; features of, 8, 46–53; foundation of, 46; importance of, 15–16, 53–54; methods of, 46; in SCAMPER model, 46; of struggling writers, 57, 64; validation through, 51–52

Execute (E) component: for acting out stories, 176; to add dialogue, 194–195, 204–205; to add information to drafts, 148; for audience awareness, 231; to compose sentences, 120; for composition planning, 104; description of, 27; to edit writing, 211; to generate writing ideas, 111; for goal setting, 273; of nonfiction writing, 253; for poetry writing, 87; to promote writing fluency, 127; of Readers' Theater, 263; for rhyming versus nonrhyming poetry, 155; sample mini-lesson in, 39; to teach nouns, 78; to teach story features, 95, 138; to teach voice, 219–220

Explicitness, 2, 68, 121

Explorations in Language Acquisition and Use (Krashen), 247

Expository writing. *See* Nonfiction writing

F

Families, as writing topics, 107–114

Fear Street (Stine), 9

Fears, regarding writing, 46, 247

Feedback, 62, 277

50 Literacy Strategies (Tompkins), 70

"Finding a Voice: Do Literary Forms Work Creatively in Teaching Poetry Writing?" (Wilson), 158

Fine-motor control, 128

First-Grade Writers: Units of Study to Help Students Plan, Organize, and Structure Their Ideas (Parsons), 42

Flashbacks, 139

Following Conventions for Writing Dialogue strategy, 199–206

Foreshadowing, 97–98

Formats: for dialogue, 202, 206; for nonfiction writing, 251–252; for poetry, 158

Free choice time, 162

Freewriting periods, 63–64

Frequently used words, 61

Frog and Toad Are Friends (Lobel), 259, 264

G

Games, 97

Gathering information, 10, 265

Generalizations, 15

Genres, 34

Gestures, 161, 246

Getting Grammar: 150 New Ways to Teach an Old Subject (Topping & Hoffman), 81

The Gingerbread Boy (Galdone), 134

The Giving Tree (Silverstein), 134

Goal setting: for editing, 183, 184, 185, 186; examples of, 18; strategies for, 267–277; of teachers versus students, 277

"Goldilocks and the Three Bears," 92, 97

Good Morning, Gorillas (Osborne), 191

Goosebumps (Stine), 9

Grammar: Color-Coding Editing strategy for, 212; graphic organizers for teaching, 76, 137*f*; importance of learning, 75; personal editing checklists for, 181–187; for struggling writers, 62, 67–68; using worksheets to teach, 75

Grandpa's Teeth (Clement), 133

Graphic organizers: benefits of using, 99; to develop students' voice, 217, 218*f*; for drafting, 115; to generate writing ideas, 107–114; for nonfiction writing, 251–252; to plan compositions, 99–106; to teach grammar, 76, 137*f*; to teach nouns, 76–81; to teach story features, 95, 96*f*, 97, 132–133, 134*f*, 135*f*

Graphs, 63–64

The Great Big Enormous Turnip (Tolstoy), 259

Green Eggs and Ham (Seuss), 259

Group discussions, 254

Group roles, 246

Growing a Poem with Interview Buddies strategy, 83–90

Growing Ideas mini-lesson, 34–40

H

Handwriting: dialogue writing and, 205; for struggling writers, 67–68, 128

Harry Potter series (Rowling), 9

The Hat (Brett), 259

Hedgie's Surprise (Brett), 259

Henry's Freedom Box (Levine), 191, 193

History lessons, 265

Hobbies, 108

Horrible Harry Moves Up to Third Grade (Kline), 191

How Writing Works: Imposing Organizational Structure Within the Writing Process (Houston), 106

Hunchback of Notre Dame (Hugo), 10

I

" 'I Thought About It All Night': Readers' Theater for Reading Fluency and Motivation" (Worthy & Prater), 265

Ideas, for writing: evaluations and, 47–51; Interest Charts strategy for, 107–114; mini-lessons for, 34–41; for poetry, 87; from struggling writers, 59–60; Think, Draw, Write, Share strategy for, 166, 168; Writing Rockets and Other Graphic Organizers strategy for, 102–105

If-then strategy, 40–41

Imagery, 237–247

Imagination, 107

Immigrants, 113

"Implementing Readers' Theater as an Approach to Classroom Fluency Instruction" (Young & Rasinski), 265–266

Indenting, 202

Indirect dialogue, 199–206

Influence of teachers, 49–50

Information gathering. *See* Gathering information

Inspiration software, 140

"Instruction in Self-Questioning as a Literacy Reading Strategy: An Exploration of Empirical Research" (Janssen), 89–90

Interactive writing, 60

Interactive Writing and Interactive Editing: Making Connections Between Writing and Reading (Swartz et al.), 70

Interactive Writing: How Language and Literacy Come Together (McCarrier et al.), 70

Interest Charts strategy, 107–114

Interview buddies, 83–90

Invented spelling, 162

Inventing, 73. *See also specific inventing strategies*

Ira Sleeps Over (Waber), 202

J

James Bond series (Fleming), 10

Journals: benefits of, 59; definition of, 59; freewriting in, 64; of struggling writers, 59, 64. *See also specific types*

K

Kean University Writing Project, 237

"Key Findings" (Donovan et al.), 277

Kidwatching, 210

Kinesthetic learning, 173–174, 177, 178

Knowledge-telling approach, 11

L

Language Experience Approach, 163, 245

Language fluency, 168, 246

Les Miserables (Hugo), 10

Let's Tell a Story strategy, 91–98

Letter recognition, 127

Letter-sound correspondence, 166, 168

Library area, of classroom, 34

Library of Congress, 10

. . . And With a Light Touch: Learning about Reading, Writing, and Teaching with First Graders (Avery), 150

Lilly's Purple Plastic Purse (Henkes), 191

Listening: to add dialogue, 197; as basis of evaluations, 46, 47; student guidelines for, 63*f*

Literacy Development in the Early Years: Helping Children Read and Write (Morrow), 140

Literature, engaging, 200, 257, 259

M

Magic School Bus Inside the Human Body (Cole & Degen), 191, 197

Magnetic letters, 61

Main characters, 136, 139

Main ideas, 103, 105, 147, 148

Making associations strategy, 21

Making Pictures strategy, 237–247

"Making RTI Work" (Renaissance Learning), 28

Manipulatives, 61

Matching activities, 224–225

Materials, assembling. *See* Assemble Materials component; Writing materials

Memories, 36, 38

Memorization: examples of, 18; of sentences, 117–118; for struggling students, 62

Mentoring, 35, 36

Mentoring Authors' Voices Through Readers' Theater strategy, 257–266

Mentoring texts: for adding dialogue, 190, 194, 195, 197; description of, 36, 37

"A Meta-analysis of Writing Instruction for Adolescent Students" (Graham & Perin), 113–114

Metacognition: acting out as, 178; assessment of, 238–240; as benefit of SCAMPER model, 29; motivation and, 267; role of, in education, 277; Think Back, Look Forward strategy for, 267–277; using portfolios to map, 238

Minds in Motion: A Kinesthetic Approach to Teaching Elementary Curriculum (Griss), 178

Mini-lessons: about imagery, 238; to add information to drafts, 142, 144; for adding dialogue, 190, 200; description of, 2, 23; for editing, 187; examples of, 34–40; for goal setting, 268–269; helpful tips for designing, 42; influence of teachers in, 49–50; objectives of, 35; to plan compositions, 102–105; purpose of, 34; for reinforcement of learning, 40–41; required number of, 14; on SCAMPER model, 24; for struggling writers, 69; to teach rhymed versus unrhymed poetry, 154–155; to teach story features, 92, 95–96, 97; to teach story planning, 104–105; to teach voice, 216–217; using students' writing in, 144; for writing fluency, 124

Minority students, 2

Mnemonics, 17, 22, 228

Modeling: for acting out stories, 175; to add dialogue, 193–194, 202–203; to add information to drafts, 144–145; for audience awareness, 228–231; benefits of, 13; to compose sentences, 118–119, 121; for composition planning, 102–103; to edit writing, 211; examples of, 18; to generate writing ideas, 109; of goal setting, 271–273; of nonfiction writing, 251–253; for poetry writing, 85, 87; of polishing strategies, 172; to promote writing fluency, 125–126; of rhyming versus nonrhyming poetry, 155; sample mini-lesson in, 37–38; in SCAMPER model, 26; of script creation for Readers' Theater, 259–262, 264; to teach nouns, 77; to teach story features, 94–95, 134–138; to teach voice, 217–219

153–159; strategies for writing, 83–90; students' resistance to writing, 83; value of writing, 83

Polishing strategies: benefits of, 172; importance of modeling, 172; skills required for, 171; for struggling writers, 61–63

Portfolios, 59, 238

Posters, 85, 86*f*, 89, 155, 164, 166

Practice (P) component: for acting out stories, 175–176; to add dialogue, 194, 204; to add information to drafts, 145–148; for audience awareness, 231; to compose sentences, 119–120; for composition planning, 103–104; description of, 26–27; to edit writing, 211; to generate writing ideas, 110–111; of goal setting, 273; of nonfiction writing, 253; for poetry writing, 87; to promote writing fluency, 126–127; of Readers' Theater, 263; for rhyming versus nonrhyming poetry, 155; sample mini-lesson in, 38–39; to teach nouns, 77–78; to teach story features, 95, 138; to teach voice, 219

Preoperational stage, of development, 209

Prepositional phrases, 75

Preprinted words, 128

Prequels, 265

Prewriting: definition of, 73; with English language learners, 105, 254–255; for nonfiction, 254–255; with struggling writers, 59, 65*t*

Prietita and the Ghost Woman (Anzaldúa), 191

Primary programs, 22–23

Primary students: benefits of invention strategies to, 73; teachers' goals for, 22–23; types of, 2–3

Primary trait rubrics, 225, 227*f*

Prince George's County Public Schools, 66

Prior knowledge, 73, 254

Problems, in stories, 136, 137*f*, 139

Procedural tools, 233

Procedural writing, 178

"Promoting Learning and Achievement Through Self-Assessment" (Andrade & Valtcheva), 158–159

Prompts, for writing, 113

Proofreading: Personal Editing Checklists strategy for, 181–187; for struggling writers, 61–63, 65*t*

Proper nouns, 80

Props, 29, 132

Proximity, teacher, 69, 132

Publishing, 62–63, 65*t*

Punctuation: in Color-Coding Editing strategy, 210–211; in dialogue, 195, 196–197, 199–206; for struggling writers, 62

Puppet shows, 97

Q

Questioning strategy: to add dialogue, 191, 200; examples of, 21; to generate writing ideas, 112; for observations of students' poetry, 154; to promote fluency, 127; to reflect on adding information, 148; for students' self-reflection, 241; to teach goal setting, 268; to teach story features, 95; to write poetry, 84–85, 87, 88*f*

Quotation marks, 196, 202, 203, 205

R

Read-alouds, 254, 258

Readers' Theater, 206, 257–266

Reading fluency, 265–266

Reading Recovery program, 117–118, 122

Reading with Meaning (Miller), 64

Reading workshops, 178

Recess Queen (O'Neill), 41

Record-keeping techniques: of conferences, 35; for retellings, 132; for writing ideas, 109

Reflect (R) component: for acting out stories, 176; to add dialogue, 195, 205; to add information to drafts, 148; for audience awareness, 232; to compose sentences, 120; for composition planning, 104–105; description of, 28; to edit writing, 211–212; to generate writing ideas, 111–112; for goal setting, 273–275; importance of, 40; of nonfiction writing, 253–254; phases of, 40; for poetry writing, 87; to promote writing fluency, 127; of Readers' Theater, 263; for rhyming versus nonrhyming poetry, 156; sample mini-lesson in, 40; for struggling writers, 66, 66*f*; to teach nouns, 78; to teach story features, 95–96, 138; to teach voice, 220

Renaissance Learning, 28

Repeated ideas, 41, 143

Reread So You Know What to Write Next strategy, 117–122

Research. *See* Gathering information

students' practice of, 38–39; in well-design programs, 56. *See also* Strategic writing; *specific strategies*

Writing Strategies Journal: for adding dialogue, 194, 195, 205; description of, 27; for nonfiction writing, 254; to record writing ideas, 109; for students' drawings, 163, 165, 166; to teach nouns, 77–78; to teach story features, 133, 138

Writing Strategies Notebook: to add dialogue, 194–195; description of, 25; for record keeping, 35, 36; to record students' editing, 210; in SCAMPER model, 24–25

Z

Zen and the Art of Motorcycle Maintenance (Pirsig), 10

Zones of proximal development: audience awareness and, 224; benefits of SCAMPER model and, 24; definition of, 98; for editing, 182, 210; imagery and, 238; of struggling writers, 55; for teaching story features, 95, 132

Name Index

A

Alexander, P., 11, 12
Allington, R., 69
Anderson, C., 35, 268
Andrade, H., 158–159
Anzaldúa, G., 191
Arredondo, D. E., 140
Assaf, L. C., 189
Atwell, N., 2, 17
Avery, C., 150

B

Bandura, A., 238
Barnhardt, S., 237
Baumann, J. F., 125
Beard El-Dinary, P., 237
Beckman, P., 21, 22, 23
Benchley, R., 9
Bereiter, C., 11, 13, 89, 106, 267
Berghoff, B., 169
Bernabei, G., 196
Bhavnagri, N., 92, 95, 97
Biancarosa, G., 1
Biemiller, A., 114
Bloom, B., 191
Bodrova, E., 95, 98
Boldt, G. M., 145
Bos, C. S., 62
Boulay, B., 158–159
Boyle, O., 240
Bradbury, R., 9
Bransford, J. D., 277
Bredekamp, S., 92
Brett, J., 259
Brice, A., 246
Brice, R., 246
Bruner, J. S., 26, 131
Burke, C., 142
Burnham, S., 10
Burns, K., 10
Buss, K., 107

C

Calkins, L., 34, 35, 143, 174,
    178, 190
Callella, T., 61
Cannon, J., 254
Capote, T., 10
Cappelli, R., 128
Cappello, M., 148
Carle, E., 124, 133, 254
Carpenter, S., 259
Carroll, J. A., 204, 207
Carver, R., 10
Cazden, C., 122
Cecil, N. L., 127
Chamot, A., 237, 241

Chard, D., 69
Chard, S., 92
Christian, I., 123
Clay, M., 118, 122, 128–129
Clement, R., 133
Cline, D. B., 92
Cohan, G. M., 10
Cole, J., 191, 197
Collins, J., 2
Collins, M., 21
Copple, C., 92
Coskie, T. L., 267
Cowley, M., 10
Creech, N., 92, 95, 97
Crimi, F., 182, 187, 209, 212
Cronin, D., 259
Culham, R., 257
Cummins, J., 196
Cunningham, J., 75, 181, 182,
    255
Cunningham, P., 69, 75, 181,
    182, 255
Cutler, L., 13

D

Danoff, B., 16
Darigan, D., 84
Davis, J., 182
Davis, R., 48
Deford D. E., 122
Degen, B., 191, 197
Delpit, L., 2
Desautel, D., 267
Dillon, J. T., 89
Donovan, M. S., 277
Dorfman, L. R., 128
Dorr, R., 163
Drucker, M. J., 177
Du, Y., 158–159
Dunsmore, K., 233
Durham, J., 173
Dutro, E., 47
Dyson, A. H., 3, 161, 169

E

Eco, U., 10
Egawa, K. A., 169
Englert, C. S., 233
Evertson, J., 48

F

Fay, K., 149
Fine, J. C., 131, 140
Fleming, I., 10
Flower, L. S., 13
Foote, S., 10
Fountas, I., 70, 83, 238, 268

Freeman, D., 37, 133
Freeman, T., 48
Frus, P., 62
Furr, D., 107

G

Galdone, P., 134
Gallas, K., 149
Gardam, B., 209
Garin, E., 55
Gentry, J. R., 3
George, J., 206–207
Gersten, R., 69
Giacobbe, M. E., 150
Glover, M., 53
Goodman, K., 98
Goodman, Y., 98, 210
Gouvdis, A., 64, 70
Graham, S., 1, 7, 9, 11, 12, 13,
    15, 16, 56, 113–114, 209, 223
Graves, D., 17, 35, 68, 107, 114,
    148, 153, 190
Gregory, K. M., 2–3
Griss, S., 173, 178
Guidry, D., 199
Gunning, T., 112
Guthrie, J., 2, 22

H

Hancock, M., 241
Haneda, M., 27
Hansen, J., 8, 45, 48, 141
Harris, K., 11, 12, 13, 15, 16,
    56, 209
Harris, K. R., 11, 56
Harste, J., 142
Harste, J. C., 169
Hartman, A., 143, 178
Harvey, S., 64, 70
Hayes, J. R., 13
Heaney, S., 158
Heard, G., 141
Hendrickson, R., 9, 10
Henkes, K., 191
Hern, C., 61
Hill, S., 182
Hoffman, S. J., 81
Holliway, R. D., 233–234
Honeycutt, R. L., 215, 221
Hoonan, B. T., 169
Horn, M., 150
Hornof, M. M., 267
Houston, G., 106
Hubbell, S., 10
Hugo, V., 10
Huitt, W., 213
Hummel, J., 213

I

Ingerson, D., 92

J

Jacobs, J., 84
Janssen, T., 89
Johns, B., 237
Johns, J., 107
Johnson, A., 191
Johnston, P. H., 123, 127, 129, 268
Jones, A., 89
Jones, L., 125
Juola-Rushton, A. M., 7, 33

K

Kamil, M., 1
Karle, C., 26
Karnowski, L., 107
Katz, L., 92
Kazin, A., 9
Kellogg, S., 259
Kelly-Gangi, C., 13, 14
Ketteman, H., 191
Kissel, B., 49, 141
Klein, A., 60, 70
Kline, S., 191
Krashen, S., 247

L

Lachtman, O. D., 191, 196
Lamb, B., 10
Lane, B., 194, 197
Lassonde, C., 21, 83, 139, 153, 215
Lawrence, J., 141
Lenski, S., 21, 26, 107, 113
Leong, D., 95, 98
Lerner, J., 237
Lester, H., 259
Leung, C. B., 75, 161
Levine, E., 191, 193
Lewis, E. B., 36
Litt, D. G., 117
Littleton, K., 9
Lobel, A., 259, 264
Lowe, J., 97
Lyons C., 122

M

Mariage, T. V., 233
Martin, B., 259
Marzano, R. J., 140, 277
Mason, L., 11
Matthew, K., 97
Matthews-Somerville, R., 8, 55
McCarrier, A., 70, 238
McCarty, L., 2–3
McCutchen, D., 11, 223, 233–234
McLaughlin, T., 61
Medcalf, N. A., 199
Meichenbaum, D., 114
Mermelstein, L., 146

Meyer

Meyer, M., 148
Miell, D., 89
Milard, E., 221
Miller, D., 64
Miller, K., 246
Moore, N. S., 223
Moore-Hart, M., 255
Morrow, L. M., 140
Murphy, J., 61
Murray, D. M., 144

N

Nathan, R., 142
Nelson, K., 193
Neuman, S. B., ix–x
Nierstheimer, S., 21, 26
Nitscheke, F., 213
Norton, D. E., 83
Norton, N.E.L., 47
Norton, S., 83
Nystrand, M., 223

O

O'Keefe, T., 210
Olson, C. B., 210
O'Neill, A., 41
Osborne, M. P., 191

P

Painter, K., 144
Pardini, T., 52
Parker, E., 52
Parnell, P., 241
Parsons, L., 187
Parsons, S., 42
Patterson, J., 13, 14
Pellegrino, J. W., 277
Peregoy, S., 240
Perin, D., 1, 11, 56, 113–114, 223
Perkins, D., 14
Piaget, J., 209, 213
Pickering, J., 277
Pinnell, G., 70, 83, 122, 238, 268
Pinter, H., 9
Pirsig, R., 10
Podlozny, A., 92
Polacco, P., 191
Polette, K., 81
Polirstok, S., 237, 245
Pollock, E., 277
Prater, K., 265
Pressley, M., 275
Prior, P., 223
Pritchard, R. J., 215, 221

R

Rasinski, T., 257, 265
Rathvon, N., 64
Ray, K. W., 53, 144, 174, 190, 194, 197, 269
Read, S., 145
Reid, R., 11

Richards

Richards, J., 21, 91, 139, 177, 179, 181, 209, 249
Richardson, J., 241
Riordan, R., 196
Risemberg, R., 9, 13, 56
Robbins, J., 237
Rodgers, T., 177, 179
Rodman, M., 36
Rogers, L., 11
Rowling, J. K., 9
Ryan, P., 254

S

Salomon, G., 14
Santangelo, T., 56
Scardamalia, M., 11, 13, 89, 106, 267
Schachner, J., 259
Schunk, D. H., 267
Scieszka, J., 259
Seuss, D., 259
Shagoury, R. E., 46, 143
Shapiro, M., 9
Sharmat, M. W., 191
Shook, R., 60, 70
Silverstein, S., 134
Slobodkina, E., 50
Snow, C. E., 1
Soderman, A. K., 2–3
Solley, B. A., 47
Spandel, V., 225, 238, 239, 247
Stine, R. L., 9
Stotsky, S., 107
Sulzby, E., 3
Sumida, A., 148
Sundeen, T., 99
Suskind, D., 48
Swartz, S., 60, 70
Swifert-Kessell, N., 125

T

Temple, C. A., 142
Thayer, E. L., 206
Tolstoy, A., 259
Tomlinson, C. A., 268
Tompkins, G., 2, 62, 70, 182, 187, 209, 212
Topping, D. H., 81
Tower, H., 48
Tracy, B., 11
Trivizas, E., 259
Tunnell, M., 84

V

Valtcheva, A., 158–159
Van Slys, K., 27
Vass, E., 89
Vaughn, S., 62, 69
Verbruggen, F., 107, 113
Verdi, G., 237
Vygotsky, L., 24, 27, 55, 95, 98, 132, 161, 182, 210, 224, 238, 249

W

Waber, B., 202, 203
Waddell, M., 254
Wallace, I. Pear, J. J., 10
Wang, X., 158–159
Watterston, B., 11
Weinrich, H., 89
Wells, G., 27

Whaley, S., 149
White, Z., 143, 178
Williams, R., 61
Wilson, A., 158
Wilson, E. E., 204, 207
Woodward, V., 142
Wortham, S., 107
Worthy, J., 265

Y

Young, C., 265
Young, C. J., 257

Z

Zakin, A., 237
Zimmerman, B. J., 9, 13, 56